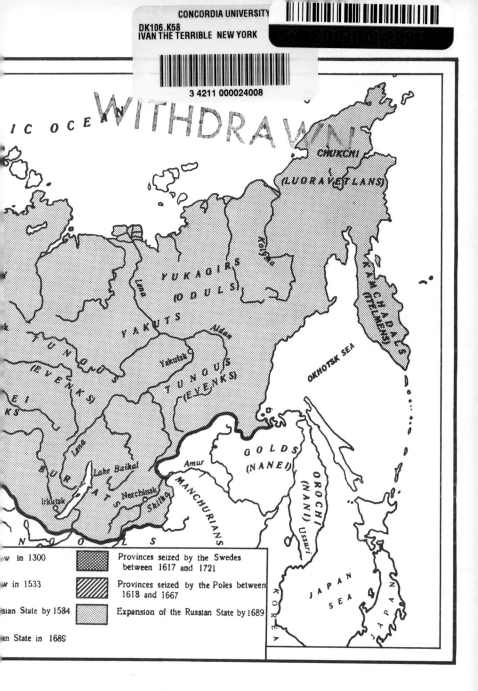

IC OCEAN

WITHDRAWN

CHUKCHI
(LUORAVETLANS)

KAMCHADALS
(ITELMENS)

YUKAGIRS
(ODULS)

YAKUTS

Yakutsk

TUNGUS
(EVENKS)

TUNGUS
(EVENKS)

OKHOTSK SEA

Kolyma

Aldan

Lena

Lena

BURYAT

Lake Baikal

Irkutsk

Nerchinsk

Shilka

GOLDS
(NANEI)

OROCHI
(NANI)

Amur

MANCHURIANS

Ussuri

KOREA

JAPAN
SEA

JAPAN

MONGOLS

w in 1300 | Provinces seized by the Swedes
                 | between 1617 and 1721

w in 1533 | Provinces seized by the Poles between
                 | 1618 and 1667

sian State by 1584 | Expansion of the Russian State by 1689

an State in 1689

EXPANSION OF THE RUSSIAN STATE IN THE XIV—XVII CENTURIES

Ivan the Terrible

JULES KOSLOW

Ivan the Terrible

 HILL AND WANG · NEW YORK

The map of the growth of Moscow 1462–1682 (from *A History of Russia* by Bernard Pares), Copyright 1953 by Alfred A. Knopf, Inc., drawn by Liam Dunne, appears by permission of Alfred A. Knopf, Inc.

Manufactured in the United States of America by American Book–Stratford Press

For Sue

CONTENTS

LIST OF ILLUSTRATIONS

Plates appear facing page 84

Ivan the Terrible

"A tyrant may be intelligent or stupid, good or evil; whatever the case, he is both all-powerful, he is frightened by conspiracies, he is flattered, he is deceived; the prisons fill, the cowardly hypocrites whisper, and the silence becomes so complete that the heart almost stops."

—*Stendhal*

I

A Grand Prince Is Born

THE BELLS of the churches and monasteries within the forbidding crenelated walls of the Kremlin rang out joyously. Soon the thousands of bells in the forty times forty churches of Moscow joined in. Throughout the city, the people crossed themselves and gave thanks to God. The Grand Duke Vasili III at last had an heir.

No one in Moscow that day was so overjoyed as Vasili himself. For more than twenty years, he had been married to Salome Sabourov, but she had not borne him any children. Vasili had not resigned himself to his grief and disappointment. As he grew older, an heir became an obsession. His destiny—and Russia's—demanded it.

Salome had tried everything—sorcery, potions, astrology—to put an end to her barrenness, but still she did not conceive. For the most part, her marriage to Vasili had been a happy one, but unless she could bear him a child she knew the time would come when she would be put aside.

In 1526, Vasili took the step Salome dreaded. He sent her to a convent, and announced his intention of taking another wife. His choice was Helena Glinsky, the daughter of a Lithuanian refugee who had found asylum in Russia.

Helena was a young, vivacious, intelligent, and beautiful woman, and Vasili had been attracted to her the first time he had seen her. She was different from the ignorant, superstitious, and cloistered Muscovite women. She had traveled in many parts of Europe, and in many ways was more West European than Slav.

1

Vasili was now in his fifties; Helena was twenty, and a rejuvenating change from the older—and barren—Salome. Accounts of the time say Vasili was deeply in love with Helena. Perhaps. Certainly she intrigued him. He shaved off his beard to make himself look younger and more Western. It was a noteworthy and, according to the religious belief of the time, dangerous step to take.

The Church opposed his intended marriage to Helena. It called it adulterous, and set in circulation rumors that Helena was not a virgin, that she had given birth to a child out of wedlock at a remote convent. Vasili was not deterred. When the Metropolitan protested against the marriage, Vasili banished him to a monastery in the far north. Maxim the Greek, the learned monk from Mt. Athos who had come to Russia to arrange the Library of the Patriarchs and to translate the sacred books into Slavonic, dared to raise his voice against the new alliance. Vasili turned him over to a group of ecclesiastics, who accused him of heresy and of falsely interpreting the Scriptures. Maxim was banished to the city of Tver.

On August 15, 1526, Vasili and Helena entered the Cathedral of the Annunciation, the smallest but most beautiful of the cathedrals in the Kremlin's Cathedral Square. In this intimate cathedral, the traditional place for the marriages and christenings of the royal family, Vasili and his bride walked over the agate and jasper mosaic floor to the altar, and in an elaborate ceremony were married.

Though they had both been sprinkled with hops before the wedding ceremony to assure fertility, they were married four years before Vasili's dream came true. Not until August 25, 1530, did Helena bear him a son—Ivan. Eighteen months later, Helena gave birth to another son—Yuri. Vasili, now ailing, could die in peace; his line was secure.

The August day of Ivan's birth was a memorable one for others than Vasili. The Grand Duke ordered the prison doors opened, and the chains of thousands of prisoners were removed and the prisoners freed. Hundreds of nobles who had fallen into disgrace were pardoned. Hermits and holy men of all kinds, among them the so-called naked ones, were invited into the Kremlin and given seats of honor at the royal table. Forgotten in the midst of the general rejoicing was the curse that Mark, the Patriarch of

Jerusalem, had thundered when he was informed of Vasili's intention to take a second wife while his first wife was still alive.

"If you should do this wicked thing," the Patriarch had said, "you will have a wicked son; your states will become prey to terrors and tears; rivers of blood will flow; the heads of the mighty will fall; your cities will be devoured by flames."

Ten days after Ivan's birth, Vasili and Helena brought the infant Ivan to the Trinity Monastery to be christened. Joseph, the hegumen of the monastery, and three monks received him from the font. Vasili confided Ivan to the prayers of St. Sergius, on whose tomb he placed his son. Then Vasili prayed fervently that the Saint would protect Ivan throughout his life, for the Grand Duke, a most devout man, was not unmindful, though he was unheeding, of the curse of Mark.

The cloud under which his son Ivan was born, and under which he would have to live his life, was a dark one. In time, the dark cloud of fear and suppression and terror would blanket all of Russia and cover everyone, nobleman and peasant alike. But now, in the pleasant days of August and September, 1530, there was only rejoicing, for the bloodline of the Ruriks was secure. A Grand Prince had been born.

In 1533, Vasili died. Vasili's twenty-year-long hesitation before he finally resolved to be rid of Salome—the barren fig tree that had to be cast out of the fields—and to remarry had a profound effect on the state of the monarchy now that he was dead. For Ivan, his oldest son, was only three years old at the time of his father's death. The tumultuous boyars, who as the most powerful, most privileged, and most blue-blooded members of the aristocracy had never become reconciled to the diminution of their power under the strong rulership of Ivan the Great and Vasili, immediately made plans to assert themselves. So also did Vasili's brothers, who believed the regency rightfully belonged to them. The opposition to the boyars was, to all outward appearance, puny: a three-year old prince and a widow who was especially vulnerable to attack because she was not only a woman but a Lithuanian, not a Russian.

However, the Church rallied behind the royal family, and Metropolitan Daniel hastened to administer to the boyars and the people the oath of allegiance to the child prince Ivan and his mother, Helena.

If the boyars and Vasili's brothers thought they had a frail obstacle to their power in Helena, they soon discovered they were mistaken. Helena, energetic and ambitious, gathered around her a strong body of supporters. Among them were her uncle, Michael Glinsky, and her lover, Prince Obolensky. Soon, however, the advisers fell into disagreement, and Helena chose to be guided by Obolensky. Michael Glinsky was thrown into prison, where he remained until his death, and his supporters were hanged from gibbets erected along the Moscow-Novgorod road.

Guided now by Prince Obolensky, Helena's rule was capricious and unenlightened. Two ineffectual wars, one with Lithuania and another with the united Tatar forces of the Crimea and Kazan, brought deprivation and suffering to the Russian people.

In 1538, Helena died, probably by poison. Obolensky was immediately overthrown by the boyars. Among the nobility a violent battle for power began, the main contestants the princely families of the Shuiskys and the Belskys.

For the next several years, the struggle continued without scruple or mercy on either side. Tyranny prevailed. Prisons filled. Anarchy supplanted oligarchy. The boyars behaved like wild beasts, the chroniclers of the time said. Russia was rent by contending factions, bathed in blood, and ruled by barbarity.

In the midst of chaos and violence, the child-prince Ivan grew up within the fortress-city of the Kremlin.

II

Childhood and Youth

IVAN was eight years old when his mother died. Throughout his life Ivan bemoaned the fate that deprived him of the strong, instructive hand of a father and the sweet, tender love of a mother during his formative years and substituted brutal, unloving boyars as guardians and tutors.

"The boyars fed us [Ivan and his younger brother, Yuri] as though we were foreigners or the most wretched menials," Ivan wrote, with bitterness, twenty-five years after his mother's death. "What sufferings did I endure through lack of clothing and through hunger! For in all things my will was not my own; everything was contrary to my will and unbefitting my tender years. . . . How can I enumerate the countless sufferings I put up with in my boyhood?"

His orphaning was a blow that shaped his entire life, for it led to a childhood marked by a degree of violence that indelibly stamped his character and sharply influenced his future thoughts and actions. He lived his early years at the center of a vicious struggle for power, within which murder, imprisonment, and torture were commonplace. In the halls of the Kremlin palace itself, boyar killed boyar and boyar henchmen seized their enemies and marched them off to prison at sword's point.

One of the most striking incidents imprinted on the young prince's mind occurred when he was twelve years of age. Followers of Prince Ivan Shuisky made a midnight raid upon the palace of the Metropolitan Josephus, who was friendly to their antagonists, the Belskys. The Metropolitan escaped from his palace and fled for refuge to the royal palace. After partially wrecking the Metropolitan's quarters, Shuisky's followers pursued the prelate to the room where the young Prince Ivan slept, and broke open the door. Awakened from sleep, Ivan saw about him a large number of fierce, armed soldiers. He fully believed—and not without cause—that they had come to murder him. His terror was unbounded. Even after the soldiers withdrew from the room, hours passed before Ivan could be pacified and the terrifying face of death removed from his mind's eye.

Dozens of other incidents—some of a terrifying nature, others merely annoying—occurred that had the cumulative effect of making violence and terror integral parts of life to him.

Spurred on by his boyar guardians and tutors, Ivan was methodically trained, as were other children of the nobility, to regard pity, kindness, and gentleness as characteristics unbefitting a prince, and arrogance, brutality, and terror as a prince's hallmarks.

One of the games Ivan was introduced to might descriptively be called splattering the dog. The sport consisted of Ivan and other young nobles climbing to the top of one of the high towers of the Kremlin wall, some of which, like the Saviour's, Trinity, and Nicholas Towers, rose to a height of well over two hundred feet, and then dropping dogs from the topmost platform. With excited shouts and whoops the children would then run down the tower stairs to view the splattered animals' bodies in the courtyard below.

In another game that Ivan relished, the victims were human. Ivan and his boyhood friends, accompanied by bodyguards, would ride their horses at full speed through the streets of Moscow flush into crowds of men, women, and children. The Moscow citizens who were lucky escaped with no more than a scare; the unlucky ones were trampled beneath the horses' hoofs.

With the exception of the injured victims or the families of those who were killed by the so-called deviltry of the nobles, the people of Moscow seemed not to be incensed by such acts. They themselves were steeped in brutal ways, and their own children engaged in games that were similar in intent to the young nobles', though different in detail.

The Austrian ambassador Heberstein tells of one of these games practiced by the youths of Moscow.

"The youths and boys," he wrote, "usually have a large open space in the city, where they assemble on holidays and can be seen and heard by the people. They assemble at a given signal, which is a certain sort of whistle; after which they run off and fight among themselves. First they strike and punch one another with their fists; but soon with their knees and feet, too, striking at random, as hard as they can, in the throat, the chest, the belly, and the genitals or wherever else they can. In the struggle for victory one will fling another down in such a way that they are often carried off half-dead. The one who is most often victor, remains last on the spot, and the one who most bravely bears blows, carries off the glory. They have this sort of competition so that the boys may get used to giving blows and receiving punches."

During the time Ivan's mother was alive, her son had been treated with the awe and respect accorded a grand prince. His every wish was granted by the multitude of boyars and retainers that swarmed through the sixty-five-and-a-half-acre enclosure within the Kremlin walls.

Awe and respect came to an abrupt end with the death of Helena. The boyars who previously had fawned upon him now either ignored him or treated him with contempt. The struggle for power, wealth, and position possessed the court around him.

Bewildered and confused by the sudden change in his position, he struck out wildly, viciously, and blindly. He expressed his fury, which was of no small proportion even when he was a child, by inflicting pain and torture on those about him who were unable to fight back.

But his brutalities and cruelties expressed only one side of his character. Another—and in many ways more significant—side found expression in sulkiness, in brooding, in inner, silent rages.

He felt deserted, despised, and utterly alone. More and more, to the very end of his life, Ivan retreated into self-pity when loneliness, failure, or guilt assailed him.

In 1564, when Ivan was thirty-four years of age, in a letter to the self-exiled Prince Kurbsky, Ivan wrote about his childhood sufferings in a white heat, as though the events had occurred on the day of writing, instead of twenty to twenty-five years before. The intervening two decades had not lessened his rage against the boyars who had victimized him or his pity for himself as their victim.

In his letter to Kurbsky he accused the boyars of having been happy that his mother had died, for, since he was only eight years old, the boyars could seize power. He accused them of not caring about Russia, but of being interested only in their own aggrandizement. "They [the boyars] did not deem us, their sovereigns [Ivan and Yuri], worthy of any loving care, but themselves ran after wealth and glory, and so leapt on one another in conflict."

Ivan further charged the boyars with massacring the supporters of his father, and of seizing possession for themselves of villages that belonged to the royal family, and of controlling the courts illegally. Nothing was sacred to the boyars, Ivan wrote; they took even his mother's personal wealth, transferring some of the valuables to the national treasury and dividing the rest among themselves.

He accused them of seizing control of the government by appointing themselves guardians of his brother and himself, of releasing from prison various boyars who had been imprisoned by Helena at the beginning of her regency, and of exiling boyars opposed to the Shuiskys' rule.

With a fiery display of anger, he recounted personal affronts. "I recall one thing," Ivan wrote, "whilst we were playing games in our childhood. Prince Ivan Vasilievich Shuisky is sitting on a bench, leaning with his elbows on our father's bed and with his leg up on a chair; and he did not even incline his head towards us, either in parental manner, or even as a master—nor was there any element of servility to be found [in his attitude towards us]." Ivan summed up such intolerable boyar behavior by writing, "How can I enumerate such countless sore sufferings as I put up with in my youth?" and cited one of these "countless sore sufferings" by recalling that "many a time did I eat late, not in accordance with my will."

He accused the boyars of being nothing more than common thieves, declaring that they stole vessels made of gold and silver from the royal treasury and then had them inscribed with their own family names.

He wrote that Prince Vasili Shuisky "began to live in the court as though it were in a Jewish synagogue," implying that he turned the court into a loud, raucous place full of confusion.

Ivan then named those who befriended him when he was a youth, and charged that the boyars sent them into exile to assure Ivan's having no friends at court. He cited the Metropolitan Daniel, who was exiled to the monastery of Volokolamsk, and also his friend and confidant Feodor Vorontsov. Ivan wrote of Vorontsov that "Prince Andrei Shuisky together with his partisans came into our refectory and in a frenzied manner having seized and put to shame before us our boyar, Feodor Semenovich Vorontsov, they bore him out from our refectory and intended to kill him. And we sent unto them Metropolitan Makary and our boyars, Ivan and Vasili Grigorievich Morozov, with our order not to kill him, and they, barely hearkening unto our order, exiled him to Kostroma."

What Ivan does not mention in his letter is that one of the perpetrators—Andrei Michaelovich Shuisky—of the action against Vorontsov was subsequently executed, by Ivan's orders, in revenge for his attacks on Vorontsov.

And so it went. Outrage upon outrage; revenge upon revenge; murder upon murder. And through it all the young Ivan seethed, brooded, educated himself in a peculiar form of statesmanship by learning well from those about him lessons in how to rule by intrigue, violence, and corruption.

"From the death of our mother unto that time for six and a half years they ceased not to practice these evil things!" Ivan wrote.

The six and a half years terminated when Ivan, at the age of thirteen, made a successful bid for authority—and succeeded, as he himself phrased it, in "putting our kingdom in order."

The order Ivan congratulated himself on obtaining at the age of thirteen did not become fact for another several years. What Ivan succeeded in accomplishing at this time was the destruction of the power of the Shuiskys in the Kremlin, and their replacement in strategic positions by the Glinskys.

The change was effected in a bold and dramatic coup. After the Christmas fetes of 1543, Ivan issued an order that the boyars should come to the court. When they had assembled, Ivan spoke to them with firmness and passion. He insisted that the boyars were misruling Russia, that they were interested only in their own advancement, and that their excesses must come to an end.

The scene was familiar—a prince dressed in his ornate robes lecturing and scolding his haughty, bearded boyars on their behavior. Ivan, the main character, however, was unusual. Here was a smooth-faced thirteen-year-old boy telling mature, tough, and wily boyars in the most dictatorial terms what he expected of them.

At the end of the lecture, Ivan ordered Andrei Shuisky to be seized. This Shuisky was not necessarily more guilty than others, but Ivan told the boyars, "Only one among you will be punished this time." Shuisky fled from the palace, was caught, and then handed over to the kennel keepers of the Kremlin. Savage dogs were turned loose, and Andrei Shuisky was literally torn to pieces. Then Ivan, forgetting his declaration that he would punish only one this time, ordered Shuisky's partisans to be executed. Thirty boyars were hanged on gibbets along the Moscow-Novgorod highway.

Under the Glinskys, Ivan's stature and prestige increased, and no longer could he complain that he was not treated with respect. However, there was no apparent change in the ruthless methods of government. Ivan and the Glinskys governed in the only way they knew how, in the way Muscovite princes had ruled for hundreds of years—by force, terror, and murder.

In 1545, Ivan suspected a plot against him on the part of certain boyars, among them his childhood friend Vorontsov and an influential boyar, Prince Ivan Kubensky. He had them thrown into prison and then beheaded. In addition, two members of Vorontsov's family were executed, and a boyar, Afanasy Buturlin, had his tongue cut out for speaking impertinently to the Grand Prince.

Ivan's handling of a delegation from Novgorod revealed much about the young prince's character. One day in May, 1546, while Ivan was hunting with a small party near Kolomna, he and his entourage were suddenly confronted by a band of armed men. The tough-looking horsemen explained that they were Novgorod musketeers and that they were on their way to Moscow to complain to the Grand Prince about their governor. It was a time-honored custom in Russia to petition the reigning prince for redress from real or imaginary wrongs. Nevertheless, Ivan was angered that his hunting was disturbed, and ordered the musketeers to move aside. Exactly what happened after Ivan gave his order is not clear, but some misunderstanding obviously ensued, for the musketeers and Ivan's men exchanged shots. As soon as the fighting started, Ivan spurred his horse, and fled. When the skirmish was over, Ivan's adherents found him in hiding some distance away. Upon realizing the danger was over, Ivan issued an order that an immediate inquiry be undertaken.

Ivan's retreat on this occasion at the threat of physical harm to himself was only one early incident in a long series throughout his life in which he showed great fear for his personal safety. The intrigues and bloodshed he had seen during his childhood had left their mark. Nevertheless, when the danger was over, he reacted by a show of bravado, and sometimes gave orders for fearful retaliation against those who had upset him. Moreover, he never forgot or forgave those who had opposed him, and even decades after the event, he would resurrect old wrongs and let the remembrance trigger an act of cruelty or bloodshed.

With the exception of an occasional hunting trip in nearby forests or carousings in the streets of Moscow with hard-riding young boyars, Ivan, for the most part, led a solitary life. With the possible exception of his early-childhood friend Vorontsov, he called no man his companion, and no one called Ivan his friend. Morbidly distrustful of all those about him, constantly watchful of hurts to his pride, and suspicious that anyone who made conciliatory overtures to him was in reality approaching him for intended treachery, he maintained an aloof relationship with everyone in the Kremlin.

For solace, Ivan turned to books. He studied them with dogged determination and against the wishes of his boyars and Church mentors, who had no patience with his desire for knowledge and who tried as best they could to deprive him of access to all printed matter except such acceptable works as the Breviary and Psalter.

For hours on end Ivan would lock himself up in his own room, refusing to see anyone. And there in the semi-darkness of the gloomy chamber so typical of the rooms in the Kremlin palace, he would read or meditate.

Few things that Ivan undertook in his lifetime were done openly, directly, and without the need for secrecy and conniving. So it was in his youth, even with such a matter as his pursuit of knowledge. His Church mentors regarded secular knowledge as sinful and corrupting; the rough boyars, though often clever in practical affairs, regarded the reading of books as a sedentary pursuit unbecoming to leaders of warriors, which the boyars considered themselves to be.

Scarcely anyone in the Kremlin was even aware that the young prince was engaged in reading books for hours on end. As for Ivan, the stealthy manner in which he had to pursue knowledge added incentive to his desire for knowledge. He had to out-trick and out-maneuver his enemies who at every turn attempted to deny and frustrate him.

His reading consisted of a few books on ancient history, a few Russian and Byzantine chronicles, and works on religious and Church matters. Bishop Paulus of Nuceria in a report on his mission to Muscovy to Pope Clement VII was one of the few contemporaries, Russian or foreign, to write down his observations of what books were available in Russia.

"Beside the books that they have of the ancient Greek doctors," Bishop Paulus wrote, "they have also the commentaries and homilies of Saint Ambrose, Augustine, Jerome, and Gregory, translated into the Illyrian or Slavonian tongue, which agrees with theirs. . . . A great number of books of holy scripture are translated into this tongue by the industry of Saint Jerome and Cyrillus. Furthermore, beside the histories of their own country, they have also books, containing the facts of great Alexander, and the Roman Emperors, and likewise of Marcus Antonius and Cleopatra."

Ivan's heavy and didactic reading matter contributed to deepening his proclivity to gloom and depression as well as to anger and violence. He constantly identified his trials and travail with the secular and Church princes he read about, and cast the boyars in traitorous and satanic roles. He built about himself a world that consisted of traitors, spies, ingrates, and deceivers that plotted endlessly against him. He cast himself in the role of the prince betrayed who one day, as God's avenging servant, would strike down all of these sinners against God, the ruler in Heaven, and himself, the ruler in Muscovy. Now he was still too young, his power too weak, but he vowed that his time would come.

In addition to his self-education, he received the kind of formal education that was typical among the Russian aristocracy of the time and had been the same for many years. Each day he had to recite new passages from the Breviary and Psalter. And each day, too, he had to repeat over and over passages from these two works that he had previously studied. No attempt was made to interpret or explain; all was endless repetition. Coupled with Ivan's native ability to memorize, these endless repetitions enabled him to store up in his mind vast numbers of word-for-word passages that remained with him until the end of his life and that he used profusely, although with innumerable errors, both in speaking and writing whenever the opportunity presented itself.

When the time came that Ivan was no longer under the thumb of men who were supposed to be his protectors, and he could openly and fearlessly display his knowledge, the court at the Kremlin was astonished that their ruler was a man of great learning. His range of information appeared to them a kind of sorcery, and they were in awe of him and uncomfortable in his presence. Furthermore, they were ashamed of their prince, who delved into ideas and concepts that neither Ivan's ruling forebears nor they were desirous of considering. An unbridgeable gap was opening between Ivan and his boyars, a gap that was to widen over the years as their ruler drifted farther and farther away from the typical conception of the rude boyar chief.

The day of the grand prince as the warrior leader was nearing an end; the day of the Czar as the Little Father was dawning.

III

Coronation and Marriage

RUSSIA of the sixteenth century was an old state and a new one. It was powerful and weak. It was united and divided. It bordered on the West and was Eastern. It was dissolute and puritanical. It was outwardly inert and restless within. It was, in sum, a totality of baffling contradictions, mystifying perplexities, and irritating anomalies.

For centuries in the wide expanse called Rus, there had been a disunited scattering of city-states, some weak and others relatively strong. There was Great Novgorod in the north, the giant commercial center, somewhat democratic in its organization, which in the middle of the ninth century invited the Varangian Rurik to rule over its domain.

"Our country is great and fertile, but under the empire of anarchy," Novgorodian ambassadors informed Rurik. "Come and govern us and reign over us."

Rurik accepted the offer. Around 862, about the time other Northmen were fighting Alfred the Great in Britain and Charles the Bald in France, he and his two brothers, Sineous and Trouvor, arrived in Great Novgorod. For over seven hundred years, the Rurik bloodline survived as rulers of, first, a part of Rus, and, later, all of it.

There was the queen city of Kiev in the south, the center of Russian cultural and artistic accomplishment in medieval days. The city declined in power around the thirteenth century, as

14

much from its bloody princely struggles as from its physical destruction by Batu Khan in 1240.

There was Vladimir, the capital of the Monomakh princes, destined for a brief period to be the religious center of Rus as well as the repository of the most beautiful church architecture in Russia. There were others—Suzdal and Rostov and Tver among them—that became weakened by constant struggles for power among their own princes and with princes of other cities.

And then there was Moscow, a newcomer among the city-states of Rus. Founded in 1147 by the Kievan prince Yuri Dolgoruki, it remained little more than a small trading center for over a century. Situated on the Moscow River, at the crossroads of the east-west and north-south trading routes, it had a scattering of log huts, warehouses, a church, and a flimsy wooden stockade, or kremlin, for protection. Partly because of its favorable geographic location and partly because of the craftiness of its princes, the city grew more powerful. By the time of Ivan I, nicknamed Ivan Kalita (Moneybags), in the middle of the fourteenth century, Moscow became the capital of Rus.

But it was a capital of an occupied land. For almost two hundred and fifty years, from the middle of the thirteenth century to near the end of the fifteenth century, the Tatars of the Golden Horde occupied the country, and ruled through their sometime allies and sometime enemies, the Moscow princes.

Under Ivan III (the Great), the Tatar rule finally was broken, partly as a result of Russian defiance but mostly because of the disintegration of the Golden Horde itself. Russia was at last free of Tatar rule, though several areas were still under Tatar hegemony; she was now free to be enslaved by her own princes.

The two grand dukes who preceded Ivan the Terrible to the throne of Rus, or Muscovy, as it was known in those days, were precursors of the kind of ruler Ivan was to be. Both grand dukes —Ivan's grandfather, Ivan III, and his father, Vasili III—were cruel, autocratic, proud, and ambitious.

When Ivan III ascended the throne in 1462, Muscovite territory consisted of about fifteen thousand square miles. He and his son Vasili expanded the domain, and by the time Vasili died in 1533 Moscow dominated more than forty thousand square miles. Yet it was more than territory that was acquired by the two assemblers of Russian land, as Ivan and his son are called; it was also prestige and power and a growing realization that the destiny of Rus was national greatness; she was to be boundless in territory, varied in population, and the inheritor of the power and glory that had resided for hundreds of years in the second Rome—Byzantium— and was no more after Byzantium's fall to the Turks in 1453.

Ivan III was obsessed with the imperial vision of making Moscow the third Rome, the inheritor of the mantle of the Eastern Roman Empire and through that empire the heir to the empire of Rome itself. He always remembered the prophecy of a Russian monk who had written to him, saying, "Know now, pious Caesar, that the sovereignty of all Christendom has been united in your own, for the two Romes have fallen, but the third does endure, and fourth there shall never be, for your Christian Empire shall last forever!"

To strengthen Russia's bid to become the Third Rome, Ivan's ecclesiastical advisers and supporters spread the fiction that Rurik's ancestry was directly traceable for fifteen generations to the Roman Emperor Augustus. For Augustus, it was claimed, had a son by the name of Prus, from whom the Lithuanian Prussians and Rurik were descended. And Ivan, of course, was a direct descendant of Rurik. Moreover, the Church insisted that the royal cap, scepter, and mantle had been given to the Russian prince Vladimir Monomakh by the Greek Emperor Constantine Monomachus at the time of his invitation to the Russian prince to share the rulership of his empire. The fact that the Greek emperor had died fifty years before Vladimir became Grand Prince of Kiev did not seem to trouble the Church fathers. The churchmen also claimed that the Metropolitan from Constantinople, upon presenting the crown, expressed the thought that it was sent from God, and that it was His wish that all Orthodox people should be under the common rule of the "Empire and of the great autocracy of great Russia."

Ivan III himself supplied the master stroke. At the time of the fall of Constantinople in 1453, the child Zoe Paleologus, the niece of John Paleologus, the last emperor of Byzantium, was taken to Rome for safekeeping, becoming a ward of the Pope. Later, when Zoe was grown, the Pope's emissaries, to try to effect a reconciliation of the Church of Rome and the Church of Russia, proposed to Ivan III that he should marry Zoe.

Ivan agreed to the marriage, craftily giving the impression that he was interested in the unification of the two churches; he was in fact interested only in the prestige of marrying the direct descendant of the Byzantine princes, and thus supplying a bond and a claim to the mantle of the Byzantine princes themselves.

In 1472, Zoe crossed the frontier into Russia. A large number of emigrants came with her from Rome, Constantinople, and Greece, and these in time became the core of Russia's diplomats, engineers, artists, and theologians. They brought with them into Russia Greek and other books, some of which formed the beginnings of the Library of the Patriarchs, others of which were probably incorporated, years later, into the legendary lost library of Ivan the Terrible.

Ivan had never set eyes on Zoe, but his emissaries had reported to him that she was not uncomely. However, her appearance, according to Italian observers, left much to be desired. One of them described her as having an ungainly figure and referred to her as "that mountain of fat." Another observer, trying to find something kindly to say about the fat princess, wrote that she could be admired greatly for "her little mouth and her gentle manner of spitting."

Ivan himself was far from handsome. He was tall and painfully thin and so stooped that he was known as Ivan Gorbaty, or Humpbacked. He was cold, imperious, and mirthless. His countenance was said to be so fierce and forbidding that his very glance caused women to faint. The boyars themselves, rough and hearty men, were said to be awe-stricken when face to face with him. He punished and tortured all those who raised the slightest opposition to him, even men of the highest rank. He publicly whipped the highest authorities of the Church and mutilated the counselors of his son Vasili when they committed some slight infraction of court etiquette.

After his marriage to Zoe Paleologus, who was renamed Sophia Fominichna, Ivan adopted the Byzantine imperial arms—the double-headed eagle—as the imperial arms of Russia, introduced into the Russian court Byzantine court customs, and even had the Church organized on Greek hierarchical lines.

The imposing title, Czar, had never been used by a Russian ruler until the time of Ivan the Terrible. Until then, Prince, Grand Prince, and especially Grand Duke were the usual titles. Ivan the Great, who had united and extended the growing Russian state and had broken the two-hundred-odd-year yoke of the Tatar Golden Horde in 1480, had refrained from calling himself more than Grand Duke, though by his achievements he would have been justified in referring to himself as Emperor. And for a time it appeared that he might do so, for he had had visions of empire, he had proclaimed himself the inheritor of the mantle of the glorious Caesars and the grandeur that had been Byzantium, had married the last Byzantine emperor's niece, had introduced the outward trappings of Byzantine royal customs into his court, and had made the Kremlin into a magnificent and imposing citadel of pomp and power.

Like Ivan the Great, his son Vasili had extended the scope and power of Rus, and had completed the building of the great edifice, the Moscow Kremlin. The autocracy was further consolidated, and the power of the ruler became even greater, so great that Heberstein, the astute and observant Austrian ambassador to Moscow at the time of Vasili, reported that "the will of the Grand Duke is the will of God, and the will of God is the Grand Duke fulfilled." It was not uncommon at the time, Heberstein continued, to speak of the Grand Duke as "God's Steward and Gentleman-of-the-Bedchamber," thus applying the phraseology of the Kremlin court to the relationship between the temporal and the divine rulers. Yet Vasili had not been bold enough to call himself Emperor, though he, too, had reason to assume the stately title.

It remained for the sixteen-year-old Ivan, who had not overthrown a centuries-long oppressor, or extended and consolidated the empire, or built anything at all until this time, to take the audacious step. And he did so with the precipitous, flamboyant gesture that was to characterize many of the great decisions of his life.

In December, 1546, boyars and high churchmen were summoned to the Cathedral of the Assumption by the Metropolitan Makary. Excitement ran high, for there had been rumors for some time that Ivan had been entertaining the idea of marriage.

After the Liturgy was said, the great boyars and churchmen, led by the Metropolitan, made their way to the Palace of Facets. Seated on his throne, Ivan met them. When they had all assembled, Ivan addressed them: "By the mercy of God, and his all-pure Mother, by the prayers and grace of the great wonder workers, Peter, Alexei, Sergei, and all the Russian wonder workers in whom I put my trust, and with your blessing, Holy Father, I propose to marry. At first I thought to marry a foreign princess, the daughter of some king or emperor, but afterwards I gave up the thought. I have no wish to marry a foreign princess, for if I marry a wife from a strange land we may not agree, and life would be hard for us. Therefore, I wish to marry in my own realm and God will bless it."

The throne room hummed with subdued but excitable whispers; from what Russian noble family would the bride be chosen? For any noble family, even the most lowly, could be the one so honored.

But Ivan had not yet finished. The master dramatic stroke was still to come. Silencing the crowd, he continued: "Before my marriage, I wish, with your blessing, O father Metropolitan, to seek the ancestral rank, such as that of our ancestors the Czars and Grand Dukes, and our kinsman Vladimir Vsevolodovich Monomakh. I wish also to be invested with that rank."

Coronation and marriage both! Here indeed was an announcement of the utmost significance. In all likelihood, Ivan's announcement that he wished to marry and that his bride would be a Russian girl, not a foreigner, meant most to the boyars personally. For under the system of selecting a bride for the prince that then prevailed and that Ivan's father himself had used, girls would be assembled in the Kremlin from all over Russia for the Prince's examination and choice. And the family from which she would be chosen would be elevated in rank and power above all other boyar families in the land. It was an unambitious boyar indeed who that day and subsequent days didn't dream that perhaps his eligible daughter might become the favored one, and that he would take his place at Ivan's side, exceeded in glory and power only by the Metropolitan and Ivan himself!

The more thoughtful boyars and churchmen—and those without eligible daughters—were more concerned with Ivan's announcement that he wished to be crowned not only as Grand Duke but also as Czar. Some of them probably knew that no other Russian ruler had ever had the audacity to insist upon such a title; others felt the title Czar had become discredited and was offensive to the national dignity of Russia, since Tatar princes, even minor ones, had used it. These included not only Tatar princes who in the past had exacted tribute from the conquered Russians but also lesser Tatar princelings who were now little more than heads of provinces or who were paying tribute to Moscow.

Ivan, however, was unconcerned with this line of reasoning. The years in which he had studied both Russian and ancient history had had their effect. From his reading he had become aware—and intrigued—by the fact that the heads of ancient Byzantium had used the title. And was not Russia destined to become the new capital of the Orthodox world and of an Eastern empire? Then it was only befitting for its head to be so named. His books, written in Slavonic, had told him, too, that the word czar denoted the kings of Judea, the rulers of Assyria, Egypt, and Babylon, and the emperors of Constantinople and Rome. He had read of such rulers as Nebuchadnezzar and Belshazzar, and they had fascinated him.

The fiction of royal lineage and destiny that had been started at the time of Ivan III was again promulgated—Ivan's bloodline traceable back to the great Augustus Caesar, the dynastic line of empire going back to the Byzantine emperors, and God's will and blessing for the success of Ivan as His choice to rule over all people under the sway of Orthodoxy.

The mass of people—even many of the nobles—were intrigued by this mélange of temporal and divine justification. Although they were ignorant and superstitious and understood little of what really was at stake, the bits and pieces they did manage to understand were a welcome relief from their poverty and misery; for this was a glorious world of powerful legends, mysterious symbols, thrilling history, and exciting dreams of power and glory to come. The Russian mystique that had been gestating for centuries was a-borning. The people themselves, even the most insignificant peasant grubbing like an animal to stay alive in the midst of his abysmal poverty, was the collective mother, Ivan was the great Little Father, and God was the midwife.

All of this was for domestic consumption—for the time being. Ivan did not attempt to communicate to foreign powers his demand to be considered an emperor. Not until almost fifteen years later—in 1561—after notable victories in the field of battle did he attempt to do so. He remembered that when his father had made a timid effort in 1514 to refer to himself as emperor in a treaty then being negotiated with the Emperor Maximilian, Vasili had been met with an abrupt rebuff. Maximilian had refused to sign unless the reference to the Russian "emperor" was deleted. Meekly, Vasili had agreed.

The Patriarch of Constantinople, however, supported Ivan's pretensions, and by a benedictory letter confirmed Ivan in his kingdom as the scion of the ancient imperial house. Thirty-six metropolitans, archbishops, and bishops of the Eastern Church joined the Metropolitan in signing the letter. The letter was received with great fanfare and rejoicing. The authenticity of the letter that caused rejoicing, however, has been questioned; some authorities find as many as thirty-five of the signatures forgeries.

Beyond question, there were some high Orthodox Church dignitaries, among them those of Alexandria and Antioch, who praised the new Czar. The Patriarch of Jerusalem went so far as to call Ivan "the head of Christendom."

The Russians' homage to Ivan's glory and the acknowledgment of his power from high Church dignitaries within and without the country were the first manifest acknowledgments of his drive for power. For a boy of sixteen, they were a strong stimulant. Since the age of thirteen, he had taken firm measures, and they were now being rewarded. The emperor's mantle, he felt, was where it belonged—on his shoulders. This was so, he further felt, not only because he was the first Russian prince who had the courage to demand that it be placed there but also because he understood the significance of establishing himself as a sovereign whose power came to him from God. During the next four decades of his rule, he forged so firmly this direct linkage between the Russian sovereign and God that it held sway over the mind, body, and soul of the Russian people for almost four hundred years.

The coronation took place in January, 1547, in the Cathedral of the Assumption, situated in the historic heart of the Kremlin, where, since its completion in 1475, coronations of Russian rulers have always been held.

The setting itself is exciting, for the Cathedral, which even today is a showplace of the Kremlin, is an awe-inspiring marvel. There are colossal columns supporting a central dome and four satellite cupolas, all of them embellished with murals that gleam with beaten gold. Thousands of religious statues line the walls in mute assemblage, fixing their eyes upon poor human sinners while at the same time extending their hands in benediction. The iconostasis, a lofty screen of silver-gilt with five rows of figures, dazzles the imagination. Gleaming filigree from which peer Madonnas and saints, their aureoles ablaze with thousands and thousands of precious stones, is the extreme of religious homage. Yet, the magnificence is not only exciting; it is somber, too. For the Cathedral, with many of its sections in shadow, expresses a deep gloom, and the thousands of figures in hieratic rigidity give the Cathedral a cryptlike appearance.

The coronation ceremony more or less followed a pattern. The procession that entered the Cathedral was led by a confessor, who carried a crucifix in one hand and with the other hand sprinkled holy water on the acolytes. Behind the confessor, Ivan walked. In his train were his brother Yuri and a large number of princes and boyars. In the Cathedral, the choir began chanting with great fervor the hymn "In Plurimos Annos." Mass was celebrated. Ivan was then led to a chair that was on an elaborately decorated platform, with steps leading up to it, situated in the middle of the Cathedral. The Metropolitan's chair was alongside Ivan's, and like the Prince's was adorned with cloth of gold. On a table in front of the platform was the regalia for the coronation.

Metropolitan Makary then proceeded with great pomp to invest Ivan with the traditional Holy Barma (a kind of broad collar made of coarse silk and adorned with gold and gems), the chain, the crown, and the cross of Monomachus, all according to the order for the coronation of Greek emperors. In the profound silence in the Cathedral, the Metropolitan then placed the crown on Ivan's head, crowning him for the first time in Russian history with the title Ivan, by the Grace of God, Czar and Autocrat of All Russia. The Metropolitan then invoked God's blessing: "May his throne flourish even as the throne of David! May his throne be ever a throne of righteousness! May he turn a terrible face to those who rebel against his power; but a smiling face to those who are his faithful subjects!"

The hymn "In Plurimos Annos" was again sung with great fervor. The processional lines were formed again and the exit from the Cathedral began. Ivan, now invested with the coronation regalia, walked upon the velvet and damask carpet towards the Cathedral door. As soon as he passed through it, the crowds, which had had difficulty in restraining their excitement, rushed towards the platform and tore away the cloth from Ivan's chair, for a memento of this glorious occasion.

Now that the coronation ceremony was over, Ivan insisted that his plans for marriage should be quickly consummated. In December, 1546, when he had told the boyars that he would not marry a foreigner but would, as his father had done for his first marriage, select a bride from among eligible Russian girls, a circular letter had gone out to noble families throughout Russia.

"When these, our letters, reach you," the circular stated, "it shall be your duty instantly to repair with your unmarried daughters, if such you have, to our lieutenant in the city for inspection. Conceal not your marriageable daughters under any pretext. Whoever shall conceal a marriageable daughter and not bring her to our lieutenant, on him shall be our great disfavor."

In the Kremlin in the meantime, preparations were under way to take care of the marriageable daughters. A huge building that had many rooms was made ready, with each room containing twelve beds.

How many girls finally arrived is unknown, but the number has been estimated to be between five hundred and fifteen hundred. When the virgins arrived, they were shown to their sleeping quarters and were given detailed instructions on how to conduct themselves. They ate at a common table and various entertainments were provided for their amusement.

Doctors and midwives were then sent to the girls to examine them. The examination was thorough, and, as one observer in the court put it, "no part of them is unsearched."

As the days went on, the number of girls constantly diminished as they were found for one reason or another to be unsuitable. Thus, from the original hundreds there remained only two hundred, then a hundred, finally ten. When the girls left, they were given presents for their trouble.

Through all this, Ivan observed them privately and listened to their conversations. Sometimes he entered their rooms at night to observe them while they were asleep, to see which of them slept quietly or unquietly. Sometimes he went to their rooms during the day, but always accompanied by an elderly courtier. Thus, he was able to observe their dispositions, their tempers, their intelligence.

Meanwhile, frenzied activity and intrigue by the fathers of the virgins was taking place throughout the Kremlin. The prize of becoming the Czar's father-in-law, and thus of having great power, was irresistible. In the past, it had not been unusual for a chosen girl to be poisoned by a rival's family before the wedding could take place.

Ivan's choice finally fell upon Anastasia Zakharina-Koshkina, whose father had died some time before but whose family was well known and popular among the Muscovites. In the traditional manner, Ivan made his choice known by one day sitting down beside her while she was dining and presenting her with a handkerchief and a ring. All the other girls still in the Kremlin were dismissed, and Anastasia Zakharina-Koshkina, or Romanov, as the family later was named, was publicly declared the bride-elect.

What kind of person was Anastasia? According to the picture of her that has emerged over the centuries, she was the sweetest, wisest, most even-tempered virgin in all Russia at the time of her marriage. As a wife, she was the paradigm of virtue, affection, and loyalty. As the Czaritsa, she was the model of wisdom, nobility, and compassion.

The picture, however, is too much a stereotype. She was undoubtedly a woman who had a good deal of common sense, which could be interpreted as wisdom, considering the times in which she lived. Yet as a product of her times she was, like other women of the nobility, unread, superstitious, provincial, and unconcerned with the miserable life of the mass of the common people.

Still, if she did not rise above her times as a woman and as a czaritsa, she did at least represent the best of what then existed. And it is because of this that an English traveler at the time referred to her as "wise and of such holiness, virtue, and government as she was honored, beloved, and feared of all her subjects. He [Ivan] being young and riotous, she ruled him with admirable affability and wisdom."

There is little doubt that Ivan's decision to marry Anastasia was the result of a deep attraction for her, and this attraction was probably due more to her character and personality than her looks, for contemporary accounts ignore a little too noticeably a description of Anastasia's beauty or physical charms. Otherwise his choice of Anastasia makes little sense. The Romanovs were not a powerful boyar family at the time, and Ivan realized no direct political advantage from the alliance. His only advantage was an indirect one; the Romanovs were not involved in the political intrigue of the period. But even so his choice of a bride was virtually limitless from the hundreds of other Russian noble families that had kept aloof from the scandalous political scene involving such families as the Shuiskys and the Belskys.

The marriage ceremony took place on February 3, 1547, in the Cathedral of the Annunciation, the smallest of the cathedrals in the Kremlin but extremely attractive because of its intimate, though elaborate, character. Like other Kremlin cathedrals, it is richly decorated; the gold enclosure of the image of the Annunciation alone contains more than eighteen pounds of pure gold, together with pearls and other precious gems.

The ceremony itself was a long, solemn occasion. For hours, hundreds of dignitaries stood upon the same magnificent agate and jasper mosaic floor of the Cathedral where Ivan's father, Vasili, had married his mother, Helena, watching the elaborate and seemingly endless nuptial rites. Finally, after the bond had been sealed, the Metropolitan turned to Ivan and Anastasia, and said: "This day, in the mystery of the Church, you have been united forever, that together you might submit to the Almighty and live in virtue, virtue for you being righteousness and grace. My lord! Love and honor your wife, and you, Christ-loving Czaritsa, obey him. As the Holy Cross is the head of the Church, so is the husband the head of his wife. Fulfilling God's commandments, you will have vision of the blessed Jerusalem and peace in Israel."

Outside the Cathedral, huge crowds had assembled from all over

Moscow and other parts of Russia, partly out of curiosity, partly out of respect, and partly because they knew that on such an occasion alms would be distributed. They were not disappointed. Ivan's retainers went among them and liberally distributed coins. Even Anastasia herself made a token gesture to the poor, handing out alms to several persons in the crowd as Ivan and she left the Cathedral to return to the Palace of Facets.

At the Palace a lavish banquet was set with every conceivable meat and fowl, delicacies, and native and imported wines and liqueurs. Innumerable toasts were made to the health and happiness of the Czar and his bride. Time and again Ivan sent bread from his table to favored guests, to honor them. Singers, dancers, acrobats, and trained bears provided constant entertainment. A procession of flunkeys kept bringing more and more food and wine to the banquet tables. Hours passed, and with each passing hour the celebration became more wild, the guests more drunk, and the conversation more ribald.

In the midst of it all, Ivan and Anastasia left, to go to their bedroom, where favored retainers waited to prepare the couple for their wedding night. Several of Ivan's uncles on his mother's side, the Glinskys, took up position at the head of the bed. One boyar helped Ivan put on his nightcap. Another boyar helped him into his nightshirt. Still another tucked a blanket around the couple.

Several days later Ivan and Anastasia deserted the Kremlin to go on their honeymoon. But it was not a honeymoon as we think of it today. It was a devotional pilgrimage, to the Trinity Monastery of the Holy Sergius, where Ivan's father had placed his infant son, after his christening, on the tomb of the Saint, and besought the Saint to help Ivan to a good and noble life.

The Monastery was about forty miles from Moscow, and Ivan and Anastasia, dressed as pilgrims, journeyed there on foot through the ice and snow. And once there, Ivan lived an ascetic life, spending entire days in prayer and communion at the tomb of St. Sergius. From the Trinity Monastery, he and Anastasia went to other monasteries to complete the pilgrimage.

After several weeks, the Czar and Czaritsa returned to the Kremlin. For one of the few times in his life, Ivan seemed to be at peace with himself. The pilgrimage had had a quieting effect upon him. Anastasia had proved to be a gentle and loving companion and wife. Ivan was in no hurry to take up the reins of government, and he allowed the Glinskys to continue to manage the affairs of state. For days on end he stayed in his Kremlin apartment with Anastasia, content just to be in her company. Ivan felt blessed and happy; his choice of a wife had been a most lucky one. At long last, love had come into his life. And it gave him peace of mind and soul. The torment and misery of his childhood seemed distant. Life was good.

IV

The Great Fire at Moscow

Moscow in 1547—the first year of Ivan's czardom—was an immense multiringed walled city, larger than London, twice the size of Florence or Prague, and with the circumference of its outer walls greater than the circle of the walls of Paris.

At the heart of Moscow was the Kremlin—the original city—in which lived the Czar, his family, his relations, and some of the richest and most powerful boyars. The ring closest to the Kremlin was the Kitaigorod, in which lived the traders, wealthy boyars, and the few foreigners then in Moscow. The next ring was the Bielgorod, in which the privileged citizens and some of the city's merchants lived. And finally, there was the outer ring, or suburbs, where the artisans and laborers had their homes.

The population was estimated at about two hundred thousand. There were more than forty thousand dwellings, almost all of them built of wood. The streets were narrow, crooked, and winding, with only a few of them paved with logs to combat the deep mud that was everpresent except in extremely dry weather.

Since Moscow was the crossroad of the north-south and east-west commerce, wagons and caravans filled its narrow streets. And in the Kitaigorod, the main trading area, the streets were lined with stalls and crowded with Moscow merchants and citizens, as well as traders from other parts of the empire and beyond.

It was an exotic city, more Oriental than Western—crowded, dirty, boisterous, and dynamic, colorful, mysterious. Dominating the area like an austere, authoritative, forbidding master was the massive Kremlin, situated as it was on a hill overlooking the city.

Almost from the time of the founding of Moscow, fires were the bane of Moscow's existence. Some were local in scope; others, however, leveled a part of the city, and in a few cases most of it.

Since almost all houses in Moscow were of wood, there was always the danger of fires. But there were other factors that made fires common—cooking of meals on poorly designed ovens, arson by deranged and disgruntled citizens, and irresponsible acts by the innumerable drunkards who constantly roamed the city. The means for fighting fire were negligible. Moreover, the Moscow citizens regarded fires with superstition, passivity, and fatalism, and in times of crisis by fire would do little more than pray fervently for divine assistance.

Shortly after Ivan's marriage, a series of fires broke out, many of them of mysterious origin. Fortunately, they did not cause widespread damage. However, in June, 1547, a fire broke out that was destined to be the worst that had ever occurred.

Immediately preceding the fire an event occurred that seemed to be a portent of bad times. Ivan and Anastasia were vacationing at a summer house in the village of Ostrovka when Ivan was informed that a delegation of seventy prominent citizens from the city of Pskov wished to have an audience with him. Their complaint: the Glinskys had appointed a vicious and brutal governor, a Prince Turuntay, to rule over the city, and he was terrorizing the inhabitants. In support of their claim, they produced witnesses and a long list of grievances, cited in detail. As representatives from the proud city of Pskov (together with Novgorod, Pskov had the most democratic form of government in Russia, and only recently had come under the jurisdiction of Moscow), they expected justice from their ruler.

Ivan was furious; his vacation with his bride was being interrupted and an action of his government was being questioned. Moreover, the city of Pskov with its long tradition of popular, democratic procedure was anathema to him, and he detested the proud, liberty-loving burghers.

Ivan scarcely heard them out. He ordered that the members of the deputation be stripped naked, bound, and laid in rows on the ground. This done, he ordered spirits to be poured over them, and he himself went among them with a taper, setting fire to their hair and beards.

What further torture was in store for the Pskov burghers will never be known, for at that moment a messenger arrived and informed Ivan that Moscow was in flames. He turned away from his prisoners, ordered his horse, and dashed off to Moscow.

In Moscow, the conflagration was frightful. A fierce wind had whipped the flames, spreading the fire to all parts of the city. In a short time, almost all of Moscow was in ashes. One account described the city as "an immense funeral pile, over which was spread a pall of thick and black smoke. The wooden edifices disappeared entirely. Those of stone and brick presented a still more gloomy aspect, with only portions of their walls standing, crumbling and blackened. The howling of the tempest, the roar of the flames, the crash of falling buildings, and the shrieks of the inhabitants, were all frequently overpowered by the explosions of the powder magazines in the arsenals of the Kremlin. To many people it seemed that the day of judgment had actually arrived, that the trump of the archangel was sounding, and that the final conflagration had arrived."

The fear of the inhabitants was unbounded, for on all sides were roaring flames, making escape almost impossible. By the thousands, the people rushed to the Moscow River, hoping to save themselves in the water. However, many of them, their clothes on fire, were burned to death before they could reach the river, and their blackened bodies littered the streets, together with the debris of the burned-out buildings. The toll in human life: seventeen hundred persons, not including children, whom the government did not include in the figures it subsequently issued.

The fire had started among the wooden churches near the suburbs and had quickly spread across Moscow to the Kremlin, which suffered irreparable damage. The Cathedral of the Assumption was partially destroyed and great damage was done to the Czar's Palace and the Cathedral of the Annunciation. The Arsenal Building was destroyed, as were the houses of the Metropolitan and the dwellings of many of the boyars living within the Kremlin. Irreplaceable sacred relics, frescoes, holy screens, and treasures of all kinds were lost.

Metropolitan Makary almost lost his life trying to save the invaluable icon of Our Lady from the Cathedral of the Assumption. Other members of the clergy found him in the Cathedral, his beard in flames, and led him towards one of the many secret passageways that led under the Kremlin walls to the Moscow River. At one point, he had to be lowered by a rope. The rope broke and the aged Metropolitan fell to a landing below. He lost consciousness and was carried to a nearby monastery.

Unlike the Metropolitan, Ivan tried no heroic acts of rescue. As soon as he arrived in Moscow from Ostrovka and saw the dangerous conflagration, he fled to a palace on the Sparrow Hills, where he remained in safety throughout the fire. Anastasia, Yuri, and other nobles joined him there.

During the night, the winds shifted, and by morning the fire had burned itself out. The extent of the disaster was incalculable: hundreds dead, thousands injured, most of the houses destroyed, the commercial area with its rich store of merchandise consumed. Lamentations for the dead filled the air. Cries of pain from injured still trapped beneath the debris mingled with the sobs of abandoned children. Many of those who were uninjured sat dumbly near their charred homes, dazed and bewildered. Others, half-mad with fear from the violent explosions that had emanated from the Kremlin arsenal, cowered among the ruins, incessantly crossing themselves and praying fervently. Looters roamed the streets, seizing anything of value that had not been consumed by the flames.

That morning Ivan visited Metropolitan Makary in the monastery. The old man had recovered consciousness, and was not as seriously injured as had at first been thought. In other monasteries near Moscow, the injured and the homeless were graciously received, their injuries were tended to, and they were given clothes and food.

During the next few days, the mood of the people changed from one of anguish and numbness to one of complaint and anger as the full import of the calamity grew upon them. With their homes destroyed, their personal possessions gone, their gardens scorched, the mass of the common people were destitute—and desperate. Rumors began to circulate that the fire was not an accident but had been caused by magic, that boyars from certain noble families had taken human hearts, soaked them in water, and with this water had sprinkled the houses and streets of Moscow, thus casting an evil spell over them. From this magic brew, the people believed, the fire had started.

This wild nonsense was accepted as truth not only because at such a desperate time a scapegoat was needed but also because it fitted in with the superstitious bent of the people. From the Czar to the humblest peasant, superstition played a vital part in the Russian's life. He believed in horoscopes, diviners, sorcery, magic, the miraculous virtues of certain herbs or certain formulae, bewitched swords, love philters, werewolves, ghosts, and vampires.

The origin of many of these superstitions went back to heathen days. But the Church, too, encouraged the continuation of innumerable superstitions by taking them seriously and convincing the people that it had powers against which magic and charms were useless.

By the fifth day after the fire had burned itself out, the frustration and anger of the people of Moscow reached a fever pitch. Ugly, vicious crowds roamed the streets and committed acts of violence and vandalism. Everywhere there was the spirit of the mob, which would not be quieted until blood had been shed, until stark death itself shamed them into becoming rational human beings again.

The Glinsky family became the scapegoat, especially Anna Glinsky, Ivan's grandmother on his mother's side, and her children. It was she, the mobs cried, who had formulated the magic of human hearts soaked in water. It was her children, they insisted, who had taken the magic water and had sprinkled it over the houses and streets of Moscow.

As a sop to the mobs, Ivan appointed the Shuiskys to investigate the charges. It is impossible to imagine a worse choice. The Shuiskys had lost their power to the Glinskys several years before, when Ivan had asserted his coming of age by literally throwing Andrei Shuisky to the dogs; ever since, they had been plotting to return to power and had succeeded in partially restoring their influence and in gaining readmission to the court. The Shuiskys made the most of their opportunity. From the day after the fire, they and their supporters had been circulating among the people, spreading and supporting the fiction that the Glinskys were the culprits. Now with Ivan's appointment of them as investigators, they became even more bold. Led by Prince Skopin-Shuisky, they gathered a huge crowd together in the square in front of the Cathedral of the Assumption.

"Who set fire to Moscow?" Prince Shuisky asked.

The response was immediate and unanimous. "The Glinskys!" the mob answered.

Attracted either by curiosity or by a desire to speak to the mob and clear his family's name, Yuri Glinsky, Ivan's uncle, and several of his servants and supporters were at the square. When he heard the threatening cry of the mob, he ran towards the Cathedral itself, for asylum. The mob pursued him. On the steps leading to the iconostasis, they caught him and killed him on the spot.

The mob, however, demanded more victims. They pursued Glinsky's servants and retainers, who had fled during the murder to Glinsky's house. There, the aroused mob killed them, wrecked the house, and took away valuable possessions.

From Glinsky's house, they fanned out over Moscow. Hundreds of disgruntled and vengeance-seeking persons joined them. Houses were broken into and their contents confiscated. Anarchy reigned.

Encouraged and inflamed by their murdering, bullying, and looting, which the authorities until now had made no effort to stop, the mobs again raised the cry: "Death to Anna Glinsky and her son Michael!"

Carrying whatever weapons they could get their hands on, as well as banners of the Church and pictures of the saints, and shouting and screaming the vengeance they would take upon Anna Glinsky and her son, they marched to the Czar's residence in Vorobyovo on the outskirts of Moscow. Arriving there, they demanded that Ivan himself hand over his grandmother and his uncle to them.

Anna Glinsky and her son Michael were in Rzhev at the time, and the mob was so told. But they refused to believe it, insisting that Ivan was harboring them.

Never one for heroic action in the face of personal danger, Ivan had barricaded himself in one of the palace's rooms. There, together with Anastasia and his closest advisers, he pondered on what course of action he should take.

Outside the palace, the mob was becoming more menacing. It was even possible that they might storm the palace, endangering the life of the royal family.

Encouraged by his advisers, Ivan made a decision. He ordered the royal guards to seize the mob's ringleaders and execute them where they were seized, as an example to the others. His order was immediately carried out. Frightened and bewildered by the sudden turn of events, the mob fled, leaving behind their guns, knives, stones, Church banners, and pictures of saints.

The mob's brief hour of power was over. But so was the power of the Glinskys, who never again regained a position of dominance in the government.

As for Ivan, he had learned at firsthand that by quickly and resolutely doing away with the leaders of the opposition, the followers would lose courage and direction. It was a lesson he would never forget.

V

First Years of the Czardom

THE calamitous fire and the threatening mobs had frightened Ivan, and at the same time had made him reflect on the ways of God and man. He brooded over the thought that the fire had seemed like the wrath of God's vengeance.

Years later he was to write of the fire, saying that "since human sin ever acerbates the Grace of God, it came to pass that—because of our sins and the intensification of God's wrath—a fiery flame burned the ruling city of Moscow, and our treacherous boyars . . . seized the moment which appeared favorable to their treacherous wickedness and incited the feeblest-witted of the people. . . ."

Ivan refused to believe that Moscow could go up in flames simply because it was a tinder box. The holocaust had indeed appeared like Armageddon. Phrenetically religious, he saw the hand of God everywhere, and sincerely believed that "because of our sins"— and he meant his own, too—God's wrath had become intensified and that He had sent "a fiery flame to burn the ruling city of Moscow."

Yet God's wrath did not free the boyars from guilt. Selfish monsters that they were, they had seized on the occasion for their own advantage. Ivan did not believe in the tale of hearts dipped in water and the magic of this water sprinkled over Moscow. But the supernatural element itself affected him, in spirit if not in detail, and helped to inflame his thoughts.

It was while Ivan was thus deeply troubled by a confusing and

35

disturbing mixture of doubts, fears, guilt, and anger that he came under the benign influence of an obscure monk, Sylvester by name, who had come from Novgorod to Moscow sometime between 1542 and 1547 and at the time of the Moscow fire was a minor priest in the Cathedral of the Annunciation.

Their first meeting took place at Vorobyovo immediately after the fire and while the mobs were terrorizing the city and demanding that the Czar turn Anna Glinsky and her son over to them for vengeance.

Sylvester probably gained access to Ivan through Metropolitan Makary, whom he knew not only in his present position but also from the days when Makary was Metropolitan of Novgorod. Sylvester was supposed to have approached Ivan while he was, as the classic account goes, "trembling in his palace at Vorobyovo, and while the virtuous Anastasia besought Heaven's aid with fervent prayer. With upraised hand, with threatening eye, he drew near to Ivan, like a man inspired by the divine afflatus, and declared to him, with an imposing gravity of demeanor: 'The thunder of God has come upon thee, O Czar, for thy idleness and evil passions. Fire from Heaven has consumed Moscow and the cup of God's wrath has been poured into the hearts of the people.'

"Finally, by the terrible effect of certain apparitions, he shook both the spirit and heart of the young prince, and having engrossed his imagination, produced a miracle. In a moment the Czar became another man; bathed in tears of repentance, he stretched forth his hand to his intrepid counselor, and begged for the power to become virtuous."

Though legend has colored this momentous first meeting so that it is difficult to know where truth begins and imagination leaves off, it is entirely possible that the basic facts were as described. Sylvester had a flair for the dramatic; he was a master of the poignant phrase, the thunderous delivery, the facial expressions that threatened and inspired at the same time, the pointed finger that transported one straight to heaven or hell.

And Ivan, on his part, was particularly susceptible at this time to a person like Sylvester. The momentous events of the past few months were enough to disturb the most mature of persons, let alone a boy of seventeen. Within the short span of a half year, he had been crowned Czar and had married, his capital had burned to the ground, and mobs had threatened not only the order of the state but his personal safety. He needed desperately the support of strong, reliable advisers. And these advisers could not come from the discredited boyars, who were politically bankrupt and whom Ivan despised and distrusted because of their miserable treatment of him during his boyhood.

Within the next few months, Sylvester became the leading adviser of the Czar, as well as his confessor. And in this short time, too, Sylvester and Alexei Adashev, an obscure retainer whom Ivan had become fond of and had elevated to the position of chamberlain, became the administrative heads of the government, with the power of ministers.

The elevation of Alexei Adashev to such power was in many respects more significant than Sylvester's rise to power. Sylvester was a priest of the Church, albeit a minor one, and carried with him the dignity, position, and power of that body. Adashev, on the other hand, did not come from the boyar class, which traditionally supplied leaders to the government, but from humble origins. Ivan thus threw tradition to the winds by reaching down among the common people, instead of into the boyar class, for a top official. It was the first of many times of uneasiness in which Ivan relied upon commoners.

Adashev was at one time an obscure clerk. In 1543, he was appointed a *postelnik,* or keeper of Ivan's bedchamber. His job, as it turned out, was not only to take care of Ivan's bed but to take care of his master's sexual needs by bringing virgins to Ivan's bedroom.

Adashev had a patient, gentle disposition, and as such had a calming influence on the temperamental Czar. He was liked by the common people, who came to know him well since he was most generous in distributing alms.

At the time of Adashev's appointment, Ivan wrote him a letter, in which, as Ivan later expressed it, he took him "out of the mire."

"Alexei, I have raised you up from among the ranks of the humble and the most insignificant of the people," Ivan wrote in his letter. "I had heard of your good deeds and have therefore chosen you above your degree, for the aid of my own soul. Though it was not your own wish, yet I have desired you, and not you alone, but others who are like you and think like you, who assuage my grief, and like you, are able to take care of the men who are entrusted to

me by God. I therefore enjoin upon you to receive petitions from
the poor and injured and to read them through with care. Have no
fear of the strong and famous, who worm their way into places of
honor and oppress and destroy the poor and weak by their superior powers. . . ."

Ivan's regeneration from his days of boyhood cruelty seemed
complete. The events since the fire all pointed to the fact that no
longer would the Czar indulge himself in the kind of vicious torture
he had inflicted on the deputation from Pskov, or in senseless brutalities like treading under his horse's hoofs innocent people in the
streets of Moscow. His home life was now stable and pleasant, with
the good Anastasia, whom he loved dearly, as his helpmate. His
government was now being run by earnest, trustworthy, and
kindly officials. His soul was now cleansed; his heart was with the
poor and the meek. His wrath was to be reserved only for evildoers, those people like the treacherous boyars who placed personal gain and the desire for power above the common good.

Excited with his conversion, Ivan wanted everyone to know
about it and to share in the glory of the light that had at last been
revealed to him. He wanted, in effect, to make a public confession.
For this purpose, he ordered that the nobles, the clergy, and the
common people be called together so that he could address them.
His order was carried out, and a large crowd assembled at the
famed grand place of execution at the Kremlin.

The young Czar first turned his attention to the Metropolitan.
"Holy Father, your zeal for virtue, your love for my country are
known to me, second my good intentions," Ivan said. "I lost my
parents too young; the boyars and the nobles, who only aspired to
domination, took no care of my person; they have usurped in my
name wealth and honors; they are enriched by injustice, and over-
whelm the people, so that no one dares to hinder their ambition.
I was, as it were, deaf and dumb; I heard not the lamentations of
the poor, and my words did not sweeten their woes."

Ivan then turned to the nobles. "You, you are delivered then to
your caprices, you rebellious subjects, you corrupted judges; how
can you now justify yourselves? What tears you have caused, what
blood you have shed, which falls upon me! But fear the judgment
of God!"

Then he addressed the common people. "Oh, you! a people that

the Almighty has confided to me, I invoke today your religion and
your love for me; show yourselves generous. It is impossible to repair the past evils, but I shall in the future wisely preserve you from
apprehension and pillage.

"Forget the sorrows that shall never be renewed, scatter every
subject of hatred and discord, let a Christian and brotherly ardor
embrace all your hearts. From this day forward, I, I will be your
judge, your defender."

The speech, as it turned out, was more than just a public confession of past sins and future plans. It revealed Ivan's knack for
popular appeal that, as time went on, was to become more obvious
and masterful. He, the Czar, would personally defend the people.
No matter how great were the abuses of the nobles, no matter how
difficult were the day-to-day conditions of their impoverished lives,
he was with them. Even more: together with God and through
God's mandate, he was their protector. In effect, he was their
Little Father, and he and they were inescapably bound together by
inseparable ties of love that God had ordained should exist between the ruler and the ruled.

The concept put him above and beyond the evil that might be
caused by their immediate masters, the nobles, or by actions of the
government. It left him blameless, even for those acts that emanated from his own royal decrees and actions. For these acts were
not inspired by the need to insure the proper functioning of government but were acts that the Little Father had to take in order to
teach, punish, and reward his children.

This was by no means all, however. Ivan was already develop-
ing the concept of the state as a political entity ruled in the final
analysis by one man—the Czar; a state in which the ruler was
above and beyond responsibility for the actions of that state. Evildoers could—and would—exist at all levels of government, and
this was natural because in government as elsewhere ordinary men
were motivated by greed and power. The Czar, however, was divinely inspired, or at least responsible only to God, and his function was to carry out the divine will.

It was a concept that in a crude form was easily understood and
welcomed by the mass of the people. For to them it meant that as
in heaven there was one ruler who, for better or worse, was their
master, so it was on earth. And both God and Czar were beyond

reproach, no matter what adversities were visited upon the people. To God and Czar they could give their love; to all others their curses and hatred.

And it meant, too, that Ivan could dispense with the support of the nobles and rely upon the allegiance and support of the mass to help him achieve the ultimate he wanted in autocratic states. He would have to share power with no one, nor have to endure interference in the compact, made by God's will, between the ruler and the ruled.

In order to achieve an autocratic state, which even in his first years of rulership Ivan was reaching towards, he could have refused to let various councils meet. However, even as a youth Ivan revealed himself to be a master political tactician. Instead of denying meetings to such bodies as the *Zabore* (the parliament), which would have needlessly flown in the face of tradition, he convoked them. The councils reflected no population groups or political points of view; they represented various administrative branches of the government. Their function was not to legislate, criticize, or propose, but to listen, to take orders, and so say *"da."* Thus, Ivan reaped the benefit of apparent representation which in reality was no representation at all.

In 1550, for instance, the Territorial Council did not propose or legislate the revision of the *Sudebnik,* or Code of Laws of Ivan III, which provided for certain judicial reforms; it merely discussed and approved the presentation of such reforms as Ivan and his advisers submitted to them.

In the thirteen years following the convocation of this council, more than a dozen other assemblies of various kinds were held. In all cases, the members were summoned at the will of Ivan, discussed and approved what was submitted to them, and then, when Ivan had finished with them, dispersed to the four corners of the empire.

The most vivid contemporary description of the rubberstamp Russian parliament as it existed in the sixteenth century was given by Giles Fletcher, an Englishman who lived in Russia during the latter part of that century. He wrote his eyewitness account of a session of the Zabore as it occurred during the regime of Feodor, Ivan's successor, but it applies equally to the time of Ivan. After describing the makeup of the Zabore, the opening ceremonies, and the seating arrangement, Fletcher wrote:

"One of the Secretaries [gives] the cause of their assembly, and the principal matters that they are to consider of. For to propound bills that every man thinks good for the public benefit (as the manner is in England) the Rus Parliament allows no such custom, nor liberty to subjects.

"The points being opened, the Patriarch with his Clergymen have the prerogative to be first asked their vote, or opinion, what they think of the points propounded by the Secretary. Whereto they answer in order, according to their degrees, but all in one form without any discourse: as having learned their lesson before, that serves their turns at all Parliaments alike, whatsoever is propounded. Commonly it is to this effect:

"That the Emperor and his Council are of great wisdom, and experience, touching the policies and public affairs of the Realm, and far better able to judge what is profitable for the commonwealth than they are, which attend upon the service of God only, and matters of religion. And therefore it may please them to proceed. That instead of their advice, they will aid them with their prayers, as their duties and vocations do require. . . ."

The fact that these assemblies were puppetlike and were maneuvered by the will of the Czar does not mean that no reforms were undertaken. Judicial reform resulted from the revision mentioned before of the Code of Laws of Ivan the Great. Over the next several years, there were other notable changes. In some places, local officials were elected to collect local taxes, and the former tax collectors—the governors—were abolished. In those places where the old system of tax collection by governors still prevailed, the people were given the right to elect assessors who could invalidate the governors' orders, and could even impeach the governors if necessary.

Certain measures to reorganize the military system were also undertaken. Heretofore, each district was also a distinct military unit. Ivan broke up these districts into units of hundreds, and appointed special officers over each of them. He formed a special infantry equipped with muskets, known as the *streltsy,* and various artillery groups.

In religious matters, the Council of the Hundred Chapters (so called because the Council wrote a hundred lengthy chapters on various outstanding religious matters of the time), in theory at least, instituted various ecclesiastical reforms. These involved measures against poor administration and excessive holdings of lands and property by the powerful monasteries. The monasteries were forced to return land ceded to them by boyars without Ivan's consent, as well as other lands acquired illegally by the Church, thus restoring to Ivan's personal fortune huge tracts of land that had been given to the Church during his boyhood. In the future, the Church was forbidden to accept patrimonial estates of the hereditary princes, and in general could not add land to their already widespread holdings without Ivan's consent.

These reforms undercut one of the Church's most formidable powers—its power through control of greater and greater land holdings. At the same time, they vastly increased the Czar's personal wealth.

VI

The Conqueror

AT THE age of twenty-two, Ivan looked every inch the imperial monarch. He was tall and thin, with broad shoulders and a well-developed chest. Like Ivan the Great, he was stooped, though not so badly. His face was somewhat hawklike, with its high forehead and beaked nose. His eyes were his most striking feature; they were close-set, intense, piercing. And it was said, as it was of his grandfather, that Ivan's very glance from his fiery eyes caused women to faint and men to turn away in embarrassment and confusion. His pointed auburn beard was thick and unkempt; his mustache was long, and, as was the custom at the time, his head shaven.

His usual expression was threatening and gloomy. On occasion, however, the fierceness disappeared from his eyes and instead they were thoughtful and dreamy, giving his face an absent-minded, faraway expression. His voice was high-pitched and strident; his laughter shrill and mirthless. It was said that no man ever really saw him look happy or laugh with genuine mirth. A sardonic smile that was often on his lips expressed his contempt for those about him.

His countenance was highly expressive, so that his moods were immediately discernible. His morbidity was profound and often of long duration. His rages were almost beyond belief. They came upon him suddenly with uncontrollable fury, and during them he would abuse and threaten everyone near him, from foreign ambassador to the meanest lackey. Sometimes his rages bordered on hysteria, depriving him of reason. At such times he would not only strike out at those near him with invective and foul language but would abuse them physically with his fists or whatever weapon was at hand.

He was high-strung, intense, volatile. He always seemed to be in a state of strain. Even when he was a young man, he did not have the appearance of a youth, for there was nothing about him that was frivolous, easygoing, devil-may-care. He seemed always to have been burdened, his very soul torn by conflicts.

An insatiable restlessness constantly drove him, tormented him, allowing him no peace or relaxation. He did not have the faculty for unburdening himself of troubles. His active, searching mind allowed him no respite from his disturbing thoughts.

Fortunately, Ivan had Anastasia. Her even-tempered, gentle, considerate, and understanding nature was balm. Undemanding and unambitious, Anastasia was indeed what Ivan himself in later life affectionately called her—his "little heifer." Ivan had enough restlessness, ambition, drive for twenty men, and did not need a wife who would prod, inspire, or goad him to carry out his imperial role. He wanted—and got—from Anastasia peace, quiet, rest. As time went on, his early attraction to her turned to love. And it was a deep love that restrained his violent nature, mellowed his fierce passions, and controlled the demon within him.

By 1552, Ivan had been Czar for five years, and, except for a couple of brief and minor excursions into the field of battle against the Kazan Tatars, he had been content to stay in the Kremlin and in nearby summer palaces close by the side of Anastasia. Through these years, he had busied himself with internal affairs of state, consolidating his power, curtailing some of the abuses of the Church and boyars, and reorganizing his army.

However, Ivan was troubled by the more or less inglorious course of his czardom; he had engaged in none of the glorious exploits about which he had dreamed ever since the days when he had read of conquering emperors in books of ancient history. Even the exploits of Ivan the Great and Vasili loomed large in comparison to his own.

In this year, however, the situation changed. The struggle against the Kazan Tatars was reaching a climax, and a whole-hearted military campaign against them was becoming a necessity. His opportunity of wearing the conqueror's mantle and glorifying himself in the world's eyes was at hand.

The struggle against the Kazan Tatars, as well as the Crimean Tatars, had a comparatively recent beginning. However, the origin of the whole Russian-Tatar conflict went back hundreds of years, to the thirteenth century, when, beginning with Genghis Khan, the Mongol hordes had established their empire over a large part of the earth. For more than two centuries, the Golden Horde ruled Russia. Then in the fifteenth century it began to crumble. By the time Ivan ascended the throne, the Golden Horde was merely a memory. Only in the east, around Kazan and Astrakhan, and in the south in the Crimea, did the Tatars still have power, blocking the growth and expansion of the restless Russian state. For years, Russian colonizers had been on the move, settling new lands, claiming new territory for Ivan the Great and Vasili, and now for Ivan. The Tatars who at one time exacted tribute from the Russians were now paying it. One such khan was Safa Gerei, the Khan of Kazan, who was of the Crimean Tatar dynasty and who had gained a foothold in Kazan. And, like him, the khans who followed him in rapid succession after his death in 1549 paid tribute to Russia.

But in time the khans became bold; they stopped paying tribute to Moscow. They even demanded that Moscow pay tribute to them, and if Moscow refused they would, as one of them expressed it in a message to the Kremlin, march on the Russian capital. "And I do not march in secret. . . . I shall take your lands, and if you follow me, you will not reach mine!"

Again there rose the specter of the shameful Tatar domination of the past. The Tatars, the Russians charged, were planning a Tatar empire that would extend from Kazan to the Caspian Sea. Actually, the Tatars were no real threat to the safety of Russia. They were disunited, weak, and no match for the Russians. They simply stood in the way of the march of Moscow towards empire, and they had to be destroyed.

Verbal threats from the khans were not new. Ever since 1539, there had been similar ones, and in some cases skirmishes had occurred between the Russians and the Tatars. In 1548 and 1549, Ivan himself had participated briefly in these battles, which on one occasion occurred at the very walls of Kazan. In each encounter the Russians had been defeated, partly because of treacherous weather that had destroyed their equipment, partly because of poor planning and poor battle tactics, and partly because, as Ivan charged in later years, of the perfidy of his generals.

Ivan was particularly incensed against Prince Kurbsky, who, he charged, had been "unwilling to fight with us against the barbarians" and had given "perfidious advice." He charged Kurbsky with being "unwilling to wait for long for a favorable opportunity," but, he said, "you spared your lives and had no thought for military victory. Only one thing did you have in mind—to return home as quickly as possible, either having won a quick victory or having been defeated. And likewise did you leave behind your excellent warriors in order to return quickly, so that as a result of this there was much spilling of Christian blood."

The Russian defeats at the hands of the Kazan Tatars was a national disgrace, and Ivan chafed at the shame of them. Moreover, the Khan now demanded tribute from Ivan, as though he were still one of the early Russian princes who at the time of Tatar supremacy was forced to stand in the dust in front of the haughty Khan of the Golden Horde astride his horse, or come begging to Sarai, the headquarters of the Horde, asking the Khan's permission to take up a prince's duties in his own land.

In a message to Ivan, the Khan had said, "You were young, but now you have reached the age of reason, state your wish—blood or love. If love, you will send gifts worthy of a prince and fifteen thousand gold pieces every year. When it may be your pleasure to fight, I am ready to advance on Moscow, and all your lands will be under the feet of my horses."

Ivan replied, as Ivan the Great had done in 1480 when he, too, defied the Tatars, by throwing the Khan's messengers into chains and by declaring that the Russians would undertake a holy war against the infidels. His expedition against them this time would be unlike previous expeditions in which the storms on the Volga had destroyed Ivan's ships and equipment and the miserable winter had disheartened his soldiers. He would plan his campaign carefully, employ the latest military equipment, even hire foreign engineers to breach with explosives the strong walls of Kazan. Furthermore, he would not make the mistake of a winter campaign; the expedition would take place in summer.

The previous expeditions, although failures, had achieved some profitable results—the capture of some Tatar land and the establishment of the town of Svyazhsk at the confluence of the Sviaga and Volga rivers, quite close to the city of Kazan. The town was destined to become the base from which the Russians would launch their attack.

The establishment during the winter of 1550–51 of the town of Svyazhsk, according to the German Heinrich Staden, who later served in the Oprichnina, was an amazing feat of construction under war conditions.

Staden wrote that Ivan "commanded that a city be erected with wooden walls, towers, and gates, like a real city, and that the beams and timbers be numbered, all of them, from top to bottom. Then the city was dismantled and the timber was placed on rafts and floated down the Volga, together with the soldiers and the heavy artillery. When he arrived near Kazan, he commanded that the city be erected and all [the fortifications] be filled with earth. He returned to Moscow, but the city was occupied by Russian men and artillery, and he called it Svyazhsk."

The Russians in the Kazan campaign in 1551 had frightened the Tatars sufficiently to make them sue for peace. It is doubtful that the Tatars sincerely made the offer; they were probably playing for time in order to enlist the aid of the Crimean Tatars and even the aid of the Sultan of Turkey. It is doubtful, too, that Ivan would have ever agreed to a peaceful settlement of differences. He had dreamed too long of wearing the conqueror's mantle, and that mantle would have to be distinguished by blood and death.

Yet both sides went through the motions. Ivan demanded, and the recently installed leader of Kazan, Shig Ali, agreed to deliver to the Russians the young Princess Suunbeka and her infant son Utemish, the nominal rulers of Kazan, as hostages to peace. That the Tatars should have been willing to send the Princess and her son to what appeared certain death was a sign either of their heartlessness or their great need to gain time. Only a little while before, Suunbeka's lover, the Crimean Tatar prince Koschak, and dozens of his followers had been executed at Ivan's orders when they had fled to him for sanctuary, having been accused by the Kazantsi of plotting the death of Utemish, seizing control of Kazan, and turning the city over to the Russians.

The story of the departure of Suunbeka and Utemish from Kazan to almost certain death at the hands of the Czar has over the years taken on a folk-tale quality, and what actually happened at the time is lost in myth. As the legend goes, almost all the people of Kazan turned out to see their beloved princess and her infant son on the day of their leaving. The air was filled with loud lamentation, and tears flowed freely. After visiting the grave of her dead husband, Sapha, where she threw herself upon his grave, the slender, beautiful Suunbeka was escorted to a richly decorated barque. Then, as thousands of Kazantsi watched sadly from the walls of their city, the barque was rowed slowly down the river by picked Tatar oarsmen. Downriver, Suunbeka, her son, and several Tatar attendants were transferred to a Russian boat, which took them on the Volga River to the Oka River, then to the Moscow River, and finally to Moscow.

Contrary to expectations, Ivan greeted the lovely Suunbeka warmly, set her and her son up in a style befitting her regal position, and persuaded her to become a Christian.

Shortly thereafter, the treacherous Shig Ali himself, who was little more than a puppet of the Russians, was ordered to come to Moscow. He agreed. He, too, was treated well, amused himself by making love to Suunbeka, and finally married her.

Through all this confusion, Ivan's envoys, the military leader Mikulinsky and Adashev, were negotiating with the Kazantsi, and for a brief time Mikulinsky was installed as the governor of Kazan. However, it was in name only, for he spent most of his time in Svyazhsk, where it was safer, since only a handful of Russian soldiers were allowed to enter Kazan.

The Kazantsi sacrifice of their princess won them the time they needed to rouse their allies. From the south the Crimean Tatars, under the leadership of their khan, Devlet-Girai, marched toward Moscow. Taking heart from this move, the Tatars drove the Russian governor and the handful of Russian soldiers out of Kazan, and a new khan, Ediger, from the Nogai Tatars, was installed as their leader.

The Crimean Tatars, supported by Turkish janissaries, appeared to be strong. Their numbers were quite large, they had cannon, and even several hundred camels, which were probably more impressive than useful. At the city of Tula, the two armies clashed. The Tatars were routed, and they fled, leaving behind huge stores of military equipment—and their camels.

It was Ivan's first military victory, and he was overjoyed. He counted much of the equipment himself, and sent excited, glowing letters of the victory to Anastasia. The camels were indeed a novelty—he had never seen one before—and he even tried to ride one. However, at his command the camel would not kneel to His Royal Highness. In anger, Ivan killed it.

Now that the Crimean Tatars were disposed of—temporarily at least—Ivan gave orders that preparations be made for the capture of Kazan. The delays had demoralized the troops, who had been languishing at Svyazhsk for months. The previous winter, scurvy had afflicted the troops and hundreds of soldiers had died from its effects. A wave of sexual debauchery had swept through the ranks, causing the Metropolitan at the time to issue a stern letter of rebuke.

"By the grace of God," the letter said, "through the wisdom of our Czar and the valor of our arms, we have been able to establish the stronghold of the Church in a hostile land. The lord has delivered Kazan into our hands. [Kazan was only nominally in Russian hands at the time.] We flourish and become famous. Germany, Lithuania, seek our friendship. In what way can we express our gratitude to the Most High, but in the keeping of His commandments? But do you keep them? The popular rumor has alarmed the sovereign's heart and my own. It is said that some of you, forgetting the wrath of God, are sunk in the sins of Sodom and Gomorrah, that many decent-looking virgins and women, released from Kazan, defile themselves with debauch among you, and that men, to please them, put a razor to their beards and in shameful effeminacy pretend not to be males. But God will punish you not only in disease but in shame. Where is your glory? Once a terror to the enemy, now you serve him as a scoff. Strong men weaken from vice and weapons are blunt when virtue has gone from the heart. It has led to villainy; there has been betrayal. . . . God, Ivan, and the Church call you to repentance. Amend your conduct or you will know the anger of the Czar and you will hear the curse of the Church."

After reading the letter to the soldiers, the Metropolitan's emissary, a priest by the name of Timothy, went among them with holy water to wash their sins away.

While military preparations were being made, Ivan arranged domestic affairs in Moscow preparatory to his leaving for Kazan. Yuri was designated head of the government in Ivan's absence. The Metropolitan was appointed his counselor.

Leaving the pregnant Anastasia, who had already given him two daughters, was a grievous necessity to Ivan. For five years he had waited for her to give him a son. He fretted at the possibility of his not being with her at the time of her delivery. As a gracious parting gesture, he turned over to Anastasia the keys to the prisons, telling her that she could use her discretion in releasing inmates. Although this appeared to be a gesture to her desire to do kind deeds, it actually was in keeping with a time-honored custom. At the birth of a royal heir, many prisoners were released. Ivan was making sure that if he himself were still at the front at the time of birth, Anastasia would be in a position to give orders for the prisoners' release.

By June, 1552, everything seemed to be ready for the advance on Kazan. The Czar himself would lead his troops into battle. Before leaving Moscow, Ivan and Anastasia went to church, where Anastasia kneeled and prayed for the health and safety of her husband and the victory of the Christian Russians over the infidel Tatars. In full sight of Ivan's comrades-in-arms, Anastasia kissed him. Then she accompanied him out the church door. Ivan mounted his horse, and together with his guard rode away to join his army at Svyazhsk.

The Russian army that had converged on Svyazhsk, some by foot and others by boat, waited for the arrival of the Czar before going into battle. It was a motley crew. The bulk of the army consisted of conscripts, men who were called up during wartime. Each town was required to furnish a specified number of such conscripts from the nonmilitary section of the population. As soldiers, these conscripts left much to be desired. They were untrained, undisciplined, and unwilling. Their greatest virtue was their stamina. They could—and did—exist on little more than a bit of flour mixed with boiling water. They slept on the ground, with nothing more than their own cloaks for protection even in the coldest winter weather.

Completely untrained for battle, they made poor offensive soldiers. Their only battle tactics—or so it seemed—consisted of rushing at the enemy en masse with loud yells and thunderous beating of drums and cymbals, and overwhelming their adversaries with the sheer force of numbers. In a siege, however, they were superb, being able to withstand the greatest privations, the fiercest cold, and the most excruciating hunger.

With the exception of the conscripts, all were on horseback. The horseman had a sword, bow and arrows, a drum—and a good pair of lungs. How important the ferocious noises and loud beating of drums were in the battles of the day was described by Giles Fletcher.

"The *Bulsha Dworaney,* or chief horseman, has a small drum of brass at his saddlebow, which he strikes when he gives the charge, or onset.

"They have drums besides of a huge bigness, which they carry with them upon a board laid on four horses, that are sparred together with chains, every drum having eight strikers or drummers, besides trumpets and shawms, which they sound after a wild manner, much different than ours. When they give any charge, or make any invasion they make a great hallow or shout altogether, as loud as they can, which with the sound of their trumpets, shawms, and drums, makes a confused and horrible noise. So they set on first discharging their arrows, then dealing with their swords, which they use in a bravery to shake, and brandish over their heads, before they come to strokes."

In addition to the newly formed *streltsy,* or musketeers, there was the warrior boyar group. The boyar officers were as resplendent as the conscripts were miserable-looking.

The high officers, Fletcher wrote, "will have their horse very richly furnished, their saddles of cloth of gold, their bridles fair bossed and tasseled with gold and silk fringe, bestudded with pearls and precious stones, themselves in very fair armor, which they call *Bullatnoy,* made of fair shining steel, yet covered commonly with cloth of gold, and edged round with ermine fur, his steel helmet on his head of a very great price, his sword, bow and arrows at his side, his spear in his hand, with another fair helmet, and his *Shestapera,* or horseman's sceptre, carried before him."

None of the soldiers or officers, except the *streltsy,* had firearms.

However, the army did have the best artillery and the most skilled artillerymen in Europe at the time. From the days of Ivan the Great, emphasis had been placed on the development and use of all kinds of this type of ordnance, and, according to the chronicles, a hundred and fifty artillery pieces—a great number for those days—were used at the battle for Kazan.

In the impending battle for Kazan, the untrained soldiers of the Czar believed they had something to fight for, and this compensated in part for their lack of skill. The Tatars were Mohammedans, and the soldiers were told—and believed—that they were fighting a battle not only for their country but for their religion. Moreover, the hatred for the Tatar was revived, and they were taking revenge for the infamy of centuries of vassalage to the khans.

But it was not necessary to go back to the time of the ascendancy of the Golden Horde to find grievances against the Tatars. There were sufficient at hand. The free lands in Siberia, to which more and more peasants were making their way, were under constant predatory raids by the Tatars. Thousands of Russian men and women from these lands and especially in the southeast of Russia, where the Nogai Tatars were powerful, were yearly taken into slavery, their crops burned, and their homes destroyed.

The khans became wealthy from the slave trade. In Kazan, fifty thousand Russians were slaves. In other Tatar khanates, additional Russians by the tens of thousands were slaves. The demand by the Turks for slaves was particularly heavy, and the prize slaves were the tall, blond, husky Russian men and the plump, blond Russian women. At times, the entire population of a town was captured, put into chains, shipped to Kaffa, the center of the slave traffic at the time. Then in the market place they were put up for sale, with their neck chains still about them.

Baron Heberstein, an excellent observer, wrote that he had heard that as many as eight hundred thousand slaves were carried off by the Tatars over a period of only a few years.

"Most of them were sold to the Turks at Kaffa; those whom they could not sell they beat to death," Heberstein wrote. "For the old and sick, for whom not much was paid, and who are no good for work, are given by the Tatars to their young men, just as they give hares to young hounds, to make them savage; they stone them to death, throw them into the sea or over a precipice, or do whatever they like with them."

Another account, this one by a Lithuanian, Michalonis Litvani, went into even greater detail about the slave trade as he observed it.

"Ships from Asia bring arms, clothes, and horses to the Crimean Tatars, and start on the homeward voyage laden with slaves. It is for this kind of merchandise alone that the Crimean markets are remarkable. . . . The stronger of these captives, branded on the forehead and the cheeks and manacled or fettered, are tortured by severe labor all day, and are shut up in dark cells at night. They are kept alive by small quantities of food, composed chiefly of the flesh of animals that have died—putrid, covered with maggots, disgusting even to dogs. Women, who are more tender, are treated in a different fashion; some of them who can sing and play are employed to amuse the guests at festivals.

"When the slaves are led out for sale they walk to the market place in single file, like storks on the wing, in whole dozens, chained together by the neck, and are there sold by auction. The auctioneer shouts loudly that they are 'the newest arrivals, simple, and not cunning, lately captured.' . . .

"This kind of merchandise is appraised with great accuracy in the Crimea, and is bought by foreign merchants at a high price, in order to be sold at a still higher rate to blacker nations, such as Saracens, Persians, Indians, Arabs, Syrians, and Assyrians.

"When a purchase is made the teeth are examined, to see that they are neither few nor discolored. At the same time the more hidden parts of the body are carefully inspected, and if a mole, excrescence, wound, or other latent defect is discovered, the bargain is rescinded. But notwithstanding these investigations the cunning slave dealers and brokers succeed in cheating the buyers; for when they have valuable boys and girls, they do not at once produce them, but first fatten them, clothe them in silk, and put powder and rouge on their cheeks, so as to sell them at a better price. Sometimes beautiful and perfect maidens of our nations bring their weight in gold. This takes place in all the towns of the peninsula, but especially in Kaffa."

Russian girls, especially the blond, fair-skinned ones, were extremely desirable for the harems of the East, and they were the most valuable slaves on the market. The story is told that the Sultan of Constantinople asked his eldest son and heir, "My son, will you conquer Crete for me?" His son replied, "What have I to do with Crete? I will conquer the land of the white Russian girls."

This slave trade between Tatar and Turk, it might be noticed, continued until the nineteenth century, and it was no uncommon sight to see the Tatars from Crimea carrying baskets with them on their horses, to be used in kidnapping Russian children, particularly girls.

In the summer of 1552, Ivan and his troops advanced upon Kazan. Like Moscow, Kazan had its kremlin, or fortress, which was large enough to hold the entire population of the city. It would have to be besieged, its walls breached, and its inhabitants overcome. The task was not an easy one. Yet, considering the size of Ivan's army, its artillery, its resources of men and material, Kazan's chances of ultimate victory were small indeed.

The Russian army consisted of from fifty to a hundred thousand men (the Russian chroniclers gave the exaggerated figure of a hundred and fifty thousand). Its equipment was made up, among other things, of a large number of cannon, the *gouli gorod,* or city that walks—an immense portable protective wooden shield with holes through which the *streltsy* could fire their muskets—and a most valuable asset in a Danish engineer who was an expert in the use of explosives. Its leading generals were Andrei Kurbsky and Vorotinsky. Ivan's military role, it turned out, was a passive one.

The Kazan forces numbered thirty thousand. Their main strength was the high, strong walls of their fortress city and the determination of the soldiers and population to defend their city and their faith.

Even while the troops were mobilizing for the attack, the Russians asked the Kazantsi to surrender. Ediger defied the Russian demand, saying bitterly, "All is ready for you here; we invite you to the feast."

The siege now began in earnest. Siege towers were moved up close to the very walls of Kazan. Cannons were placed in position. Ammunition was distributed to the *streltsy.* Bows and arrows were made ready. Swords were sharpened.

Tradesmen who had flocked to Svyazhsk by the hundreds, setting up stalls that made the town resemble a country fair, now moved up with the besiegers, too. Long-bearded priests in their long, black cassocks carried crosses high in the air and blessed the soldiers. Candles were burned in honor of various patron saints. The Russian camp was huge, bustling, noisy.

There was no element of surprise involved in the Russian siege. The Tatars knew every move of the Russians; the Russians made no effort to conceal their plans for an attack.

On the morning of the general advance, the city of Kazan was—to outward appearances—strangely inactive. The Kazantsi made no move to block the advancing Russians or to fire upon them. There was such a forbidding stillness about the Tatar city that the advancing Russian soldiers shivered with fear at the ominous silence. The Russians advanced into the outskirts of Kazan. There was still no opposition. They advanced almost to the walls of the kremlin. They had still not come across a single Tatar defender or inhabitant.

Then suddenly the ominous silence was shattered. The gates of the kremlin opened, and fifteen thousand screaming Kazantsi warriors, some on foot and others on horses but all of them brandishing swords and scimitars, swarmed out of the fortress. For a brief moment, the Russian lines froze; the sight of the ferocious sword-swinging Tatar horde paralyzed them. Then the Russians panicked. They dropped their bows and arrows and fled. The *streltsy,* after making a timid show of resistance by firing a few shots, threw away their weapons and ran for their lives. On the battlements of the fortress, thousands of other Kazantsi soldiers fired arrows into the disorganized Russian ranks.

Then as suddenly as the Russians had panicked, they recovered. The shock of the Tatar onslaught lost its first power. Officers rounded up and regrouped their men. The Russians stood their ground. The Kazantsi, unwilling to engage the Russians away from their protective walls, slowly retreated to their kremlin. The massive iron gates were closed. The battle was over.

The Russians had lost many men, but so had the Tatars. Prisoners had been taken by both sides. Psychologically, the Tatars had won the battle. Militarily, it had been a stalemate.

The following day, however, the Russians were attacked by a phenomenon they could not fight. A fearful storm broke. Wind and rain with the fury of a hurricane lashed at the Russian encampment. Tents were blown away. Warehouses with their precious supplies were leveled. Ammunition was destroyed. Food stocks were washed into the river. On the river itself, the Russian flotilla was dispersed, and most of the boats lost. Hundreds of Russian soldiers were drowned.

When the storm finally ended, the Russians tried to count their losses; they were incalculable. At this moment had the Kazantsi attacked, the Russians would have been overcome. They were virtually helpless. But the Kazantsi, because they were unaware of the extent of the Russian losses or because they had stubbornly based their plans on a defense behind their walls, did not attack.

It was an event that could have proved disastrous to the morale of the soldiers, and for that matter to the course of the entire campaign. However, Ivan was to prove on this occasion—as he was to prove on other occasions in the future when faced with an adverse situation—that he had the fanatic stubbornness, single-mindedness of purpose, and organizational genius of which great leaders are made. He immediately ordered the army contractors and merchants to resupply the army with the greatest possible speed. Significantly, he specifically commanded them to set in a supply of winter clothing. He gathered together his staff and laid plans for a new type of attack on the walls of Kazan, a plan in which the Danish engineer and his skill with explosives would be the main feature.

To improve the morale of the soldiers, he had a wonder-working cross sent to him from Moscow, which he told the soldiers—and himself—would bring God's blessing for the success of their crusade to replace the Mohammedan crescent with the Christian cross on the mosques within the city of Kazan.

Throughout the next weeks, while their army was being resupplied, the Russians made minor attacks on the city, utilizing whatever equipment they could salvage from the storm's wreckage. Siege towers were erected, and were put into action. Balls from their cannons battered away at the mud-and-timber walls of the kremlin, which withstood the artillery attacks better than stone walls.

Once in a while the Kazantsi sent out parties to probe the Russian lines, and minor skirmishes resulted with prisoners taken by both sides. When the Russians captured prisoners, they were tied to stakes facing the walls of the fortress, and were instructed to shout to their countrymen to surrender. A shower of arrows answered their cries. The Kazantsi preferred to have their countrymen die quickly by their own clean Moslem hands than by slow torture at the hands of the unclean Christians.

Again and again Ivan asked the Kazantsi to surrender, promising to spare their lives if they did so. Ostensibly he made the offer to stop the needless shedding of blood; actually the offer was made to gain time.

Though faced with overwhelming Russian forces, the Kazantsi believed they could successfully defend themselves. Many times in the past the Russians had been at their walls, and they had been driven away by Tatar arrows. Moreover, they were told by their leaders—and they believed them—that in spite of Ivan's promises they would be massacred by the Russians if they surrendered, and that it was better to die gloriously as warriors than to die miserably as slaves.

The Kazantsi were defiant. From the top of their battlements, they spat and cursed at the infidel Russians and the White Czar. They poured boiling water on groups of Russians whom Ivan, in an attempt to shake the Kazantsi, had sent up to their very walls to chant incessantly, "Surrender! Surrender!" They held weird rites to terrify the ignorant, superstitious Russian soldiers. Tatar women lifted up their garments, and presenting their buttocks, jeeringly yelled, "Look, White Czar, this is how you will take Kazan!"

The Russians continually probed for sections along the fortress wall that could be shattered by explosives. Several times huge holes were made in the wall, and on one occasion a break was made large enough for a Russian party to enter the fortress. But the party was beaten back. Repeated failures, though, were giving the Russians experience. The undermining of sections of the wall continued, and the effects of the explosives became more and more pronounced.

In addition, a huge forty-foot-high platform loaded with artillery was moved to a position in front of the wall. Ten large cannon and dozens of small ones poured shot into the city. Musketeers behind protective wooden shields sniped at the inhabitants. The confusion and fear caused was greater than the loss of life. The shells were not particularly effective and the marksmanship of the musketeers was not nearly so accurate as that of archers.

Nevertheless, the Kazantsi kept to their homes, the more timid of them burrowing into holes in the ground.

Towards the end of September, the tempo of Russian activity increased. Raiding parties entered the city through small breaches in the fortress walls. Once inside the city, they looted, burned, killed as many Tatars as they could take by surprise, and then quickly retreated to their own lines. The explosions became more frequent and more effective, and on the last day of September a huge breach was made in the wall. On this occasion, the Tatars swarmed out of their fortress, battled the Russians on their own ground, and then, after a particularly bloody battle, retreated back to their citadel.

The invasion the Russians had so long planned was only days away. Everything possible was done to prepare for it. The chill of the early October days and especially the nights was already giving the Russians a foretaste of the bitter winter that lay ahead. Ivan, the generals, the common soldiers realized that the decisive moment had come.

Early on the morning of October 2, while the Russian camp bustled with last minute preparations, Ivan withdrew to his tent, to pray for divine guidance. Time passed, and he did not come out. The generals became restive, and sent messengers to inquire when the Czar would leave his tent and lead the final assault against the infidels. Ivan ignored the messengers, and continued to pray before the image of St. Sergius, his patron. The leading general, Vorotinsky, decided to wait no longer. He gave the order to set off the greatest accumulation of explosives ever assembled under the walls. There was a frightening explosion. The walls crumbled; Russian soldiers waited for the signal to swarm through the breach.

A messenger was again sent to the Czar, urgently requesting his presence at the front. The messenger was stopped at the entrance of the tent. Ivan could not be disturbed. Even as the explosion had gone off, Ivan had been paying rapt attention to the priest chanting, "There shall be one fold and one Shepherd." At the sound of the frightful explosion, the priest had stopped. Ivan ordered him to continue the service.

The command was given to breach the walls, and outside Ivan's tent cries of "God be with us! God be with us!" resounded through the crisp autumn air as the soldiers ran toward the citadel. Again a messenger was sent to the Czar, who rushed in shouting, "Come, O Ivan! Your troops wait for you! Come at once, O Ivan! to sustain the hearts of your servants!"

But Ivan, kneeling before the icon of St. Sergius, continued his long-drawn-out devotions. It was only later, when the banners of the victorious Russians were already flying over the ramparts of the fortress, that Ivan bestirred himself: he pressed his lips in reverent devotion to the picture of St. Sergius, had holy water sprinkled over him, asked the attending priest to bless him now that he was "going forth to suffer for the true faith," mounted his horse, and dashed to the already doomed city.

By the time Ivan reached the fortress, the leading columns of the Russian forces were within. The Kazantsi put up a furious fight, but they were hopelessly outnumbered. The carnage was frightful. All Kazantsi soldiers and male inhabitants were marked for death. Only women and children were spared, to be sold into slavery. The Russians went from street to street and from house to house flushing out the defenders.

The battle—and the campaign—was over. From the highest tower in Kazan, the double-headed imperial eagle of Russia now rippled in the breeze. And in the streets and houses and shops, the soldiers, with Ivan's permission, looted and raped at will.

Ivan ordered a *Te Deum* to be sung. With his own hands, he planted a large cross on the very spot the standard of the Khan of Kazan had waved during the battle, and commanded that a Christian church be erected there to celebrate the "triumph of the Cross over Islam." With banners and icons held aloft by his victorious troops, he then led a triumphal procession around the walls of the conquered city, consecrating it to the name of Christ.

Ivan the Czar was now Ivan the Conqueror.

VII

Glory and Power

As the conqueror of Kazan, Ivan's fame spread throughout Russia and his prestige and power soared to unassailable heights. In song and verse and story, his glorious victory was celebrated throughout the land. The most miserable, obscure peasant felt a sense of participation in his Christian Czar's victory over Islam. Everywhere, pride in being a Russian was manifest, for the conquest of the Tatar khanate was considered a national achievement. The sleeping bear had at last awakened and with a ferocious shake of its ponderous body had risen to its full gigantic stature. Adulation of the Czar was boundless, for it was Ivan, their Little Father, their most magnificent leader, who had performed the miracle.

At the age of twenty-two, Ivan became, in effect, an epic hero.

For a week or so after the momentous victory, Ivan stayed in Kazan. He was in the best of spirits, enjoying to the fullest his new role as conqueror. For one of the few times in his life, he was buoyant and gay. He went among the common soldiers, clapped them affectionately on their shoulders and proudly called them his Macedonians and worthy successors of Dmitri Donskoi.

Ivan's generals made him feel that he, too, was comparable to the great Alexander and to the national hero Dmitri Donskoi. Vorotinsky told him that it was "through your valor and good fortune that victory has been achieved and Kazan is ours." Vorotinsky said this even though Ivan had not led his troops into battle. But this was not unusual for Russian rulers. Ever since the thirteenth cen-

60

tury, when the tradition of prince as warrior was beginning to come to an end, few of them had ever done so. Even Dmitri Donskoi, the first Russian ruler to take a stand against the Tatars and defeat them, at the battle of Kulikovo in 1380, had run away two years later when Tamerlane had ordered Tokhtamysh, a descendant of Genghis Khan, to march upon Moscow. Only after the people of Moscow themselves had fought the invaders, and winter had caused the Tatars to withdraw, did Dmitri return to the Kremlin.

It was enough for the generals and the soldiers to know that their Czar was with them, inspiring them with his noble presence.

Mellowed by his great moment of triumph and glory, Ivan embraced the Tatar leader, Ediger, and, after forcing him to repent in public, promised him his life, and even had him converted to Christianity. Expressing the sentiment that "even though the Tatars are not Christians, yet they are men," he ordered his priests to circulate among the survivors to convince them that they should become Christians in order to be better men. Many accepted the priests' advice, and were baptized.

Ivan, after inspecting the fallen bastion of Islam, insisted that its mosques be destroyed and Christian churches be built in their stead. Then in a magnanimous—and practical—move, he pardoned all Tatars, and invited them to return from the forests, where many of them had fled, and to take up the regular course of their lives again within Kazan. He appointed a governor and various officials to administer the new addition to the Rus empire, and assigned five thousand soldiers to garrison the city.

At the end of the week, Ivan called his generals and advisers together and informed them that he was returning to Moscow, to be by the side of Anastasia, who was momentarily expecting the birth of his child. The boyars pleaded with him to remain in Kazan. They pointed out that the situation was far from settled, that thousands of Kazantsi and neighboring Tatars were still in a state of rebellion, and that his presence in Kazan was necessary at least through the winter in order to consolidate the victory and so prevent future trouble.

Ivan was adamant. He insisted that he wanted to be with Anastasia, and made preparations to leave Kazan. Ivan was anxious to return to Moscow for other reasons, too: he had had enough of rough soldiers, miserable Tatars, and the stink of death, and was impatient to receive the adulation he felt sure awaited him from the mass of the Russian people for their conquering hero.

He was not disappointed. News of the great victory had preceded him, and his journey from Kazan to Moscow was a continuous march of triumph. Cheering, sobbing, praying men and women gave him a hero's welcome at every hamlet, town, and city he passed through. In Nizhny Novgorod, for instance, the entire city turned out to do him homage, and as he alighted from the boat in which he was being rowed down the Volga, the people fell to their knees and bowed their heads in reverent tribute. Then, as the story is told, "they burst into tears of joy, so great was their delight at the overthrow of Kazan."

From Nizhny Novgorod, Ivan proceeded on horseback toward Moscow. Near the city of Vladimir, he was met by an emissary from Moscow, a boyar named Trakhanyot, who breathlessly informed him that Anastasia had given birth to a boy. Ecstatic with happiness, Ivan leaped from his horse, embraced the messenger, and whooped with delight. Impulsively, he took off his royal cloak and gave it and his horse to Trakhanyot as presents.

Though excited and pleased by the good news, Ivan did not immediately hurry to Anastasia. Master as he was of the dramatic, he wanted to keep the people of Moscow tense and eager, so that he would have the full advantage of suspense in his homecoming. Furthermore, he wished to pay his proper respects to his patron St. Sergius and to pray to God for the health and welfare of his heir.

Thus, he tarried for a long time in Vladimir, making repeated visits to the cathedral, and spending long hours in prayer. In Suzdal, he did the same, while his entourage waited impatiently for him to continue the journey. At the Trinity Monastery, before the tomb of St. Sergius, he offered thanksgiving and prayer. Then, unhurriedly, he held long conversations with the priests, especially the former Metropolitan Joseph and Maxim the Greek, the remarkable scholar who had been banished from Moscow many years before and now, as one Church chronicler wrote, "lingered on in confinement to a cheerless old age." Congratulations on his victory and safe return were given to him by his brother Yuri and other boyars who had hastened to the Monastery, and who were to accompany him on his triumphal march into Moscow.

The following morning Ivan set off for Moscow. The entire city was wild with pent-up excitement and expectation at seeing their Czar, their hero, and the father of the newborn heir. Huge crowds in holiday mood swarmed into the streets, and fought like people possessed to kiss Ivan's hand or foot or even to get a glimpse of him. The hero's reception was even more overwhelming than Ivan had imagined it would be. A delirium of joy seemed to have seized the people.

The official welcome for Ivan was held by the Church, attended by the Metropolitan, the bishops, and all the priests of Moscow. They had brought with them their holy images and were lined up under their sacred banners. Ivan made a speech in which he recounted his victory, attributing it to the prayers of the prelate himself. With a display of humbleness, he prostrated himself in front of the procession. Metropolitan Makary complimented Ivan on his safe return, and thanked him in the name of all Russia for the victory. Then Makary and all the priests fell to their knees and bowed their heads into the dust in homage to the Czar.

Ivan removed his armor and put on the royal robes. The crown of Monomachus was brought to him, and he placed it upon his head. Then the monks held aloft the holy images and crosses, and the procession, with slow, solemn steps, walked toward the Cathedral of the Assumption, where Mass was held.

At long last Ivan was free to visit Anastasia in the Palace of Facets, and to see for the first time his infant son, whom he had already decided to call Dmitri, possibly after Dmitri Donskoi. Several weeks later Ivan and Anastasia made a pilgrimage to the Trinity Monastery to give thanks for the birth of their son and to have him baptized.

Anastasia, fate, and God had been good to him. At the age of twenty-two, he had attained glory and power. Ivan's cup was full.

VIII

Ivan the Good

THE thirteen years from Ivan's ascendancy to czardom in 1547, to 1560 might be called Ivan's good period. It was not that the stern, moody Czar was so good but that he was good in comparison to the cruel, bloodthirsty, tyrannical, maddeningly complex man and monarch he became after 1560, and as a consequence of which he has been labelled by history Ivan the Terrible.

Yet during this later period he was not terrible, or dread, as the Russian epithet *grozny* is more accurately translated. Had it been his fate to die before 1560 he would have been characterized as a typical stern autocrat of the time, no more—and in some respects less—terrible than his counterparts in other parts of Europe and Asia. And it is to these other rulers of his time—and within the events of the time—that he must be compared. For this was the century of Henry VIII of England, Catherine de Medici, and Philip II of Spain, and of the Inquisition and the Massacre of St. Bartholomew. And it was more than a century before the Salem witch burnings in the American colonies.

Throughout the relatively benign 1550's in Russia, Ivan was not troublefree. Political difficulties and personal tragedies constantly plagued him, slowly hardening his already stern character and embittering his already mirthless personality.

The conquest of Kazan did not, as Ivan's advisers had feared, mark the end of Tatar resistance. Almost from the moment of Ivan's departure from the fallen city, defiance and even armed rebellion broke out not only among the remnants of the Kazantsi army but among Mongol tribes who had formely paid tribute to the Khan of Kazan and now refused to pay tribute to the White Czar of Moscow.

The Russian garrison in Kazan, having had the tacit permission of the Czar immediately after the fall of the city to loot and rape, continued to act as unbridled conquerors instead of pacifiers. The authorities that Ivan had installed in Kazan were somewhat less than honest, capable administrators and caused more friction than they healed. Finally, the very spirit of the Tatars was such that they could not readily submit to the Russian yoke. They were fierce, proud warriors whose traditions were extremely meaningful to them and whose history, they felt, was more glorious than the history of the abject Russians who had groveled at the feet of their ancestors for two hundred and fifty years.

Stern, cruel measures were applied to counteract the Tatar rebelliousness. At Christmastide, scarcely more than two months after the fall of the city, scores of Kazantsi accused of rebellious activities were hanged on gibbets in the heart of the city as a lesson to the rest of the people. The people were not affected. Collecting whatever arms they could, they openly defied the Russians, and in one encounter killed almost a thousand musketeers and Cossack members of the garrison in a battle near the city. Brazenly the Tatars built a fortress less than fifty miles from Kazan and threatened to recapture their city and take revenge for their dead fellow-countrymen and their wives and daughters that the Russians had sold into slavery. Ivan sent his generals, Kurbsky, Mikulinsky, and Sheremetiev, to put down the rebellious Tatars. In twenty different battles, more than ten thousand Tatars were killed, thousands were taken prisoners, and huge amounts of booty were delivered up to Ivan at the Kremlin.

In the long run, the resistance of the Tatars came to naught. They were too weak; Russia too strong. Their day in the sun had passed, and they were in the twilight of their once great power. Eventually they were pacified, and huge numbers of them were assimilated into the Russian groups, so that before another century had passed it was estimated that seventeen per cent of upper class people of Moscow, for instance, had Tatar or Eastern blood in them.

Still, the several years that elapsed after the capture of Kazan were trying ones for the Czar. Even the capture of Astrakhan in 1556, the last important stronghold of the Tatars on the Volga River, and the annexation of the entire Volga region by this blow and others, such as the pacification of the migratory Nogai Tatars, did not lessen the sting of their defiance. And certainly, Ivan reasoned, their defiance should have come to an end when the Volga River, the main artery of Eastern commerce, passed, from its source to its mouth, into Russian hands.

Petulantly and bitterly, Ivan was to write in later years that much of the Kazantsi rebelliousness was due to the treachery of his generals, and that instead of organizing the city they plundered it. He even retracted the complimentary words he had expressed at the time of the capture by writing that all the generals, "like servants, acted from compulsion and not of their own will, and furthermore with grumbling."

Thus, in Ivan's mind, though not in the minds of the mass of the Russians, the military campaign that assumed the proportion of a holy crusade became a humdrum military exploit characterized by the usual backbiting, faultfinding, charges and countercharges of inefficiency, self-glorification, and lack of consideration for the common soldier. "At the very capture of the town," Ivan wrote later to Kurbsky, "were you not about to destroy in vain the Orthodox soldiery—and you would have done so had I not restrained you—by joining battle at an unfavorable time?"

Tortuously, he analyzed every event and every person with whom he came in contact. He accepted no one at face value. He believed in no one's intrinsic worth. He considered all his advisers potential traitors.

Much of this became obvious only as he grew older, but even as a young man he gave manifestations of his later personality traits. He did so especially during the events that occurred in March, 1553, when he suddenly became seriously ill.

At first, Ivan believed he was a victim of the plague that had been raging in northern Russia and had killed a large section of the population especially in and around the cities of Pskov and Novgorod. There, the deaths had been so numerous—one estimate gives the figure of a half million—that there were not enough healthy people left to carry on the cities' normal functions, or, as some accounts have it, to bury the dead.

However, the plague had not come to Moscow, and the doctors assured Ivan that he did not have the disease. They described his ailment as the "fiery fever," but they did not know its cause or its cure. They did know, however, that the Czar had a dangerous illness, possibly a fatal one.

As Ivan lay on what he fearfully thought might be his deathbed, he was concerned, in addition to his own health, with his succession; the hereditary right of succeeding to the throne was not firmly established in Russia, primogeniture having been established only recently. It is quite possible, too, that he thought of his own childhood, when the boyars, taking advantage of the death of Helena, had so miserably ignored and insulted him and his brother Yuri, and he now hoped that by binding them in an oath the Czarevich Dmitri might be spared the suffering he had undergone.

He ordered his closest relatives, his most influential advisers, and the most powerful boyars to assemble in his bedroom.

He then asked them to kiss the cross and pledge allegiance to the infant Czarevich. Their response was totally unexpected. With only a few exceptions, they refused, as they expressed it, "to kiss the cross for the Zakharin-Romanov." Instead, either by affirmation or by their silence they said they would support Ivan's cousin, Prince Vladimir Staritsky, who was the son of Andrei, the fifth eldest son of Ivan the Great and, therefore, the fourth eldest brother of Vasili III, for the throne. Vladimir had openly declared himself a candidate and had rallied their support.

Ivan was stunned. Then in a rage he insisted that each of them declare his own intention. The embarrassment and confusion that resulted is not difficult to imagine. Even on what appeared to be his deathbed, Ivan was a fearful man to confront. Finally, he turned to his closest advisers, Sylvester and Adashev. "Do you, too, support the pretender Vladimir?" Ivan asked. Their silence was their affirmation. The records are confused on whether or not they openly refused to take the oath for Dmitri; it is clear that they did nothing to oppose Vladimir, and by assuming what they hoped was a neutral position they condemned themselves in Ivan's eyes. It was a condemnation that was to have dire results, in time, for both of them.

In the meantime, Prince Vladimir and his closest supporters were continuing to rally support. Vladimir dipped deeply into his treasury to shower expensive gifts on possible supporters. He made promises of land and wealth, as well as threats of punishment, to those few boyars who would not willingly come over to his side.

Outside the apparently dying Czar's bedroom, within earshot of Ivan, wrangling among boyars over the succession went on far into the night after their assembly by the Czar. Some of the questions raised were by no means easy to answer. The entire system of succession was cloudy and loose, its precedents a maze of conflicting traditions and practices. Time and again in the history of Russia bitter and bloody battles had raged between contenders for the throne upon the death of a grand duke, and had resulted in some of them being murdered, others exiled, and one, Vasili II, being blinded.

Vladimir's adherents insisted stubbornly that they could not pledge their allegiance to Dmitri, since as an infant he was unable to rule, and anarchy would result from the struggle between contesting boyar factions. They pointed to the long and bloody battle that only recently had taken place between the Shuiskys and the Belskys during Ivan's minority. And certainly they could not support Anastasia or any of her kin, since the Zakharin-Romanovs were not sovereign princes or of the very highest noble families. The adherents of Ivan and his son Dmitri insisted, on the other hand, that only Dmitri's claim to the throne was valid, and that it was their dying Czar's wish that he be given the crown.

During the fierce debate, Ivan again appealed to the boyars. "If you do not kiss the cross for my son Dmitri that means you have another sovereign already in mind—you, who kissed the cross for me, and more than once, too! And do you now mean to seek another ruler instead of me? . . . I will force you to take the oath! I command you to serve my son Dmitri, and not the Zakharins at all. . . . You have forgotten your souls and are not willing to serve us and our sons, even though you have already kissed the cross upon it once before now. Have you suddenly forgotten that? He who is unwilling to serve my son now is unwilling to serve the great one either—myself. . . . But if you really need us no more, then this lies like a sin and a weight upon your souls."

The tide of the debate turned somewhat in Ivan's favor. Some of the boyars agreed, though reluctantly, to take the oath; some in fear of retribution should the Czar recover, others to spare him grief and agitation at such a crucial moment of his illness.

Sylvester now attempted to assume the role of conciliator. He begged Ivan to admit Prince Vladimir to his bedroom, and to confer with him on a possible solution to the impasse. Ivan's adherents resisted the suggestion.

Ivan then called the most powerful boyars together again, and as they stood around his bed, he said: "Boyars, you have pledged your soul's salvation that you are ready to serve us and our son. But now the boyars do not want to see my son sovereign, and, should the will of God be fulfilled and I shall live no longer, then think of what you have sworn to me and my son, and do not give the other boyars any chance of injuring my son in any way. Take him away to foreign lands, to which God will guide you." And then specifically speaking to the members of Anastasia's family, he said: "Why are you Zakharins so frightened? Or do you think the boyars will spare you? You will be the first to be killed, for you will die for my son and his mother. But for all that, you will not abandon my wife to the insults of the boyars!"

The speech had a profound effect on the boyars. Those in the room who had not kissed the cross, now did so; those who had kissed it before, kissed it again. Upon hearing how Ivan had persuaded the boyars in his bedroom to bow to his will, the boyars in the anteroom, including Prince Vladimir, now came in like chastened children, and one by one kneeled and kissed the cross.

To all intents and purposes, the incident was closed. Ivan, for the time being, did not take any steps of reprisal against the boyars who had opposed his will. However, it was a lesson in politics, loyalty, friendship, and boyar intrigue and greed that he never forgot—or forgave. The rupture between the Czar and his boyars, which had begun when he was a small child, was well on its way to becoming an open breach.

More than ten years later, in writing to Kurbsky, Ivan recounted the events that occurred during his illness in 1553 with as much bitterness and unforgiveness as if they had just happened.

"It fell to our lot, as indeed it falls to the lot of all men, to be afflicted with sickness and to be sorely ill; and then did those who are called by you 'well-wishers' rise up like drunken men with the

priest Sylvester and with your chief Alexei, thinking that we were
no longer alive, having forgotten our good deeds and even their
souls, too, and having forgotten that they had kissed the cross in
allegiance to our father and to us, vowing to seek no other sovereign but our children. Yet they desired to raise to the throne
Prince Vladimir, who is far removed from us in the line of succession; while our infant, given to us by God, did they, like Herod,
desire to destroy (and how could they fail to destroy him!), having
raised Prince Vladimir to the throne. For even though it was said
in the ancient secular writings, yet none the less is the following
fitting: 'Czar does not bow down to czar; but when one dies, the
other rules.' If then we, while still alive, enjoyed such 'well-
wishing' from our subjects, what will it be like after our death!
But again thanks to God's mercy we recovered, and thus was this
counsel scattered. But the priest Sylvester and Alexei ceased not
from that time forth to counsel all that was evil and to inflict on
me still harsher oppression, conceiving persecutions of various
kinds against our true well-wishers, while indulging every whim
of Prince Vladimir; and likewise they stirred up great hatred
against our Czaritsa Anastasia and likened her to all impious
czaritsas; as for our children, they were not able even to call them
to mind."

The following day the fever disappeared. In a few more days
Ivan recovered his strength, and, as he had vowed during his illness should he recover, he made preparations for a pilgrimage to
various monasteries to offer up his devotions.

Accompanied by Anastasia and his infant son Dmitri, Ivan first
visited the Trinity Monastery, where he had a long conversation
with Maxim the Greek. The meeting had been arranged by Sylvester, who hoped that the learned Greek, who was his own teacher
and master, would have a soothing effect upon the Czar as well as
being instrumental in healing the wound caused by Sylvester's
betrayal of Ivan during his illness.

Maxim was a most controversial character. He was an Albanian
by birth, who as a young man had come under the influence of
Savonarola, and like him he had the fervor of the prophet, was
dogmatic and unyielding, and insisted that man had to choose between pleasure and absolute faith. Having grown up at a monastery
at Mt. Athos, he was a firm believer in the Orthodox faith. His

education was varied and exacting and the influences upon him were broad and varied. He had been exposed to the culture of renaissance Italy and the various intellectual and spiritual currents of Florence during the time of the Medici. He had a deep and profound respect for learning and, as he saw them, Christian ethics and political justice.

He had come to Russia at the invitation of Vasili III, to undertake various assignments as a theologian and scholar. He soon became a severe critic of Russian theological, political, and social practices. However, he was a stranger in a strange land and, in spite of his great erudition and penetrating intellect, never could grasp the peculiarities of Russian life and customs. As a non-Russian intellectual, he could not understand or sympathize with that confusing mystery called the Russian soul, and had no patience with the Russians' penchant at that time for the sorcery, magic, ghosts, werewolves, and goblins that had persisted from their heathen past.

His literary efforts to correct and revise various religious texts were attacked most severely by Church authorities as violating tradition and robbing the Church of the sacredness and mystery that mystical renderings of its rites and liturgy expressed. Form was more important to the Church fathers than content, and they were not in the least concerned with his kind of fanatical devotion to accuracy of text in the Scriptures—accuracy that he insisted the Russians had violated.

The Church fathers reproached him for his meddling with sacred works. "By your amendments," they wrote, "you provoke the venerable miracle workers who shed luster upon our land. Through the sacred books in their present state they won God's approval and, by His grace, were granted holiness and the gift of working miracles."

Maxim answered them by first quoting St. Paul: " '. . . the manifestation of the Spirit is given to every man to profit withal. For to one is given by the Spirit the word of wisdom; to another the word of knowledge by the same Spirit; to another faith by the same Spirit; to another the gifts of healing by the same Spirit; to another the working of miracles; to another prophecy; to another discerning of spirits; to another divers kinds of tongues; to another the interpretation of tongues; but all these worketh that one and the selfsame Spirit, dividing to every man severally as he will.' "

He then continued his instruction: "You see, then, that not all the gifts of the Spirit are granted to one man. The gift of healing and of working wonders was granted to the holy Russian miracle workers by reason of their humility, mildness, and holy life; but the gift of interpreting languages and the gift of prophecy were denied them: to others, however—as, for instance, to me, though I was born the chief of sinners—was granted the gift of understanding languages and expressing ideas; do not, then, be surprised if I correct clerical errors that were hidden from them."

The clerics were not convinced. They were not interested in intellectual arguments and justifications, and were equally uninterested in linguistic accuracies for accuracy's sake. Maxim became a thorn in their side, a thorn whose point they would blunt. Their determination to do so became stronger when Maxim wrote a violent attack on various practices of the Church, putting his remarks in Christ's own mouth.

"Ye have angered Me with your harmonious anthems and the sound of your sweet bells, the richly adorned pictures and the fragrance of your incense. All this is the product of godless and wrongful usury, of the plundering of other's property. The sacrifices that ye make to Me are wet with the tears of orphans, with the blood of the poor and wretched. What does it profit Me if ye picture Me crowned with an aureole of golden rays if I am perishing among you of hunger and frost, while ye partake of sweet dishes and adorn yourselves with costly garments? It was not for the ringing of bells, not for hymns of praise nor for costly myrrh, that I came down to earth; not for this did I take upon myself suffering and death."

For a while, Vasili himself protected the learned Greek. However, when Maxim began to attack the political and social structure of the Muscovite state, this was too much for the autocratic Russian grand duke. Charges were made that Maxim was engaged in traitorous activities with Vasili's enemies. Courageous in his intellectual beliefs, Maxim was a coward when it came to his personal safety, and he defended himself by admitting to the truth of the charges. He named the conspirators—actual or imaginary— and they were summarily executed. Maxim's life was spared, and he was exiled to a monastery in a remote part of Russia, where he continued his studies and writing.

He continued in exile for twenty-four years until Sylvester had him freed. He was not allowed to leave Russia, however, and he took up residence in the Trinity Monastery.

This was the man, then, that Ivan, at Sylvester's request, was to converse with and—Sylvester hoped—be influenced by. Ivan was on his guard. He was impressed by Maxim's learning. Throughout his life, Ivan was to forgive much because of a person's erudition. Yet Maxim was not just a scholar but a clever and insidious critic of the political and social order. And at criticism of his government, Ivan, like his father, drew the line. His first concern was the sanctity of the autocratic state, and he would brook neither criticism nor interference that threatened its safety.

Ivan's caution was not ill-founded. After the usual preliminary courtesies, Maxim, obviously prompted beforehand by Sylvester, turned the conversation to a project that was close to Sylvester's— and Adashev's—heart; a conclusive campaign against the Kazan Tatars to be followed by a campaign against the Crimean Tatars.

"The fulfilment of unwise promises is not acceptable to God," Maxim said. "God would be much more pleased if, as a token of gratitude for the miracle of your health, you would undertake a new campaign against the Tatar. God is everywhere and you could find Him at Kazan as easily as at Kirilov."

Maxim had underestimated the Czar; Ivan was not taken in by the Greek's attempt to link a campaign against the Tatar's with God's will. The conversation between them became somewhat less than cordial. In desperation, Maxim then begged the Czar not to continue with his pilgrimage: the exertion would be too great for a man who had just got up from a sickbed; the roads were almost impassable; the weather was vile.

Ivan insisted that he had to be true to the vow he had taken at the time of his illness. He was especially anxious to visit St. Cyril, where his mother had gone while she was pregnant with him, and nothing would deter him from his purpose.

Maxim then tried his final—and he hoped most devastating— warning. If Ivan continued his pilgrimage, his infant son Dmitri would die. This was the kind of prophecy that would certainly put the greatest fear into the Czar's heart. Ivan was unimpressed.

Maxim's purpose in conjuring up such a warning was too obvious. The conversation came to an abrupt end.

And now as if to spite Sylvester, Adashev, Maxim, and all those who would interfere with his plans and try to divert him from his pledged purpose, he made extremely elaborate preparations for the pilgrimage. In addition to Anastasia, the infant Dmitri, and his brother Yuri, a large retinue of intimates would accompany him, including Kurbsky and other military men, whom Sylvester would rather have had at the front fighting Tatars.

Soon after the Easter services, which Ivan observed in the Kremlin, the pilgrimage began. The weather was miserable— damp, windy, and cold. The first stop was the Pesnoshsky Monastery, and Ivan made part of the journey there by boat up the Volga.

At the Monastery, Ivan had another notable conversation, this time with an old anchorite named Vassian Toporkov, who had formerly been a monk at the monstery of Volokolamsk, and then had been appointed Bishop of Kolomna. After about seventeen years in this position, he had been dismissed in 1542 for "cunning and cruelty," and for the ten years preceding Ivan's visit had been living at the Pesnoshsky Monastery.

Although it is not clear whether their meeting was by accident or design, the latter is possible, for Ivan seemed determined as part of the pilgrimage to make himself known to the people and places that he associated with his parents, Vasili and Helena. And just as he wished to visit the place where Helena had gone while pregnant with him, so he may have desired to speak to the old anchorite who at one time, before he had fallen into disgrace and oblivion, had been an intimate of Vasili.

Accompanied by Kurbsky, Ivan entered Vassian's cell. Kurbsky subsequently recorded the conversation between monk and Czar.

"How should I govern so that I might keep my great and powerful subjects in submission?" Ivan asked.

"If you wish to be an autocrat, keep no adviser who is wiser than yourself," the anchorite replied, "for you are firmly established in sovereignty and hold all things in your hands. But if you have men about you who are wiser than you, then of necessity you must be obedient to them."

Ivan was greatly pleased by the reply. The clever, ingratiating monk had spoken words that fitted perfectly Ivan's growing aware-

ness of a ruler's relationship with his advisers. His disillusionment
with them had been growing for some time, and the events that
had occurred during his recent illness were fresh in his mind.

Ivan kissed the anchorite's hand, and said, "If my own father
were still alive, he could not have given me better advice."

Vassian's advice to Ivan, according to Kurbsky, had a profound
effect on the Czar, and Kurbsky claimed that from that time on
Ivan decided to become an autocrat. Of course the monk's advice
did no such thing. Ivan never wanted to be anything but an autocrat, and his actions and outlook until this moment were constantly
strengthening this position. Furthermore, there was no other form
of rulership that Ivan could turn from or turn towards, since
autocracy, in one form or another, had been in existence in Russia
for generations, and he was ignorant of the other more enlightened
governments—such as that of England—that existed at the time.
It never had been—nor would it ever be—Ivan's wish to institute
a non-autocratic form of government; his political thoughts and
actions until the day he died were concentrated on how best to
perfect and strengthen an authoritarian state. It was his particular
genius, evil though it may appear, to develop for his kind of state
the necessary forms and methods. And these forms and methods,
with refinements and adjustments, became standards for Russian
rulers from his time to the present day.

The pilgrimage was a popular triumph for the Czar. Everywhere
he went the people turned out to cheer him, and to pray for his
health and welfare. Their adulation and respect were more touching to him than his victory march to Moscow the previous year
after the fall of Kazan. Then he had ridden the wave of military
victory, and the people praised him as a conquering hero. Now they
worshipped him as the Czar. The distinction was not lost on Ivan.
Now he had a solid base of support; let the treacherous boyars
beware!

Even though the pilgrimage was a popular triumph, it resulted
in personal tragedy. Dmitri fell ill, and died. The difficult journey
under primitive conditions in the chill and dampness of a northern
Russian spring had been too much for the infant. Maxim's prophecy had come true. The struggle at the time of Ivan's illness over
the succession now became tragically ironic.

It was a crushing blow to Ivan. He had already lost one child—

Anna, his first born. Maria, his second born, was alive. She died during the next year. But in the order of things at the time, princesses were quite unimportant. It was the male heirs that mattered. Upon Dmitri's death, Ivan ordered that all speed be made to return to Moscow, where the Czarevich could be properly buried in the traditional way and in the traditional burial place of the royal family—the Cathedral of the Archangel Michael in the Kremlin.

But Ivan's bitter cup was not yet full. On the journey home, Anastasia became ill. Had the difficult trip been too much for her also? Had the death of Dmitri crushed her, destroying her will to live? No one knows. Yet from this time on—although she recovered from this illness—Anastasia was never again healthy and robust. She became listless, and the slightest exertion tired her. She seemed to be wasting away.

IX

The English Come to Russia

SOME months after Ivan's return from his disastrous pilgrimage, the routine of the Kremlin was interrupted by the arrival of a messenger from the St. Nicholas Monastery in the far north. The messenger brought the news that a strange foreign ship had entered the mouth of the Dvina River, and its captain, Richard Chancellor, requested an audience with the Czar. When Ivan ascertained that it was an English ship, his curiosity was aroused, and he gave orders that sleighs, horses, guides, and other necessities should be given the captain to bring him to Moscow.

The story of how Captain Richard Chancellor happened to find himself at the far distant monastery goes back a year or so before, to 1552, when the English decided to try to find a way to the East by a northeast sea route. Navigators had gone as far as Lapland's North Cape, but beyond that point stretched a vast unknown.

The Italian Cabots, who had been hired by the English, and specifically Sebastian Cabot, had advised that an expedition by this route might prove successful in reaching the East, and suggested that a company be formed to make the attempt. The company that was established was "The Mysterie and Company of the Merchants Adventurers of the Citie of London, for the Discoverie of Lands, Territories, Isles, Dominions, and Seignories unknown." Three ships were outfitted, and in May, 1553, the ships with crews totaling a hundred and twelve men, under the general command of Sir Hugh Willoughby, left London headed toward the mysterious and treacherous northern waters.

During the course of the voyage, two of the ships were forced to land on the northeast coast of the Kola Peninsula, where Willoughby and all his men died from hunger and the cold. The other ship—the *Edward Bonaventure*—under the command of Captain Richard Chancellor, put up at Vardo, the rendezvous previously agreed upon should the three ships become separated. Chancellor stayed on at Vardo for several days, and then decided to sail on without the companion ships. Subsequently, the *Edward Bonaventure* entered the Bay of St. Nicholas, and anchored where the city of Archangel is now situated. Chancellor was surprised to discover that he was in Russian territory.

At first the natives there were frightened, and fled, refusing to have anything to do with the men from the strange ship. Then, as the account goes, "they, being in great fear, as men half dead, prostrated themselves before him [Chancellor], offering to kiss his feet." Chancellor "comforting them by sign and gestures," reassured them of his peaceful intentions, and requested that he be brought before their sovereign. He felt quite secure in making such a request, for in his pocket he had a letter from the highest English authorities addressed to "all the princes and lords, to all the judges of the earth . . . whoever possess any high authority in all the regions under the vast sky" to give the adventurers their aid and treat them well.

The *Edward Bonaventure* had anchored in Russian waters in late August, 1553, but it wasn't until December that Chancellor and his company of merchants and sailors arrived in Moscow. When they requested an audience with the sovereign, little did they realize that he was fifteen hundred miles away, and that they would have to travel over vast stretches of ice and snow and almost impassable roads to reach him!

When they finally arrived in Moscow, they were kept waiting for almost two weeks before Ivan agreed to see them. The Germans, Dutch, Persians, Arabians, and others who were already trading with Russia were accustomed to this kind of Russian diplomacy, but the English were surprised. It was not that they weren't treated cordially; they were. But after such a long journey they expected a prompter audience. To while away time, Chancellor and his companions walked around the city of Moscow, which they found fascinating in a bizarre kind of way, and to their amazement as large as the "Citie of London with the suburbs thereof."

In the Kremlin, Ivan was perhaps more anxious to meet the English than they him, but he could not outwardly show his anxiety, for he was the ruler of the vast, powerful empire of Russia, and these men were from a small island off the coast of Europe. Nevertheless, when he finally deigned to admit them to the Kremlin, he displayed himself to them in his finest dress, the hall was lavishly ornamented, and the Czar's numerous retainers were dressed in their most elaborate ceremonial costumes.

As the English recounted the momentous meeting, Chancellor and his party "being entered within the gates of the court, there sat a very honorable company of courtiers, to the number of one hundred, all appareled in cloth of gold, down to their ankles. And being conducted into the chamber of presence, our men began to wonder at the majesty of the Emperor: his seat was aloft, in a very royal throne, having on his head a diadem or crown of gold, appareled with a robe all of goldsmith's work, and in his hand he held a scepter garnished and beset with precious stones; and besides all other notes and appearances of honor, there was a majesty in his countenance proportionable with the excellency of his estate. On the one side of him stood his chief secretary, on the other the great commander of silence, both of them arrayed also in cloth of gold. And there sat the Council of one hundred and fifty in number, all in like sort arrayed, and of great state.

"This so honorable assembly, so great a majesty of the Emperor, and of the place might well have amazed our men and dashed them out of countenance, but Master Chancellor, nothing dismayed, saluted, and did his duty to the Emperor, after the manner of England and delivered unto him the letters of our king, Edward the Sixth."

Ivan received the letters, said that Chancellor and his men were welcome, politely inquired about the health of the King, and, as Chancellor reported, "upon the which I was required to depart, for I had charge not to speak to the Duke but when he spoke to me." That afternoon Ivan gave a sumptuous banquet in honor of his visitors.

Chancellor and his companions made a good personal impression on Ivan, though it is unlikely that the Czar was greatly impressed by the power they represented. Still, he acceded to their requests to establish trade relations, and Chancellor returned to England with letters from the Czar to King Edward promising that British subjects could visit safely and trade freely with Russia.

In the meantime, King Edward had died. Queen Mary, his successor, was just as anxious to see trade established with Russia, and gave her approval for a charter for this purpose to the Merchant Adventurers, which now became known as the Muscovy, or Russia, Company. Plans were now made to send another expedition to Russia, and this time special agents, headed by George Killingworth, who were well informed on trade and commerce would go to Moscow.

The instructions given to Killingworth and the others were a masterpiece of English thoroughness and self-interest. They were instructed to study Russian customs and people, as well as Russian taxes, coinage, weights and measures. They were especially warned to obey scrupulously the Russian laws and to protect their fellow Englishmen. If possible, they were to open trading centers in Moscow and other Russian cities, and to note carefully Russian needs and desires for various kinds of merchandise as well as the types and quality of goods existing in that country. They were also told "to use all ways and means possible to learn how men may pass from Russia either by land or by sea to Cathay."

Chancellor, Killingworth, and other agents of the Russia Company set off together for Russia in 1555, and arrived there without incident. Their reception by Ivan was cordial, and Ivan was surprised to find their letters to him were not signed by King Edward but by Philip and Mary, "King and Queen of England, France, Naples, Jerusalem and Ireland, Princes of Spaine and Sicilie, Archdukes of Austria, Dukes of Milan and Brabant." This time he was impressed. He made sure that in the future the English would address him as "The right High, right Mighty, and right Excellent Prince, garnished with all gifts of Nature of God's grace, Ivan the son of Vasili, Emperor of all Russia, Great Duke of Vladimir, Moscow, and Novgorod, King of Kazan [and a host of other cities and territories], Commander of the north part, and Lord of many other Countries."

After many conferences with Ivan and his advisers, arrangements were successfully concluded for commerce between the two countries. The English were given a monopoly of trade in the White Sea, and were permitted to establish business houses at Kholmogory, Vologda, and other cities. In addition, the English could trade in Russia without paying the usual Russian fees; their goods were protected from seizure, except for debt or crime; they were under the jurisdiction of their own officers, and violations of Russian law could not be settled by Russian officials, only by the Czar himself; trade disputes were to be settled quickly; and no individual Englishman could be arrested for debt if the head of the Company guaranteed payment.

The terms were extremely favorable to the English. Killingworth, whose five-foot-long beard had so thoroughly delighted Ivan that he had insisted upon running his hand through it, was overjoyed at the British negotiators' success. He wrote to the Russia Company's headquarters in London that all this had been gained for three or four years, "and in this space we shall know the country and the merchants, and which way to save ourselves best, and where to plant our houses, and where to seek for wares."

Ivan had agreed to these hard terms because he was farsighted enough to know that it was to his advantage to have an outlet to the West through the White Sea, and thus be in a position to receive goods and supplies, as well as military and technical experts in case of future struggles against such hereditary enemies as the German Order, Sweden, and Poland. Yet he had agreed unenthusiastically, describing England's stiff price for friendship and trade as being "heavier than tribute."

In July, 1556, Chancellor again set sail for England, with four ships full of Russian merchandise, presents of rich cloth and furs from Ivan to the Queen, and with the first Russian ambassador to England—Osip Napeia—and several Russian traveling companions on board.

As the ships approached the Scottish coast, a heavy storm sprang up, the ships foundered, and most of the crew and passengers were drowned. Napeia was saved, but several of his fellow Russians perished. Chancellor himself, so the story goes, was drowned saving the Russian ambassador's life. Most of the cargo was lost, and most of what was saved the Scots took for themselves. After a long delay, Napeia went to London to meet the merchants and royalty, who extended themselves to give the ambassador from such a faraway land an impressive reception.

"He was received twelve miles from London by fourscore merchants with chains of gold and goodly apparel who conducted him to a house and made him a riding garment," one account stated. "The next day he had not only the hunting of the fox and such-like sport shown him, but also by the Queen Majesty's command, he was received and embraced by the right honorable Viscount Montague and divers lusty knights, esquires, gentlemen, and yeomen who led him to the City where was presented to him a gelding, richly trapped together with a footcloth of Orient crimson velvet. The Lord Mayor accompanied with all the aldermen in scarlet did receive him, with all sorts of officers to attend upon him, as to such an ambassador of honor doth pertain."

It is extremely doubtful that any of the participating dignitaries had the faintest idea about Russia or its ruler. Ignorance about Russia was as great in England as Russian ignorance about England. Ivan may at first have thought England was a small, unimportant island off the coast of Europe, but Holinshed's *Chronicles,* in recording the arrival of Napeia stated: "About this time (1556–57) came to London an ambassador to the Queene from the Emperor of Cathaie, Muscouia, and Russeland."

The British, however, seemed to learn quickly about Russian wile. Less than a year after Napeia's arrival, the records of the Russia Company have this entry: "We do not find the Ambassador now at last so comfortable to reason as we had thought. He is very mistrustful and thinks every man will beguile him. Therefore, you have need to take heed how you have to do with him, or with any such, and to make your bargains plain, and to set them down in writing. For they be subtle people, and do not always speak the truth, and think other men to be like themselves."

X

Death of Anastasia

THOUGH in frail health from 1553 on, Anastasia gave birth to three children in addition to the three she had already borne. Less than a year after the death of Dmitri, Russia had a new heir in the Czarevich Ivan. In 1556, Evdokia was born, but she died in 1558. And in 1558 Anastasia gave birth to her last child—Feodor.

With her constant childbearing and her failing health, Anastasia spent more and more time in the *terem,* the women's quarters of the Kremlin. Yet she was always close to Ivan when he needed her, and her gentle disposition, unaffected by her cares, continued to have a soothing influence upon him. He needed her, for he was assuming more responsibilities and relying less upon his advisers, though the time for a definite rupture between him and his closest intimates was still to come. Moreover, he was having trouble with the Tatars and his immediate Western neighbors.

The Crimean Tatars, encouraged and supported by the Turkish Sultan, were continually threatening the tranquillity of Russian territory. Predatory raids were made constantly. In the summer of 1555, a large battle developed. The Tatars were beaten, and they retreated to their peninsula, to regroup for future raids.

To the west, King Sigismund of the Polish-Lithuanian empire looked on with trepidation at the fast-growing Russian state. Though most of Europe cared little about the capture of Kazan and Astrakhan and the consolidation of the Volga region, Poland did. And when, soon after these victories, Wisnkowiecki, the leader of a large group of Cossacks in the south of Russia, transferred his loyalty from the Polish king to Ivan, Sigismund's concern over Russia's growing power increased. Ever since Ivan's coronation, Sigismund had refused to recognize him by his new title of Czar and Autocrat of All Russia, and instructed that all documents to the ruler be addressed as they had been for centuries, "His Majesty, the Grand Duke of Moscow." By this slight, the Polish king helped to worsen Russian-Polish relations, which had been strained for a long time. Russia insisted more urgently than ever that Lithuanian land annexed by Poland be turned bac to Russia. Poland steadfastly refused. The restless Russian Cza would not wait much longer for satisfaction.

Ivan also worried Sweden and the German Order. Sweden was alarmed over Ivan's ambitions in the Baltic area, recent Russian moves to establish trade with England, and Russia's renewed interest in the far north. The German Order, which held a weakened position of power in Livonia on the Baltic coast, was alarmed because it was in the direct path of Russian expansion to the Baltic. For Ivan, anticipating Peter the Great's massive campaigns for an outlet to the sea, was preparing to move in that direction. The Teutonic Knights had been obstructing such moves for centuries, and in alliance with Sweden and Poland had the foresight during these centuries to try to keep Russia in isolation. They even went so far as to prevent whenever they could the passage to Moscow of Western scholars and technicians on the not too frequent occasions when Russian rulers decided to lessen the isolation they themselves were imposing upon Russia.

Ivan's growing determination to expand to the Baltic Sea was not shared by all of his advisers, especially Sylvester, Adashev, and Kurbsky. Sylvester constantly exerted pressure on Ivan to turn towards the south, to conquer the Crimean Tatars. Here, he argued, was a holy cause for Orthodox Russia—the smashing of the last important Mohammedan group on what was supposed to be historic Russian territory. Ivan refused to consider the move; and his reasons were valid. By carrying out a large-scale campaign, which was the only kind of campaign that could decisively defeat the Tatars, he would have to give up his plans for the Baltic area. Russia was in no position to carry on two widely separated campaigns at the same time. The powerful Turkish Sultan would certainly bring the full weight of his massive empire in support of

Ivan III ("the Great")

Ivan IV ("the Terrible"), from a painting by Vasnetsov

Study of Ivan the Terrible

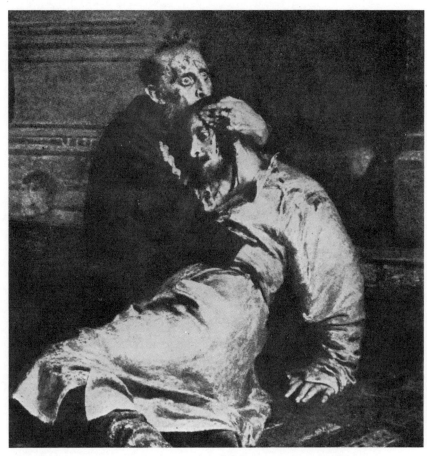

Ivan the Terrible with the dying Czarevich

Reception of an ambassador in the Kremlin

Sir Jerome Bowes

Armed boyars in the early sixteenth century

Armament of a Russian foot soldier

Russian bathhouse

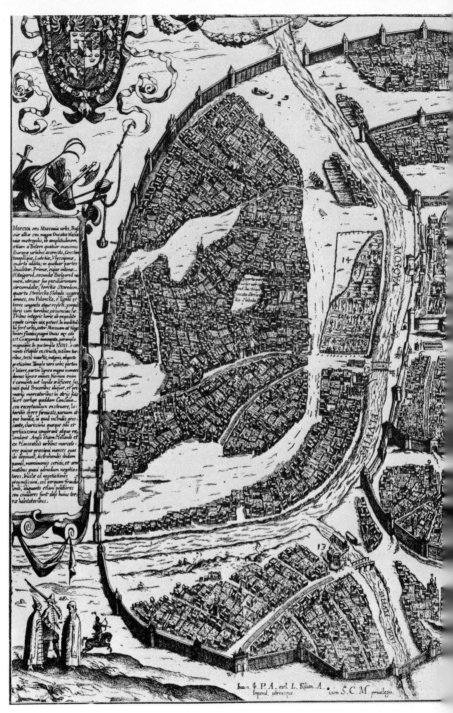

Moscow in 1610

Growth of Moscow, 1462-1682

Southern wall of the Kremlin

Cathedral of St. Basil the Blessed

Tower of Ivan the Great in the Kremlin

Interior of the Cathedral of the Assumption

the Tatars. Ivan wanted no struggle that would involve the Moslem world against Russia. The disorganized, weakened, historical anomaly that was the Teutonic Order was a much more tempting, and apparently easier, adversary.

Ivan's critics did not give up easily; they continued not only to urge the Czar to change his mind about an assault on the Crimean Tatars but they actively opposed his plans to expand westward. Part of their opposition—at least that of Sylvester and others in the Church—was based on the fear that intimate contact with the unorthodox Christian West would weaken the Church's position in Orthodox Russia as well as strengthen the Pope in Rome's long-standing desire to bring the two Christian churches under one rule—the Pope's. Others—both Church and non-Church elements —opposed Ivan because they firmly believed Russia's destiny lay in expanding to the south and east, and that Western European ideas and culture, which would flow into Russia in the wake of Russian expansion westward, would weaken and ultimately destroy the unique Russian character and tradition. Still others, as well as members of the aforementioned groups, feared that Russian moves in the West would bring into play an alliance of European states against Russia.

Ivan did not take kindly to this kind of opposition. It was not because he favored the weakening of Russian isolation. He understood quite clearly the danger of Western ideas to the Russian system and especially to the autocracy. His patience was tried because his foes did not understand—or pretended they did not understand —the dangers involved in a full-scale campaign against the Crimean Tatars and their allies the Turks. Also, he could brook no resistance once his mind was made up. Criticism then ceased to be criticism and became attacks on Russia and the Czar; in short— treason.

Ivan's will prevailed. The conquest of Livonia became a fixed Russian policy. The immediate problem was to find a pretext for ordering the Russian troops to begin to march. The pretext that was finally dragged up out of the past was one fitting an *opéra bouffe*. Years before, Russia had demanded that certain Livonian areas pay ten pounds of honey as an annual tribute. For a time it was paid, then as the years went by the tribute was forgotten by Livonians and Russians alike. Now Ivan revived the demand for tribute, but asked that instead of honey it should be in coin, and of a substantial amount. The Livonians delayed, pleading poverty. In former days, one of Ivan's predecessors had sent them a whip as a reminder of their obligations. Now Ivan sent ambassadors who sternly warned them of the consequences if they refused to respond favorably. In 1557, the Livonians sent a delegation to Moscow to beg for the Czar's patience. Ivan refused to see them; Adashev was appointed to hear them out, and then sent them packing. Russian troops were already preparing for action.

When the Russians marched into Livonia, there were in addition to Russian troops a large contingent of Tatars, recruited from the recently conquered territories to the east. The Russians met only feeble resistance. Leaders of the Teutonic Order, such as Furstenberg and Kettler, tried to rally their forces, but the Livonian response was spotty. In some places, the defenders fought bravely; in other places the will to fight was almost nonexistent, and in many instances there were cases of outright cowardice and betrayal.

City after city fell to Ivan's forces—Narva, Neuhaus, Dorpat, and Fellin. At Fellin, the Teutonic Order had rallied the best of its knights, but to no avail. The Russians, under Kurbsky, cut them to ribbons.

The Order tried negotiations several times, and on occasion they managed to effect temporary truces. But their days were numbered; the decadent Order was no match for the Russians. Their defense would have to be undertaken by stronger powers. At first, their appeals to other powers for aid were treated coldly. Eventually, however, realization of the full import of the Russian advance dawned upon Sweden, Denmark, Poland, and even the Pope in Rome. It became obvious that the intervention of the states most intimately concerned with the consequences of a Russian victory was only a matter of time.

If Ivan thought that because his first march against the Livonians was a success, the campaign would be short and fast, he was sadly mistaken. He was to spend the rest of his life battling a combination of powers in the Livonian area. The conquest of Livonia was to become the obsession of Ivan's life—and the tragedy of his czardom.

But in the beginning of what was to become a twenty-five-year struggle, victories came quickly. Russian standards flew over city after city in the Baltic area.

The Russians and the Tatars, if the German records and others are to be taken at face value, acted like monsters. Prisoners were marched through the towns and beaten with iron rods. Others were tortured and their bodies then thrown into the fields to be devoured by wild animals and birds of prey.

"I do not believe that such wailing, screams, and cries for help can have been heard among the Germans in a lifetime," one contemporary account stated. Another account noted: "In short, who can find the heart to relate all the cruelty of the said bloodthirsty Tatar tyrant, despite the fact that he afterwards wrote from Moscow to the Livonian Estates, more out of treachery than with good intent, like unto a crocodile, that 'what had happened in Livonia grieved him.' "

The Englishman Jerome Horsey wrote: "O, the lamentable outcries and cruel slaughters, drowning and burning, ravishing of women and maids, stripping them naked without mercy or regard of the frozen weather, tying and binding them by three and by four at their horses' tails, dragging them, some alive, some dead, all bloodying the ways and streets full of carcasses of the aged men and women and infants; some goodly persons clad in velvet, damask, and silks, with jewels, gold, and pearls hid about them. . . . There was infinite numbers thus sent and dragged into Russia."

In the fall of 1559, during one of the truce periods, Ivan and Anastasia decided to make another of their many pilgrimages. In spite of the almost impassable state of the roads, they set out to the monastery at Mozhaisk. During the trip, Anastasia complained of not feeling well, but they went on. Shortly after they arrived at Mozhaisk, Anastasia's illness worsened. There were no medical supplies available, and Ivan decided to return to the Kremlin, first angrily upbraiding Sylvester and Adashev and others in his party for failing to prepare for such an emergency. Sylvester replied by criticizing the Czar for taking the journey and, as he had done at the time of Dmitri's illness, suggested that Anastasia's present ailment was God's punishment for Ivan's indocility and stubbornness. Tactlessly, he threw in as an example of Ivan's stubbornness the present Russian policy in Livonia and the refusal of the Czar to battle the Crimean Tatars. Ivan retorted by accusing Sylvester and his associates of purposely neglecting to bring medical supplies, and even hinted that Anastasia was ill not because of a disease but because she had been poisoned.

Although the nature of Anastasia's illness was unknown, it was certainly a serious one. For ten months she lingered on, becoming progressively worse. On August 7, 1560, the Czaritsa died.

Ivan was crushed. Nothing that had happened to him in an already full life—he was not yet thirty—had had such a profound effect upon him, not even Dmitri's death. Anastasia had been his great love—his only love. And in his fashion, and in the fashion of the time, he had been faithful to that love. His affairs with other women during his marriage had been brief and inconsequential, undertaken because of his restless nature rather than because of any coolness toward Anastasia. Even his drinking and roistering were insignificant, considering the rough times in which he lived. Anastasia had been his constant companion, both in the Kremlin and in the numerous pilgrimages he had made. And he had enjoyed her company, seeking her out whenever he was not involved with official business.

At the news of the Czaritsa's death, the bells of Moscow tolled mournfully. And at her funeral all of Moscow turned out, and wept honest tears of grief for the most beloved Czaritsa Russia had had until that time.

Ivan himself lost no time in giving large sums of money to churches and monasteries in her memory. But nothing could assuage his sorrow. At times, his grief made him moody and silent, so that he would see no one for days at a time. At other times, he stormed and raged and struck everyone in sight, loudly proclaiming the abyss of sorrow in which he suffered. He refused to see his children, and sent them to a separate palace away from the Kremlin. In fits of anger at his miserable fate, he smashed furniture, destroyed mementos of his life with Anastasia, and even inflicted bodily harm upon himself by banging his head upon the floor, often in full sight of the court. He ordered virgins to be brought to his bedroom and there debauched them.

Probably none of the unrestrained things he did after Anastasia's death was as wild as his proposal of marriage to Catherine, King Sigismund's sister, only a week after Anastasia's interment. The

King answered by sending him what he implied was the only suitable female for the Russian ruler—a white mare. Incensed, Ivan informed the King that he had ordered a hole dug in the Kremlin grounds—for Sigismund's head.

No excess was too great for him in his attempt to forget his sorrow. Whatever restraint Anastasia's love had had on him was now gone. It was not that the Czar's character changed after Anastasia's death; rather, it was that he returned to the original complex and violent nature that Anastasia had kept in check for thirteen years.

Long after the initial sting of Anastasia's death had disappeared, Ivan acted as though her death had occurred the previous week. For instance, seventeen years later, in 1577, Ivan could write to Kurbsky: "And why did you separate me from my wife? If only you had not taken from me my young wife, then there would have been no 'sacrifices to Cronus.' You will say: 'that I was unable to endure [the loss of my wife] and that I did not preserve my purity,' —well, we are all human."

Of course Kurbsky didn't take Anastasia from Ivan, nor did the other advisers and boyars that Ivan similarly accused. His hint at the time of Anastasia's illness that poison might have been put into her wine was a refusal to believe that God could be so unjust as to strike down his beloved. It was typical of Ivan to see treachery everywhere about him, and to refuse to recognize that he, like other men, could be the victim of life's adversities and tragedies.

As he grew older, he considered himself different from other men, unique in his relationship to God. He rebelled against the idea that man's fate was his, and searched for a concept of himself as a being somewhere between man and God. As the omnipotent ruler of the Russian mass, he was above them; as God's appointed scourge of sinful man while man was on this earth, he had a relationship to Him that put him close to the Divine. Yet all this did not fit into a pattern that made sense, even to Ivan himself, and he scourged himself as much as his subjects to try to make sense out of it. His self-torture became painful to see, and at times his misery, expressing itself in outrageous cruelty to others, made him appear deranged. For try as he would, he couldn't be God, and he refused to be mere man. His position was untenable. But it was a position that he played both ways. He placed himself close to

God when it was politic to do so in order to defend himself to himself; he placed himself with man when it was to his interest to defend himself to others. Thus, his cavalier remark to Kurbsky, who had accused him of unrestrained debauchery following Anastasia's death, that he, after all, was only human becomes understandable.

Ivan wanted everyone to share his grief over Anastasia. He insisted, illogically, that his personal tragedy was theirs as well. And when they wouldn't take on his grief because they couldn't, he upbraided them, denouncing them as betraying their professed friendship to him. From this point it was an easy step for him to transfer personal betrayal to betrayal of Russia itself.

"I suffered offense in that you did not deem me worthy of your love, for you grieved not with me for our Czaritsa and our children," Ivan wrote to Kurbsky.

With increased bitterness and animosity, Ivan built up in his mind a case of perfidy against the closest of his advisers. The hint that poison had been used against Anastasia now became a direct accusation that the boyars had killed her because they had always hated her.

His attempt to prove that they despised the gentle Czaritsa was weak, and he seized upon whatever remark the boyars had ever made to or about Anastasia to justify his accusation.

In a long, rambling indictment, Ivan wrote to Kurbsky: "How shall I recall the hard journey to the ruling city from Mozhaisk with our ailing Czaritsa Anastasia? Owing to one single little word [he did not say what the word was] did she rank as worthless in their eyes. But as for prayers and journeying to desert places [i.e. hermitages], gifts and vows to the saints for the salvation of our soul, for our bodily health and for all our well-being and for that of our Czaritsa and our children—all these things were taken completely from us by your cunning scheming. And as for medical skill, for our health's sake, there was no mention of it at that time."

By word, letter, and in direct conversation, as with, among others, the Lithuanian ambassador, in 1572, Ivan insisted that Anastasia did not die of illness but was murdered.

Sylvester, Adashev, Kurbsky, and others hotly denied the charges of harassing Anastasia. They professed their love and respect for the Czaritsa. As for murdering her, they expressed horror at the idea that the Czar would even consider the charge.

Kurbsky, for instance, not only denied the insidious charges but countered with charges of his own against Ivan's policy, developed after Anastasia's death, of executing those who opposed him, even his closest advisers and relatives. After writing that he did not harass Anastasia or plot to destroy her, Kurbsky wrote: ". . . even if I am laden with sins and unworthy, none the less I was born of noble parents, of the family of the Grand Prince of Smolensk, Feodor Rostislavich . . . and princes of that generation are not accustomed to eat their own bodies and to drink the blood of their brothers, as has long since been the habit of certain other families. . . ."

The family he was alluding to is not difficult to determine.

Ivan's aroused animosity toward his closest advisers, particularly Sylvester and Adashev, was to have far-reaching consequences. And it was only a question of time until he would move against his counselors. Their supposed role in contributing to—or directly effecting—Anastasia's death was the lever he would use. But the issues were deeper, more basic. Their refusal to cease their criticism of his Livonian campaign was intolerable to him. Their power and prestige had grown too great for him to bear. Their stature in the eyes of the people robbed him, so he thought, of the undivided loyalty and love of his subjects. And their alliance with the greedy, selfish, backward boyars was a drag on the full development of Russia as a great power.

XI

Fall of the Mighty

WHEN Ivan chose as his closest advisers relatively obscure individuals—Sylvester, a minor clerical figure, and Adashev, the son of a petty government official—he was breaking a boyar-ruler tradition that had existed for centuries in Russia.

The close alliance of boyar and grand duke, so far as the Muscovite dynasty was concerned, began with the emergence of Moscow in the thirteenth century as a leading power among the many small dukedoms that then existed. Attracted by the opportunities that Moscow had to offer, large numbers of boyars migrated to that city from other parts of Russia. They came there not only from nearby centers but from such faraway places as Kiev and Chernigov and even from the Germanized districts in the West and from various Tatar areas. By the middle of the fifteenth century, the most ambitious and powerful boyars were living in and around Moscow, offering their services and support to its ruler. Their ranks included influential boyar families with national backgrounds that were not only Russian but German, Lithuanian, Finnish, Greek, and Tatar. Their number totaled more than two hundred powerful titled families, and in wealth and influence they often overshadowed the older families, many of whom could trace their origin back to Rurik himself.

The boyars who now threw in their lot with the grand duke of Moscow were allowed to keep their estates when they came to Moscow, and those who had powerful family names but for one reason or another had lost their land were given holdings. Away from their native and traditional homes, the boyars firmly attached themselves to the Moscow grand duke. In the confused period during which the Moscow grand dukes were vying for power with neighboring princes on the one hand and alternately cooperating with and defying the Tatar overlords, the military and administrative contributions of the boyars were welcome and often necessary.

The relation between the older boyar families and this group of boyars whom they considered to be interlopers became strained as time went on, and long-drawn-out disputes arose over seniority of rights and privileges. *Miestnichestvo,* the system of holding position by rank, became firmly established. A boyar would accept a position in the government or army, for instance, only when he felt that he would not be humiliated and subordinated to another boyar of equal or less distinguished rank. This led to a tangled situation. For now a new class of boyars of high lineage, the descendants of the princes who had transferred their loyalty to Moscow, assumed positions of great power. They constantly reminded the reigning grand duke of Moscow that they were of as great and powerful bloodlines as his own, and therefore were entitled to the rights and privileges befitting members of highest royalty.

In the earlier days, the Moscow grand duke embraced all his boyar associates, relied upon them completely, and did little without their advice and consent. Situations developed in which the boyars themselves took over the government because the reigning grand duke appeared incapable of performing his task.

So great was the reliance on the boyars that, in effect, there existed in Russia a joint rule of grand duke and boyar. Dmitri Donskoi, for example, on his deathbed told his sons to "love your boyars, honor them, and do nothing without their counsel," and told his boyars, "I have loved you all, and held you all in honor. With you I have rejoiced, and with you I have sorrowed, and under me you have been known, not as boyars, but as princes of my land."

However, as Moscow in time became the head of Russia, and Russia became a greater and more powerful country, the claims of certain boyars that they were equal to the ruler because of their equally high family lineage were no longer acceptable. Both Ivan the Great and Vasili III, the important forebears of Ivan the Terrible, and rulers who already had developed ideas on the role of autocracy, did as much as they were able to do in limiting the power and prestige of the boyars. On occasion, they went so far as to ignore their advice, and relied to some extent upon government officials not of royal blood. When the boyars protested, both Ivan the Great and Vasili felt in a strong enough position to exile them to remote monasteries or, although less frequently, to have them executed. Some of the boyars, unwilling to take an inferior position, tried to exile themselves to neighboring Poland and Lithuania. This was considered desertion, and if the grand duke was successful in apprehending them, they were charged with treason to the state.

More clear in his objectives, more determined in his methods, and more powerful in his role as supreme autocrat than his predecessors, Ivan intensified the drive against the boyars. For years, he harassed them, denied them their privileges, ostentatiously ignored their counsel, refused them positions in the government, and denounced them as selfish, greedy, degenerate hangers-on.

Some boyars refused to submit to Ivan's despotic and high-handed moves, and fought a constant, dangerous battle with him—dangerous because their defeat often meant the loss of their lives as well as their estates. Other boyars attempted to flee to remote parts of Russia, sometimes even taking with them their retainers and their serfs. Still others—a very small number—tried to emigrate to other countries, mainly Poland and Lithuania, where they sought out the ruling prince or king and offered their services. Interestingly enough, the dissidents did not try to form an organized movement against the Czar. Intrigue, maneuver, yes; rebellion, no. Each would scheme for his individual advantage, but they were too jealous of one another to unite for rebellion.

Ivan's decision to move more decisively against them was taken around 1560, and coincided with Anastasia's death. His campaign at this time, though, was an indirect one. Sylvester and Adashev, who were not of the powerful boyar class but who had formed alliances with the boyars, were his victims. That Ivan would not have acted as he did had his "little heifer not been taken," as Ivan complained, is difficult to believe, for the very nature of his regime up to this time made his subsequent action almost inevitable. What is possible is that Anastasia might have restrained Ivan for several more years, but it was the fast-moving events of the time, not Anastasia's death, that were most instrumental in forcing Ivan's hand.

His warlike policy had become his paramount interest and concern. In effect, from the time of the Livonian invasion to the time of his death, Russia was on a war footing. To Ivan, the interests—and rights—of anyone were secondary to the war.

Sylvester and Adashev were in a particularly vulnerable position. Ever since 1553, when they had not supported Ivan in his battle to have the boyars take the oath for Dmitri, the Czar had looked upon them with suspicion. Until then, Sylvester had been his chief adviser, and the young Ivan had leaned upon him strongly. Adashev—the gentle Adashev—in his position, among others, as receiver of the people's petitions for redress of wrongs, was a shining beacon of goodness, softening the otherwise austere, harsh Russian regime.

Both of them had had Ivan's ear in the early days, and Ivan had been quite content to listen to their advice and act upon their recommendations. He was young, in love, and not yet intent upon following his star. As the years went on, however, he chafed under their continual advice, and Sylvester's remonstrances against the Czar's immoral actions angered him. Though Ivan did not dismiss them after their lack of support in 1553, his relations with them cooled.

As for Sylvester and Adashev, it became more and more difficult for them to sway their leader, and they became embittered because he resisted them. Whether or not they transferred some of their resentment to Anastasia is not known. There is only Ivan's word for it, and he was known to invent situations to fit an idea and to manufacture grievances to justify a point of view.

Sylvester especially felt himself to be not only the moral tutor of the Czar but of all Russia. He thought himself appointed, too, to instruct in all matters of day-to-day living, and dispensed advice on everything from dietary matters to how often and how hard a husband should beat his wife to make sure she obeyed him.

He believed himself the appointed mentor of the people's spiritual, physical, and material life. His book, *Domostroy* (*The Good Householder*), reflected his view of the lives he thought men should lead, and also pointed out some of the social conditions of the times. His purpose in writing the book was to reform the personal habits of the Russian people, and to give them moral and spiritual guidance. In the book, he promulgated rules of conduct by which he advised the citizens on manners and the women on how to keep their households in order and what foods should be eaten and on what days. He even listed various recipes for preparing food and drink.

As to the punishment that a husband should inflict on his wife to keep her faithful and obedient, the husband was instructed to be firm at all times. To be sure, he was urged not to chastise his wife in public but to take her aside and in private strip her of her shift and ply the whip upon her shoulders, without too much force. He was to do this as a matter of fatherly instruction, without anger and, if possible, with gentleness. After he had punished her, he was not to carry a grievance against her but was instructed to act in a friendly and cheerful manner, so that the dispute would not carry over to the bedroom and interfere with their sexual relations.

He exhorted the woman never to be idle. Her hands were to be active at all times at some household task or other. By keeping busy she would keep out of trouble and would not have thoughts that would lead her into mischief. She was not to engage in idle chatter, especially with her neighbors, and was to avoid at all costs gossip of any kind. She was forbidden strong drink, though an occasional glass of beer was tolerated.

He gave specific instructions on personal manners: how to behave at table and in other places, and how a person should "blow his nose, and spit without noise, taking care to turn away from the company, and put his foot over the place."

His spiritual advice included warnings on the evil of coming late for matins or missing Mass and instruction on when and how to sing in church. He advised that for the good of the soul alms should be given to beggars, food and drink should never be denied a suppliant at one's door, and compassion should be shown one's fellowman.

Although both Sylvester and Adashev fell under a cloud and though Ivan railed against them, accusing them of "trying to shear him of power" and attempting "to rule the Czardom," they were for their time men of superior intelligence and advanced social viewpoints, and enlightened in their personal relations with the mass of the people. These qualities were overshadowed by their alliance with the backward and tyrannical boyars, and by their lack of political vision. They were lumped with typical representatives of the nobility, like Kurbsky, and their names, like his, were soiled after their disgrace by Ivan's vindictiveness.

There were few persons of their position in all Russia of whom it could be said that they cared a whit whether the insignificant peasant lived or died, was well fed or starved, free or slave. Though the story smacks of legend, it is said that Adashev had such compassion for unfortunates that he kept ten lepers in his house and washed them with his own hands. Sylvester in his book wrote that "just as a man is bound to love his own soul, it is likewise necessary that he should feed his servants and the poor."

Sylvester's strict moral principles were designed not to enslave men but to restrict their excesses. Behind the strict moralizing that makes him seem like a Puritan preacher, there was a firm belief that private and public morals should be above reproach in order to effect the improvement so necessary in the state of man and society. And as for social justice, many of his actions and some of his theories were far ahead of his contemporaries'.

Like other Russian priests, he was married, and in his *Domostroy* wrote as the patriarch of his personal family as well as the patriarch of the entire family of Russian people.

"Not only have I freed my own slaves and given them land," Sylvester wrote, "but I have also bought back others out of slavery and presented them with their freedom. All our former slaves are free and live in comfort, and our domestic servants have remained with us of their own free will. To many abandoned orphans and poor people, both male and female, I have given food and drink, even to slaves in Novgorod and here in Moscow, until they were grown up, and I have given them an education according to their abilities.

"Many have I taught to read, write, and sing, others I taught to paint holy pictures, yet others to make books, and to many I taught various kinds of trade.

"Thy mother has provided sustenance for deserted and poor maidens and widows, she has taught them crafts and housekeeping, given them dowries and married them; and for men, too, she has found good wives. And now all of them, by God's help, are free men. Many of them have become priests, clerks, or officials or, according to their capacity, their natural disposition, and the will of God, have chosen another walk in life and become artisans. . . . And God has been good to us, so that we have suffered neither shame nor loss from our pupils and servants, nor have we had any quarrel with anybody. From all this God has so far protected us; but even when annoyance or loss has been caused us by any of our pupils, we have borne it, and nobody has heard anything about it. But God has requited us. And thou too, my child, do thou act likewise. Endure all injuries, for God will requite thee for it all."

As a man of God, he insisted that the Czar himself live the kind of life that Sylvester believed was correct for the leader of the people—pious, righteous, just, and restrained. Ivan would not—and could not—change his nature to do so. Sylvester's constant preaching at him to mend his evil ways irritated Ivan, and in time infuriated him.

Adashev, on his part, confused power and friendship. He considered himself not only Ivan's handpicked minister but the Czar's personal friend. And as a friend he continually interfered in Ivan's private affairs. He had not been pleased with Ivan's marriage to Anastasia, not because he disliked her but because he felt Ivan had married beneath himself. He felt slighted when Ivan refused to confide in him, and was jealous of Ivan's other advisers. But though Adashev considered himself Ivan's most intimate friend, Ivan never considered Adashev an intimate friend at all. Ivan was incapable of intimate friendship; his very nature rebelled at sharing himself with another person, which intimate friendship demands. Only with Anastasia had he been able to do so, and she was the first and last person with whom he ever had such a relationship. And Adashev did not understand this until it was too late, if then. For undoubtedly Adashev went into disgrace feeling that Ivan had betrayed their supposed friendship, rather than understanding fully that it was the political chasm existing between them that had finally driven them apart.

The final break between Ivan and his two closest advisers was less violent than was Ivan's way later in his czardom, when the executioner's axe was constantly red with the blood of erstwhile advisers and friends. Sylvester was sent into exile to a remote monastery by the White Sea, where he spent the rest of his life—alone, disgraced, forgotten. After a mock trial, in which Adashev was not allowed to be present or defend himself, he was imprisoned in Dorpat, and two months later, "that dog that I lifted off the dunghill," as Ivan later referred to him, died, probably by his own hand.

XII

The Turning Point

A YEAR after Anastasia's death and a few days before his thirty-first birthday, Ivan remarried. His new bride, the daughter of the Circassian Prince Temgryuk from the northern Caucasus, was immediately baptized Maria, and, with her relatives, took up residence in the Kremlin.

Maria was the exact opposite of Anastasia. The "wild Circassian," as she was called, was illiterate, half savage, violent, and passionate. She was a woman of great beauty and loose morals. She understood nothing about her husband's affairs of state, and cared less. Ivan's violent nature did not offend her; she had been raised among violent men. His moodiness did not disturb her; her wifely function was not to criticize, restrain, inspire. She had been taught that her only function was to please a husband, fit herself unobtrusively into his life, and produce heirs.

Ivan did not love Maria, and why he married her is a question that has never been answered. She had no special qualities, no important family background. Perhaps his rebuff by Sigismund had soured Ivan's taste for a great princess from a great royal family. Perhaps he wished to have a wife who was so completely different from his gentle Anastasia that she would never remind him of his first wife. Perhaps he had given in to a wild whim that the half-savage Maria as the Czaritsa of All Russia would be a monstrous joke upon the dozens of powerful boyars who were pushing their daughters forward so that the widowed Czar might take one of them as his wife. Perhaps marriage meant nothing more to him now than a formality that had to be attended to, and a wild Circassian woman in his bed would be intriguing. Perhaps it was a gesture to appease the rebellious Tatar groups. Perhaps—

Whatever the reason, Ivan married Maria, and then ignored her. During his thirteen years with Anastasia, he had kept his desire for women more or less in check because of his love for the Czaritsa; now he indulged himself with women whenever the mood struck him. As in his youth, he had any virgin that struck his fancy brought to his private quarters in the Kremlin. Like an Eastern potentate, he kept a harem, and one of the functions of his new-found intimates was to beg, borrow, or buy girls from various parts of the empire and beyond the borders to fill his seraglio.

With no Anastasia to restrain him and no Sylvester to admonish him and no Adashev to offer friendly counsel, Ivan's actions became more unpredictable, more unfathomable, more violent.

Though he had spared Sylvester's and Adashev's lives, soon after their exile he took revenge upon those closely associated—or that he claimed were closely associated—with them. A friend of Adashev's, a saintly religious fanatic named Mary Magdalena, who had weighted her body down with chains and was spending her widow's life in fasting and prayer, was seized, together with her five sons. They were executed. Then Adashev's cousins and brother-in-law were arrested. The charge—guilt by association. They, too, were handed over to the executioner. Sylvester and Adashev followers in the government were plucked out of their posts and sent into exile or executed. Even the army felt Ivan's wrath. Generals who were suspected of too great sympathy with the exiled ministers or who had family connections with Adashev were purged.

The unpredictable and strange actions in Ivan's political life matched those of his personal life. Just how he would move next in the political arena no one could venture to suggest with any degree of certainty. And probably the most perplexing of any of his political actions was his false abdication, which took place in 1564.

Events had moved rapidly since Anastasia's death and Sylvester's and Adashev's disgrace. The Teutonic Knights had been defeated in battle after battle, and their Grand Master Kettler had renounced his post. Sweden had entered the fray by taking the city of Revel. King Sigismund of Poland made himself the ruler of Livonia, and

Kettler, now the Duke of Courland, became his vassal. The same Catherine whom Ivan had asked in marriage was married off to John, Duke of Finland and heir to Sweden's throne, and now a bond was established between Poland and Sweden.

An anomalous situation now existed in which Ivan was at war with Livonia but not with Poland, though Sigismund was the ruler of both. In 1562 and 1563, Ivan put into the field huge numbers of troops, composed to a large extent of Tatars. His victories continued, and as city after city fell Ivan added to his already long title of Emperor. Huge amounts of booty flowed into Ivan's treasury as the victorious Russian troops confiscated the cities' treasuries and the personal possessions and wealth of the citizens. Triumphant Moslem Tatar troops helped their Russian comrades in arms destroy the Latin churches. Orthodox icons and crosses became very much in evidence in the newly conquered cities.

In Polotsk, which fell in February, 1563, Catholic monks were killed, and Jews were forcibly christened. Those who resisted were killed. Moslems joined Orthodox Christians in razing Protestant churches.

Russian and Tatar troops continued their march through the Lithuanian countryside. Resistance was feeble and sporadic. For a while it seemed that all of Lithuania would fall to the Russian Czar. Then, unexpectedly, Ivan agreed to a truce with Lithuania. He ordered that the coffin he had had made for King Sigismund's body be thrown onto a scrap pile.

Ivan's victories had not made him happy or content. Instead, he fell into deep fits of depression on the one hand and violent rages on the other. He now carried with him at all times a long staff with an iron point, which he insisted he needed to defend himself from physical attacks by his enemies and which he used, when enraged, on whoever was at hand.

His suspicions became outlandish and almost completely irrational. He saw treachery everywhere. He insisted more and more on complete submission to his authority, and his counselors, afraid for their lives should they cross the willful Czar, kept their distance. They had discovered that it was useless to give him any advice, for he twisted their words and accused them of disaffection, conspiracy, and treason. Honest, sincere advisers either left his service or were dismissed, so that Ivan now had about him advisers who were nothing but lackeys, who fawned upon their master like beaten dogs.

He repeatedly raised the question of boyar treachery, fulminating at every opportunity against their supposed plots and schemes to thwart him. The number of nobles fleeing into exile increased. Even boyars who had staunchly supported him during his illness in 1553 and since then had risen to Ivan's defense no matter what unjust acts he committed were not safe from his wrath. So it was, for instance, with Prince Ivan Sheremetiev, one of his leading generals. Sheremetiev was thrown into a dungeon and tortured, and his wealth ordered confiscated. When none was found, because he had given it all to the poor, Ivan visited the chained Sheremetiev in the dungeon and accused him of treachery.

For a few weeks in 1563, his vicious mood was briefly lightened by the birth of a son. But after five weeks the infant died, and the Czar's bitterness increased. In the same year, his brother Yuri died. Ivan was deeply affected by his death. Yuri had never opposed Ivan or shown the slightest ambition for power. Ivan had been genuinely fond of his slightly defective brother, the more because Yuri had always shown Anastasia the greatest courtesy and respect. Ivan had a lavish funeral in his brother's honor, and at the funeral shed tears of genuine sorrow. Ulyana, Yuri's wife, voluntarily entered a convent, and Ivan urged her to live a luxurious life there. When Ulyana said that she honestly wished to renounce material things and lead a simple, cloistered life, Ivan ordered her to do as he commanded. Ulyana firmly resisted his orders, insisting she could only be content in living a nun's life. Infuriated at being thwarted, Ivan ordered her executed.

In 1564, Ivan received a blow that shook him deeply. Prince Andrei Kurbsky fled to Poland. Kurbsky had been one of his closest advisers and a leading general whose military talents Ivan had relied upon at Kazan and now in Livonia.

Here was real treason, Ivan reasoned, conclusive proof that his condemnation of the boyars was justified. His suspicions of a boyars' conspiracy increased to the point where not a noble, in his mind's eye, was free of guilt. The situation was intolerable. The very Kremlin itself became hateful to him, for throughout its vast expanse lurked hidden enemies and possible assassins.

In December, 1564, Ivan suddenly abandoned the Kremlin.

Together with the Czaritsa Maria, his children, and a few members
of his court, he got into a sleigh and drove away, leaving no word
why he was going away, where he was going, or for how long he
would be gone. Behind the royal sleigh, hundreds of sleighs followed, laden with the Czar's prized possessions, treasure chests,
sacred images and crosses, clothing, furniture, and provisions.

It was obvious that this was not another of the Czar's frequent
pilgrimages or an ordinary pleasure trip, for the departure had
been too secretive and the amount of baggage too extensive. All
Moscow soon heard about it, and wondered what had happened to
cause the Czar to depart so precipitously.

When word got back to Moscow that the Czar's party had
passed his favorite monastery—the Trinity—but had not stopped
there, the populace's wonder increased. Where was the Czar going
—and why?

At last they heard that the Czar and his party had stopped at
the village of Alexandrov. For days they waited for some word
from their Little Father. Ivan was mute. As the days passed,
wonder turned to consternation, and then consternation turned to
fear and despair. The people felt deserted, helpless, and leaderless.
The boyars trembled at what plans Ivan might have in store for
them, and feared the anger of the people, who were now grumbling
that they might have to live under the rule of the hated boyars if
their Czar deserted them. The shops closed, commerce ceased, and
speeches against the boyars were openly made in the streets.

A month later, when Ivan felt that the stir caused by his sudden
departure from the capital had reached its climax, he issued two
letters, one addressed to the boyars, clergy, and government officials and another to the ordinary citizens of Moscow. In the
former, he spoke angrily about the usurpation of authority and
illegal acts of the boyars during his minority. He accused the
Church and government officials as well as the boyars, individually
and as groups, of failing to defend their Czar, the motherland, and
the mass of Russian people. He indicted them as thieves, and
charged them with stealing land and wealth from the Czar. He accused them, especially the clergy, of giving refuge to criminals, and
using influence with the crown to help them escape punishment. It
was because of all these vile activities that he had decided, "with

great sorrow in his heart," to abandon his rulership. Now he would reside in the wilderness and go wherever "God shall direct."

In the latter letter, which was addressed to the merchants, poor clergy, and common people in general and which, he had instructed, was to be read aloud to them in the Red Square in front of the Kremlin walls, he told them that he was not angry with them and that they should not be afraid, and assured them of his continued affection and good will.

At first everyone was stunned by the Czar's announcement of his abdication. Then among the common people loud wailings and cries shook the Square. They wrung their hands and, crossing themselves, asked for divine help in bringing back to them their beloved Czar. Interminable and violent discussions took place among the boyars and the clergy over what was to be done to resolve the crisis.

It was finally decided that the Metropolitan, the bishops, certain older boyars, and a few merchants should undertake a mission to Alexandrov, to beg the Czar not to desert his subjects and his throne. The delegation was told to inform the Czar that if he would return to the Kremlin they themselves would help him hunt down and kill all conspirators and traitors who had dared to oppose the Czar and who were plotting the destruction of their country.

In January, 1565, the delegation left for the Czar's summer place in Alexandrov, which by now had been converted into an armed fortress. When they arrived and were ushered into the Czar's presence, they were astounded at his appearance: his usually bright, piercing eyes were dull, his beard was sparse and gray, his face was drawn and lined, his carriage stooped. He appeared to be on the verge of a mental and physical breakdown.

The delegates first prostrated themselves before the Czar, and then presented him with a petition. "If, Sire," it read, "you do despise what is temporal and transient, and will take no thought for your great land and its cities, nor the countless masses of your devoted people, be mindful at least of the holy, miracle-working pictures and of the one Christian faith, which through your abdication is faced with utter ruin or the revilings of heretics. But should treason and malice in our land cause you, O Sire, affliction of which we have no knowledge, it is for you to punish the guilty ones severely or to show them mercy; your wise laws and ordinances will set all things right again."

Ivan was overjoyed. At last, representatives of the boyars, the clergy, government officials, merchants, common people—all of them had come begging him to take the law into his own hands, do what he would according to his own plans without criticism or opposition. He accepted their petition, and dismissed them.

However, he did not immediately return to the Kremlin. With his mastery of showmanship and sense of the dramatic, he made Moscow and Russia wait for his return. The longer he delayed, he reasoned, the more eager everyone would be to acquiesce in his most extravagant demands. Disputes, dissension, charges of treason and disloyalty that now raged among his advisers only strengthened his own hand. He allowed another month to go by before he returned.

When in February he arrived in Moscow, two months after his departure, the people of Moscow kneeled in the snow by the tens of thousands, blessing their Little Father and giving thanks to God that their Czar had finally returned to protect and lead them. As was the custom, most of the people who lined the streets that day did not dare lift their eyes to look at the Czar. The few who did dare, however, saw in the royal sleigh a stranger, for the Czar, according to a description of him at the time, now looked like a completely different person: he was unkempt, with long hair and a beard that was awry, his mouth was twisted, his brow was furrowed, and his eyes had the look of a demented man.

A meeting of the Council was summoned, and Ivan presented his conditions for resuming the throne: in the future he would be free to banish from the court anyone who was disloyal or disobedient to the Czar; he would be free to execute certain specified persons and to expropriate their property for the benefit of his own treasury. In all these matters, he was to act as he saw fit, and no one—boyar, cleric, government official—could interfere in any way.

Meekly, the Council agreed to all of Ivan's demands. Ivan's coup d'etat was complete. He now could proceed, with the consent of the governed, to establish himself as supreme and unlimited dictator.

He lost no time in doing so.

XIII

The Oprichnina

WHAT had happened during those two months at Alexandrov to change Ivan's appearance so drastically? He had left the Kremlin a youthful and robust thirty-four, and had returned with the looks of an old man, haggard and demented.

Like all power-motivated men, Ivan was a reckless gambler, and in deserting the Kremlin and abdicating the throne he was playing for high stakes. There was no certainty that he would be called back; there was a strong possibility that the boyars would take advantage of his abdication to seize control of the state, send soldiers to Alexandrov, and under one pretext or another kill him.

Ivan always had an overwhelming fear for his personal safety, and he was tortured by the possibility that the risk he was taking might mean his life if he should lose. Apparently this is why he had turned his summer place at Alexandrov into an armed fortress, for otherwise there would have been no need to do so. He had had nightmares and hallucinations during his stay at Alexandrov, and they undoubtedly revolved about his fears that he might meet the fate of so many other Russian nobles—a rendezvous with the executioner.

Yet what had happened at the summer place was above and beyond all this. He had undergone a crisis at Alexandrov that had sprung from his very nature, but it had been triggered by a special, all-important decision he had made that would not only change the structure and operation of the state and drastically affect its millions of inhabitants but would necessitate the greatest exertion and dedication on his part. The decision: to make Russia a strict authoritarian state with himself as absolute dictator.

As Ivan saw it, conditions in Russia had reached such a critical point that he, as the supreme leader, had to take the most extreme measures to save the throne and the country. He believed the boyars were ruining Russia by insisting on their entrenched privileges and rights, and that they would go to any lengths to maintain them. And now that he had pledged Russia to a fight to the death to conquer the western lands and thus assure Russia her place in the sun, when everything had to be done for the winning of the war, the boyars, because of their resistance and intransigence, were particularly dangerous.

Still, this political reasoning, valid to an extent, was not the whole truth—and Ivan knew it. Ivan was neither a fool nor a charlatan. He was brilliant, dedicated, and—above all—ambitious. He was a master at deceiving others; but he constantly searched within himself for the truth. In this situation the truth was that he was using this political reasoning to justify his personal ambition for unlimited power.

Ivan's ideas and plans for a dictatorship had not come to him on the spur of the moment or without the influence and instruction of prior events. In a sense, the very history of Russia itself until his time was a gradual building-up process for his action. The two hundred-odd years of Tatar subjection, in which the authoritarian khans had acted with proverbial Oriental despotism, had had their influence. The ways of despotism had penetrated in a subtle way into the very fabric of Russian governmental life and into the relation of the Russian princes and their subjects. In only a few places, such as in Novgorod, was there a democratic tradition, a body of literature, philosophy, or law that concerned itself with the rights of men. The very early paternalistic relation of ruler and ruled, exemplified by such rulers as the pre-Tatar Prince Vladimir Monomakh, had been destroyed by centuries of Tatar domination and the subservience of Russian royalty as vassals to their Eastern masters. After the Tatar domination had ended, the ruling grand dukes in many ways became more despotic than their former masters.

Another factor, specific in plan and intent, that possibly influenced Ivan was the presentation of a petition by a government official named Peresvetov to Ivan some time before the capture of Kazan. In this petition, the knowledgeable Russian-Lithuanian Peresvetov, who had been in the service of various foreign governments—Hungarian, Polish, Walachian—proposed that the power of the Czar should be increased, to coincide with an increase in the power and prestige of the army. The central point of the proposed reorganization was to deny the nobles the right to have their own private military retinues, and to make certain that the army should be completely under the control and jurisdiction of the Czar. Peresvetov urged that the state be reorganized on the basis of military discipline. In this military state, administration should be strict, and justice should be stern and quick. Many of his specific proposals, by design or coincidence, were used subsequently by Ivan.

That Ivan lost no time in putting into practice the unlimited power guaranteed to him by his successful coup d'etat was demonstrated the day after the Council had bowed to his will; he placed all accused traitors under a court ban, and gave orders that various adherents of Prince Kurbsky should be seized. Without a trial or formalities of any kind, Ivan had six "traitors" beheaded; the seventh was impaled.

The dictatorship had begun.

And so had the terror. But terror was not enough. What Ivan foresaw was an area of operations that was completely under his domination, and in which no other force but his own could operate. It was to be a separate private state within the Russian state complex in which there was no other authority—political, administrative, or judicial—except the Czar's.

The Oprichnina was the answer.

The term Oprichnina itself was not new; it had been used in the ancient days of appanage to mean certain districts separated from others, especially those districts given in perpetuity to princes' widows. Ivan merely borrowed the term for his separatist state.

As Ivan conceived it, the Oprichnina was both a territory and an institution. As a territory, it embraced—eventually—half the land area of Russia, though its various sections were not contiguous. As an institution, it had a separate organization. The court entourage was no longer based upon inherited position, but was selected by Ivan, and consisted of chosen boyars, retainers, guards, government personnel; in other words, the usual functionaries of a court.

He began to set up this state within a state, or state alongside another state, by hand-picking a thousand men and assigning them to certain streets and wards in the quarter of Moscow known as the White City. The inhabitants of this quarter were evicted from their homes and resettled in other parts of the city.

In order to support this new court, he took for himself some twenty cities and town-districts, together with other districts, and assigned them to the members of his new organization—the Oprichniki, or as Ivan called them, court people. As in Moscow, the inhabitants of these cities, towns, and districts were resettled in non-Oprichnina areas.

Frightful hardships were endured by the dispossessed inhabitants. At one time, more than twelve thousand heads of families together with their wives and children were forced out of their homes, and, carrying whatever few possessions they could manage to salvage, had to walk hundreds of miles through the snow in the middle of winter to other areas assigned them. In many cases, these new areas were completely undeveloped, consisting of nothing more than virgin forest.

The Oprichnina area, as already mentioned, was not a province or state of contiguous districts. As the organization grew, it became a collection of cities, towns, and districts scattered over the country, though principally in the northern and central parts of Russia.

The areas not assigned to the Oprichnina were made over to various boyars known as *zemskie boyaré,* or provincial boyars, who had the responsibility of administering them. This section of Russia was known as the Zemschina, or provincial section. In effect, what now existed was a country that was divided into two parts—the Oprichnina and the Zemschina.

Among other of Ivan's purposes in setting up such a complicated and elaborate structure was that of breaking the influence and power of the old boyar groups by dispossessing them of their lands, and thus impoverishing them. He refused to admit many of them to his new court, and when he annexed their lands he regarded them as conquered territory. The newly landless boyars who were forced to go to frontier areas or other undeveloped sections of Russia where there was no tradition of appanage found themselves helpless and powerless. He filled their positions with his Oprichniki, who were completely loyal to and dependent upon the Czar.

For years Ivan continued this mass shifting of the population from one area to another. Ivan euphemistically referred to it as "sorting out folks," but his victims called it expropriation of their lands and holdings for the personal benefit and gain of the Czar. Their resentment towards their expropriator knew no bounds. And when Ivan compounded his action of expropriation by systematic extermination of the more stubborn boyars through sudden raids by his Oprichniki, the resentment of those who managed to survive turned to hatred.

Ivan gave as the justification for his actions the fact that the boyars had ruined Russia by possessing for themselves the peasants, land, and property of the state, and thus deprived the government of its means of existence. Ivan's actions, which introduced something resembling anarchy into the country and rocked it to its very foundations, were further justified by Ivan's insistence that such extreme measures were necessary to stamp out treason, which he saw everywhere. And in the name of stamping out treason, his loyal Oprichniki were given a free hand to terrorize, torture, and execute.

By setting up his own private state, Ivan now had what he considered a secure political sanctuary, where his rebellious boyars could not penetrate. In addition, he had a personal sanctuary, where he was safe from their murderous swords. The fear that he might be assassinated became an obsession with him, dominating his thoughts and actions till the day he died. In 1572, he had drawn up a will in which he pictured himself as a persecuted man, the target of evildoers, who had forced him to become an exile in his own country and a wanderer in the wilderness. "Through the multitude of my sins hath the wrath of God descended upon me," he wrote, "so that the boyars, of their conceit, have driven me from my possessions, and I wander through all the lands." It was this never-ending fear that was to underlie the episode in which he later became involved with Elizabeth I of England.

The Oprichniki became, in effect, his personal bodyguard as well as a vigilant police force that scoured the country to stamp out traitors and malcontents. And when in time the hand-picked one thousand Oprichniki increased to over six thousand, Ivan had a corps of unswervingly loyal, tough, and ruthless men whose power was unchallenged and who were feared and hated.

The formation of the Oprichnina, complex as it was in conception and odious as it was in its ruthless operation, was the result of a cold, calculated plan to strengthen the state militarily, strategically, administratively, and financially. By expropriating the land of the boyars—and land, together with the peasants on it, was the main wealth of the country—Ivan strengthened the central state apparatus. By waging what can well be termed a class war against the boyars, Ivan had a propaganda weapon that endeared him to the mass of the Russian people, who hated the selfish, greedy, merciless boyars. By establishing a police that in many ways was more powerful than the army itself, a police obedient only to him, he put the autocracy in a strategic position that was almost unassailable. And by creating a new group he was assuring the state of administrators whose only loyalty was to the autocracy and not, as in the case of the boyars, loyalty to their class, their sections of the country, their traditions.

The Oprichnina, as it developed, was more than just a state within a state or an organization to further Ivan's plans. It developed a character, a ritual, an esprit typical of a fanatical political party or brotherhood. Its members were more devoted to their cause than to their own families, friends, or, for that matter, their own personal advancement. They were constantly involved in a war against enemies, traitors, conspirators, and malcontents. Every means justified the ends, although they were hard put to explain exactly what the ends were except to mouth slogans about stamping out treason, killing the greedy boyars, and protecting the safety and well-being of their beloved Czar. Terror was justified because it produced results beneficial to the state and Czar, and so was torture, expropriation, mass exile, murder of individuals, extermination of entire families, and eventually even the extermination of the population of an entire city. There were no laws of restraint that were applicable to them. There were no limits that were set for them. All that mattered was the achievement of individual tasks that in the aggregate advanced the general objectives. It mattered not at all that vile methods were used in completing the tasks that would—and this they were blindly convinced of—achieve the bright new day of complete autocratic rule. And this, of course, led to outrages and crimes against the human being that were almost beyond belief. These were days, in truth, in which monsters in the shape of men walked that piece of earth known as Mother Russia, and no amount of rationalizing about advancing historical, political, or territorial ambitions can wipe out the crimes committed in her name.

The Oprichnik was proud of his organization and of being a member of it. Upon his initiation, he kissed the cross and took an oath in which he renounced, in a fashion, the material things of the world in order to advance the welfare of the Czar, and swore to put the Czar and state above any consideration of self, friends, or family relations. He ostentatiously wore a special uniform that was entirely black, and rode on a black horse that had black trappings. On the Oprichnik's saddlebow there was a dog's head and a broom; the dog's head to signify that the Oprichnik devoured his enemies, and the broom to signify that it was his function to sweep treason from the land.

Attracted by the Oprichnina's stern discipline, its semi-mystical ritual, its distinctive uniform, its rough and tough methods, and the pride and show of being among the Czar's elect, the men who gravitated toward the Oprichnina and those the Czar picked personally were brutal thugs and cut-throats, vicious sadists, adventurers, fanatics, and opportunists. They readily responded to Ivan's order, put by Alexei Tolstoy as: "Kill the cattle, saber the peasants, catch the girls, set the village on fire; follow me, my boys, spare no one!"

Ivan now surrounded himself with intimates selected from the Oprichnina. His former advisers were dismissed, exiled, or executed. These new advisers and intimates were far removed from the Sylvesters, Adashevs, and Kurbskys. Their qualifications were cunning, utter disregard for human life and dignity, unqualified loyalty, the ability to take orders without questions of any kind, and a fanatical devotion to Ivan's cause.

The chief adviser-executioner was Maliuta Skuratov. He was a vicious, insensitive, sadistic gauleiter, who welcomed the most distasteful assignments from his master, and carried them out firmly and efficiently. In time, his very name became synonymous with torture and death. Other Oprichnina leaders included Prince Viazemsky; the Princes Alexei and Feodor Basmanov, a father-

and-son team of murderers; Vasili Gryaznoy, the Archimandrite of the Chudov Monastery; and the enigmatic Nikita Romanovich Zakharin.

Ivan was a stern taskmaster. Proud of the institution he had created, he insisted that his followers be efficient and methodical. His temper, which was always at the bursting point, became out of hand when he discovered blunders or neglect on the part of an Oprichnik, and he would chastise him by striking him with his iron-pointed staff or, in severe cases of insubordination, turn an offending Oprichnik over to the executioner.

Yet, strict as he was with his Oprichniki, he established a camaraderie and a personal rapport with them, which he could never establish with the boyars. He enjoyed being with them, and sought out their company at every opportunity. Most of the Oprichniki were young, robust men of lower-class backgrounds, and their carefree, boisterous ways made him feel young, too. When he was among them, he was able to shed his normally gloomy feelings, and lose himself in wild bouts of drinking, in which he would sing, dance, and engage in horseplay.

Though Ivan found a great deal of pleasure and satisfaction in being among the virile, reckless, brutal Oprichniki, he had little satisfaction from the results of his grand scheme. The elaborate plan failed to crush the boyars; it merely scattered them. And by the thousands they licked their wounds in faraway places, waiting for the day when they could move back again to Moscow and other centers and regain their positions of power and prestige. The crushing of the boyars became more of an ideal than a reality, even though hundreds were put to death.

Outside the boyar class, there was no group in Russia at the time that was capable of carrying on the administration of the state. The mass of the people were illiterate and backward. The clergy could have been called upon, but a state administered by churchmen was unthinkable to Ivan. He had had enough of Sylvesters and their moralizing. Moreover, the Church had its function to perform, and to divert it from its spiritual tasks would have been to secularize it, and this Ivan refused to consider. The dilemma that Ivan faced, and that he never was able to solve, was how to dispense with the boyars' power on the one hand and use their administrative ability on the other. What the establishment of the Oprichnina accomplished, therefore, was merely the separation of the country, with the two parts existing side by side, though not jointly. How long or how well this confusing situation could last was a question that constantly plagued Ivan, and one for which he had no answer.

To crush the boyars Ivan would have had to alter radically the social structure of Russian society by lifting out of the mire the overwhelming majority of the people, who were leading bestial, degrading lives in poverty, filth, disease, and ignorance. This called for a social reformer, and Ivan hadn't the faintest desire to be one. The miserable lot of the Russian masses was no concern of his. Since the Russian mass was a supine, listless, completely beaten group who made no powerful demands, he had no pressure upon him to do anything for them. The few faint grumblings of the masses were completely overshadowed by their devotion and respect for the Czar as a figure.

Thus what developed was a situation in which the Oprichnina became a check against the boyars, not their destroyer. It functioned as a police force, not as a revolutionary group. Its energies were directed against people, not a system. As such it became the bulwark of autocracy, and in the long run it made little change in the basic system of government that had existed for hundreds of years in Russia—and was to exist for three hundred and fifty years more.

The political ideas and practices surrounding the Oprichnina, however, were only one side of its story; the other side was the human misery and suffering it caused. And it was this power of the Oprichnina to cause suffering that made the reign of Ivan so horrible and gave him the epithet "the Terrible."

Rumors, stories, and accounts of the Oprichnina terror began to flow over the borders of Russia to the outside world. When Russian ambassadors in European countries were questioned about the Oprichnina and its reign of terror, in many cases they were unable to explain its complicated origin and purpose. In other cases they were unwilling to do so. The Russian ambassador to Warsaw, for instance, was asked by King Sigismund, "What is the Oprichnina?" Stonefaced, he replied, "There is no such thing."

A very few foreigners, however, before many years had gone by, did understand to an extent what Ivan had done to Russia with his Oprichnina. One such person was Giles Fletcher, who arrived in Russia a few years after Ivan's death. He wrote: "This tyrannical practice of making a general schism and public division among the subjects of his whole realm proceeded (as should seem) from an extreme doubt and desperate fear which he had conceived of most of his nobility and gentlemen of his realm, in his wars with the Polonian and Chrim Tatar. What time he grew into a vehement suspicion (conceived of the ill success of his affairs), that they practiced treason with the Polonian and Chrim. Whereupon he executed some, and devised his way to be rid of the rest.

"And this wicked policy and tyrannous practice (though now it be ceased) has so troubled that country, and filled it so full of grudge and mortal hatred ever since, that it will not be quenched (as it seems now) till it burn again into a civil flame."

In Russia, however, a few enlightened and humane men raised their voices ever so quietly and secretively—to speak loudly or openly meant detection, with the result that they would never speak again—against the Oprichnina terror. "The Czar does continually stir up murderous strife," one critic wrote, "and does send the men of one town against the men of another town, and does many a time bid his own portion of the state ravish the other portion, and spoil its houses, and deliver it over unto death. Thus, the Czar has raised up against himself sore anger and lamentation in all the world, by reason of the many blood-sheddings and executions which he has commanded."

Some critics, unable to understand the complex situation, believed the Oprichnina was a huge, cruel game, played by a willful Czar. "All the state has he sundered in twain, as it were with an axe, and thereby has he disturbed all men," one observer wrote. "He plays with God's people, and stakes against himself all such as do conspire."

People lived in mortal terror of the sight of the black-uniformed Oprichniki on their black horses, and referred to them as "the blackness of Hell," and "as dark as the night." As if out of nowhere they suddenly descended upon a house, seized its inhabitants, killed them on the spot, and then, after taking whatever valuables were there, burned it.

Heinrich Staden, a German adventurer who served in the Oprichnina, wrote of one such episode in which he participated.

Staden and his men made a raid upon a noble's house, and "from the windows of the women's apartments stones came showering down upon us. Calling my servant Teshata I quickly ran up the stairs with an axe in my hand. At the top of the stairs I was met by the Princess who wanted to throw herself at my feet, but terrified by my frightful appearance she rushed back into her chamber. I struck her in the back with my axe and she dropped on the threshold. I stepped over her dead body and made familiar with her maidservants."

Russian nobles who had fled their country viewed with horror the excesses that were taking place there. Although when they were in Russia they were brutal to their own serfs and completely callous to their sufferings and poverty, they now shed tears for the misery and cruelty life had become in their native land. In the courts of the Western kings where they had fled for refuge, and where they felt themselves now defenders of right and justice, they condemned Ivan and his Oprichniki as barbarians and murderers. Kurbsky, for instance, from his Polish sanctuary, wrote that the Oprichniki were "children of darkness," and that the "bloodthirsty Oprichniki were hundreds of thousands of times worse than hangmen."

For the most part, Ivan ignored the critics, except Kurbsky. In fact, it is doubtful that much of what they had to say ever reached him; Ivan had by now cut himself off almost completely from his former life in the Kremlin. His wife Maria was little more than a convenience, an ornament called Czaritsa. Since 1563, she had borne him no more heirs, and this displeased him. As time went on, he spent less and less time in the Kremlin, for it had become for him a distasteful place. The formal court life of the Kremlin was a round of ceremonies and traditions, things he told himself he disliked. For weeks on end, he stayed at one of several fortified lodges, that had been constructed for him in the Oprichnina quarter of Moscow, and, in time, at the new palace at Alexandrov, which he had ordered built for him and his Oprichnina henchmen.

And here Ivan and his Oprichniki led a strange, bewildering life in a fortified palace, which was a weird combination of governmental office, monastery, drinking hall, charnel house, and brothel.

XIV

Alexandrov

IVAN's palace outside Alexandrov, a small town southwest of the city of Vladimir and about a hundred miles from Moscow, was a large structure with all the accoutrements of a medieval fortress. Underneath the palace, there were dungeons, dark recesses, and winding passageways. For protection there were barricades at every possible approach to the grounds, a deep moat, and high palisades around the palace and the auxiliary buildings in which artisans, servants, falconers, dogboys, and others lived. Guards were always on duty in the dense woods in which the palace was situated.

One aspect of life—and only one, for there were others—inside this secluded and highly fortified lair was akin to the kind of life in some of the monasteries that existed at the time. The monasteries in this "land of monasteries," as Giles Fletcher called Russia, varied considerably. Some were truly retreats from the world of affairs, where monks fasted, prayed, and led exemplary spiritual lives. Others, such as the Trinity Monastery, were vast enterprises. The Trinity, for example, had at one time over a hundred thousand serfs, together with the land to which they were attached. The Monastery itself was surrounded by a wall a mile in circumference, upon which were eight huge towers. Still other monasteries were centers of riotous living. Vodka flowed freely, for the monasteries were the chief manufacturers of intoxicating liquors. Women were permitted within their walls, and they were readily available for amorous purposes. Young boys, mainly orphans, were taken to them not for religious instruction but for sexual perversion.

118

Monks and nuns were often quartered in the same building, and their life there was somewhat less than chaste. Noblemen used these monasteries for retreats, where they would indulge themselves in what has euphemistically been described as "luxurious solitude."

Ivan insisted that he and the specially selected three hundred Oprichniki that surrounded him at Alexandrov should lead a monastic life. He had had enough of royal ceremony and ritual at the Kremlin. His soul, he said, cried out for spiritual sustenance. And the statement, in a sense, was sincere. The Czar was extremely pious. He never felt more at peace with himself, the world, and his Maker than when he was deeply immersed in prayer and Church ritual.

From the beginning of his residence at Alexandrov, he set up what might be called a brotherhood, complete with a charter of association, which he himself wrote. Ivan assumed the title of abbot, and assigned various other monastic functions to his Oprichniki henchmen. Prince Viazemsky, for instance, was made cellarer and Skuratov became sacristan. Everyone, even the Czar, wore black cassocks and monastic skull caps. Ivan himself often performed the various necessary monastery chores. Together with his sons, he scaled the belfry each morning to ring the bells for Mass, read the offices in church, and sang in the choir. No one was more fervent in obeisances to the altar than the monk-Czar, and his forehead was constantly covered with bruises from banging it on the floor.

Yet Ivan's Church interest were not confined strictly to observance and practice of ritual. As a profoundly intellectual man with a keen, penetrating mind, he enjoyed nothing better than to argue, especially on theological subjects, and had, as one contemporary of his put it, "an especial shrewdness and remembrance of God's Writ."

There were times in Ivan's life when he even arranged formal debates on theology. In 1570 with all solemnity, he arranged a debate in his palace on the subject of Orthodoxy versus Protestantism with the Bohemian evangelist Rokita, the chaplain of the Polish Embassy in Moscow. In the audience were foreign ambassadors, members of the higher clergy, and prominent boyars. Ivan spoke first, and made a strong attack on the Protestant theologian's teachings. At the conclusion of his presentation, Ivan

invited Rokita to defend his case "with boldness and freedom."
After Rokita spoke in defense of Protestantism, Ivan wrote out a
lengthy refutation of his opponent's arguments.

Ivan's temper, however, was such that his intellectual discussions sometimes ended violently. On one occasion, in 1577, he
got into an argument with a Protestant minister in Livonia. The
minister argued, among other things, that Luther was like St. Paul.
Furious at this comparison, Ivan ordered that the minister be
executed, then changed his mind, hit him over the head with his
riding crop, spurred his horse, and, as he was riding away,
shouted, "Go to the devil with your Luther!"

At Alexandrov, however, Ivan indulged himself in few intellectual religious exercises. As head of the monastery, he kept himself busy performing his self-assigned job as abbot, and supervising
the activities of the brothers. Ivan set up a rigid and rigorous
routine of religious observances.

A typical day began at four o'clock in the morning. Ivan and his
children rang the bell for matins, and all the brothers had to come
immediately to the church. A brother who missed matins was
punished by imprisonment for eight days. Services lasted for several hours, usually until seven, during which time Ivan chanted,
read, prayed, and prostrated himself over and over again.

At eight o'clock, the brothers were summoned for Mass. At
twelve o'clock, dinner was served in the refectory, and Ivan read
to the assembled brothers from one or another Church book. At
eight in the evening, there was vespers, and at midnight everyone
was called to prayers.

After midnight prayers, Ivan went into his bedroom, where
three blind men, expert storytellers, waited for him. It was their
job to tell him tales until he fell asleep.

Actually, however, the monastery at Alexandrov was no monastery; it was a parody of a monastery. And Ivan was no dedicated
abbot; he was Czar Ivan the Terrible playing at being an abbot.
For together with, or alongside, the life of black cassocks and
monastic skull caps and elaborate day-to-day Church observances,
there was another life being led at Alexandrov.

Now that the Czar spent his time at the fortified palace and
only rarely made a visit to the Kremlin in Moscow, Alexandrov in
fact, if not in name, was the capital of Russia, and, as such, the

place where final decisions of government were made. The Moscow-Alexandrov road was a well-ridden one, with numerous governmental officials among the travelers.

Ivan had not retreated from the world and his responsibility as head of Russia; he had merely pushed away that part of the world that he disliked, and had organized a different personal world for himself. It was a world more in keeping with his temperament and desires and one in which he was complete master, beholden to no one or to any forms or traditions he found distasteful. It was a world, too, where he could indulge himself in a never-ending quest to appease the restless, wild, ferocious demons that had always pursued him. Life at Alexandrov reflected these elements of Ivan's personality as well as his penchant for piety and the monastic atmosphere, and surrounded by his young, lusty, and savage Oprichniki, Ivan indulged himself in almost every conceivable kind of excess.

Fasting and abstention from drink were not characteristics of the Alexandrov monastery. Quite the opposite. The dining tables were loaded with the most exotic foods—roast swans, peacocks, sturgeon, and pastries of all kinds—and rare wines imported from various parts of Europe and Asia. Meals lasted for hours, with an army of servants constantly in attendance upon the three hundred or so Oprichniki who took their meals in common. Sometimes Ivan, like the head abbot that he was, would take his meals in private. At other times he would join his brothers. In true monastery fashion, the leftovers were taken to the public square and distributed among the poor.

There was no lack of entertainment. In the underground dungeons, there was always a good supply of prisoners, and the torture chambers were equipped with the most intricate and elaborate instruments for inflicting pain and death. One of Ivan's favorite pastimes was to visit the underground cells and watch prisoners confess their crimes, prodded toward the truth, as it were, by one or another of these instruments. There was the rack that broke bones; the iron cage in which suspects were burned alive; the iron hooks that tore away huge pieces of flesh; the pits in which prisoners were buried alive; and, of course, the knout, which was a particularly ingenious weapon of torture.

The knout has been described as "a whip made of parchment

cooked in milk and so hard that its strokes were like those of a sword. Practiced executioners could kill a man with three strokes. There were few instances of any one surviving thirty." An eye-witness has given this account of a knouting:

"The patient strips himself to his waist, taking off his shirt, and leaves nothing on but his breeches; or if a woman, nothing but her petticoat. This done, he ascends a sort of scaffold, where his feet are fastened to the floor; his hands are put over the shoulders of a strong man, who with his hands holds him fast to his breast, so that he cannot stir; then the executioner advances three or four steps, as if he was running, till he comes within reach of the of-fender, and gives him his first stroke on the middle of his back; then he retreats three or four steps, and comes forward again, al-ways with such dexterity that he never gives two strokes upon the same place. He repeats this motion as many times as there are blows ordered to be given by his sentence, the blood running in abundance all this while from the patient's back. This is the moder-ate knout. When the sentence orders the knout between the moderate and the severe, one may see small pieces of flesh taken off at every stroke of the executioner; when it is ordered to be given with the utmost severity, it is often mortal; for then the executioner, striking the flanks under the ribs, cuts the flesh to the very bowels."

Bears were used for entertainment, and they performed con-stantly at Alexandrov. On occasion they were brought into the dining hall after the meal was finished, and there they performed amazing acrobatic feats as well as grotesque pantomimes. Some-times they were pitted against dogs in a fight to the finish, and at other times against human antagonists. If the bear did not succeed in hugging or clawing his victim to death, the injured antagonist was rewarded with a generous gift; if the man was killed his family received an indemnity and the Czar ordered a monastery to re-member his name and to pray for his soul.

One of the most exciting contests was staged by bringing a prisoner from the underground dungeons to the dining hall, and there pitting him against a bear. To make the fight more equal, the prisoner was given a spear. If the bear lost, his trainer was in dis-grace, and the prisoner sometimes won his freedom.

When the Czar was in an extremely playful frame of mind, he

would have the bear-keepers let loose their bears in the courtyard, and then would be highly amused as his close friends and attendants scurried for their lives. On one occasion, he had seven priests who had been arrested for treasonable activities sentenced to fight their way to freedom by engaging seven bears. Only one was pardoned.

The Austrian envoy Heberstein recounts that bears were used not only to amuse the Russians but to amuse foreign ambassadors. "Bears are kept confined in a very large house used for that purpose, in which the prince is accustomed to exhibit games for the amusement of ambassadors. He has some men of the lowest condition, who, by the command and under the observation of the prince, attack the bears with pitch forks, and provoke them to fight; and if in the encounter they happen to be wounded by the irritated and maddened bears, they run to the prince, crying, 'See, my lord, we are wounded.' To which the prince replies, 'Go, I will show you favor,' and then he orders them to be taken care of, and clothes and certain measures of corn to be given them."

Ivan surrounded himself, as did other nobles, with jesters. Alexandrov was full of them, and they supplied relief from the pietistic atmosphere on the one hand and the charnel house atmosphere on the other. Their humor was of the most obscene kind, and practical jokes were their stock in trade. Ivan himself was a confirmed practical joker, and often played the role of jester. His practical jokes were of the most vicious kind, and usually resulted in bodily injury.

The court jesters themselves were often the victims of Ivan's cruel jokes, and many of them were mutilated or killed as a result of this or that particular prank. Few court jesters lived to a ripe old age.

One of his most famous jesters, Gvozdev, was clowning while Ivan was at table. The Czar had been drinking heavily, and was in a most playful humor. Suddenly, Ivan poured his bowl of boiling-hot soup over Gvozdev's head. The jester cried out in pain. Enraged at such impertinence, Ivan stabbed him, and then, feeling sorry for the jester, he ordered that the doctor be called. When he arrived, Ivan said, "Cure my faithful servant. I have played with him imprudently."

"So imprudently," the doctor replied, "that neither God nor your Majesty will ever make him play again in this world."

Although no one at Alexandrov had the temerity to criticize the Czar's buffoonery, some of the boyars from places of safety outside the country severely criticized the Czar's proclivity to play, as well as his fascination for tumblers, jugglers, jesters, and bears. For instance, Kurbsky scathingly denounced Ivan for the life he led. He wrote that instead of surrounding himself with "chosen and holy men, who tell you the truth without shame," and "divinely inspired books and holy prayers, which your immortal soul once enjoyed and by which your royal ears were sanctified," Ivan now surrounded himself with "buffoons with all sorts of pipes and devilish songs hateful to God, which defile and close the ears for the approach to theology."

After Anastasia's death, Ivan never again was in love. Extreme in all his passions, and violent in expressing them, all restraint was now gone in his relationship with women. Like most Russians of his time, he viewed women as immature, inferior beings whose main functions were to satisfy men's sexual passions and to bear children. If they were women of nobility, they were sequestered in *terems,* or women's quarters, where they whiled away their time. If they were peasant women, their place was beside the ox, and like beasts of burden they toiled from dawn to dusk.

At Alexandrov, and for the rest of his life, Ivan treated women contemptuously. There was no tradition in Russia of chivalry towards women. There was no "Roman de la Rose," no ballad from lovesick swain to his fair lady, no softening code of manners to curb the brutal, arrogant man and uplift the ignorant, illiterate, cowlike woman. And in the realm of royalty, there was no glittering court where women maneuvered behind the scenes while outwardly they played the role of grand coquettes. There were no court balls, no soirées, no artists attached to the court, no mingling of the sexes. The court of Russia was a man's court; the women were never seen publicly, isolated as they were in the *terems.* Many a foreign ambassador spent months at the Russian court and never saw the Czaritsa. Even court doctors were often not allowed to see their women patients, and had to examine them from behind a curtain.

Ivan's penchant for practical jokes extended itself to women, too. One of his favorite burlesques was put on when, at his orders, his minions seized a group of peasant women and brought them to Alexandrov. They were then stripped naked and ushered into the courtyard. At a given signal, they were told to run for their lives while Oprichnik marksmen used them as human targets.

Any woman who caught Ivan's fancy was fair game for his royal couch. His Oprichnik advisers and comrades were always on the lookout for women they believed would please their leader, and, almost daily, women were kidnapped and brought to Ivan for his inspection. If he found a woman particularly pleasing, she was installed as a regular member of his harem, which contained from fifty to sixty women and which on many occasions accompanied him when he made extended journeys. If the woman was not pleasing enough to become a regular member of the harem, she was used, payed for her docility, and sent away.

Mass sexual orgies were common, and usually accompanied a night of immoderate drinking and eating in which the entire order of brethren participated. Jugglers, acrobats, singers, and jesters amused the drunken carousers, bears were put through their amazing tricks and pantomimes, and servants passed among the participants and poured wine into large gold-leafed goblets and filled gold and gem-encrusted plates with exotic foods. The orgies of Ivan's third Rome put into the shade the maddest excesses of the first Rome. They continued for hours and only came to an end when Ivan managed to stagger to the belfry and ring the bells for matins.

And there in the church, Ivan would castigate himself like a typical monk of the times for his sins, calling himself, as he did in a letter to the Archimandrite and monks of the Monastery of St. Cyril some years later, "a stinking dog living in drunkenness, adultery, murder, and brigandage."

XV

Background for Terror: The Czar and His People

T HE REIGN of terror that existed for almost a decade in Russia during Ivan's regime was not the result of a sudden violent political and social event or upheaval, such as the terror that existed in France after 1789. It was an outgrowth of the mores that then prevailed in Russia, and was incited, domestically, by Ivan's drive against entrenched boyar power in order to achieve a completely autocratic state and, in foreign affairs, by Ivan's incessant wars and his determination to take the most extreme measures to make sure that no one would interfere with his winning them.

At no time during this period was there opposition from the Russian masses, because what was happening was not in fundamental contradiction to Russian life. There were only sporadic grumblings from the boyars and ineffectual pleas of "God have mercy upon us" from the clergy.

Almost every foreigner who visited Russia in the sixteenth century was shocked by the cruelty that permeated Russian life. From the highest noble to the lowest slave, all practiced it and all were victims of it. Fletcher, for instance, wrote that "as themselves are very hardly and cruelly dealt with all by their chief magistrates and other superiors, so are they as cruel one against the other, specially over their inferior and such as are under them. So that the basest and wretchedest *Christanoe* (as they call him) that stoops and crouches like a dog to the gentleman, and licks up the dust that lies at his feet is an intolerable tyrant where he has the advantage. By this means the whole country is filled with rapine and murder. They make no account of the life of a man."

Even two hundred years after Ivan's time, this condition prevailed, and was so described by a visiting Englishman, Dr. Edward Clarke, who wrote that "ere the sun dawns in Russia, flagellation begins; and throughout its vast empire cudgels are going, in every department of its population, from morning until night."

Ivan's reign of terror was an extension into the political scene of the brutality, violence, and disregard for human life that dominated all of Russian society. Moreover, it was an extension on a national scale of the thousands of reigns of terror that existed locally in almost every boyar holding and in almost every peasant household.

Though the boyars complained bitterly against the harsh and brutal measures that Ivan took against them, they themselves were no less harsh and brutal to their underlings. They were, in effect, slave-masters who had a complete disdain for human life and an insolent attitude towards human dignity. The limited scope of their direct influence and power merely meant that the crimes that they individually committed did not have the great breadth and scope of the ruler's. In the aggregate, however, their brutality when added to the Czar's made all of Russia a place of misery, slavery, and death.

The terror could be so widespread and so profound because, in reality, there was only one branch of government in Russia that had any power; it was the executive, consisting of the Czar. The legislative and judicial branches were mere shadows, without prestige, power, or autonomy. The various councils that were called into being from time to time at the Czar's whim and at the Czar's command were councils that merely gave their blessings to the Little Father and said *"da"* to the various proposals the Czar put before them. Whatever results came from them were the results the Czar wanted. The councils neither debated nor legislated; they agreed with the Czar. On the rare occasions when they tried to show some independent life, the Czar dismissed them.

The Code of 1550 was supposed to guarantee certain fundamental rights and fixed procedures, but actually contributed little to the definition and dispensation of justice. Justice was what Ivan considered it to be, and its dispensation depended upon his will. The written laws, such as there were, were so ambiguous and confusing, and so often honored more in the breach than in the observance, that, in effect, Giles Fletcher's observation that "there is no written law in Russia" was correct.

George Tuberville, the secretary to Thomas Randolph, envoy of Queen Elizabeth I of England to Russia in 1568, wrote this verse on law and life in Russia as he observed it:

> In such a squage soil, where laws do bear no sway,
> But all is at the king his will, to save or else to sway,
> And that sans cause, God wot, if so his mind be such:
> But what mean I with kinds to deal, we ought no saints to touch.
> Conceive the rest yourself, and deem what lives they lead,
> Where lust is law, and subjects live continually in dread;
> And where the best estates have none assurance good,
> Of land, of lives, nor nothing falls unto the next of blood:
> But all of custom doth unto the prince redown,
> And all the whole revenue comes unto the king his crown.

Punishment was severe for even the most trivial of misdemeanors. The Czar could—and did—condemn to death a person for disrespect, such as failure to take off one's hat and bow in the presence of the Czar. One court record recounts the torture and execution of a drunken young man who, as the Czar was driving by, expressed his disrespect of Ivan by lifting up his frock, his only article of clothing, turning his back, and bending over and grasping his ankles. Ivan was not amused.

In punishing debtors, the debtor was stripped, and then tied up in a public place and exposed to passers-by. Over a period of thirty or forty days, he was beaten three times a day. If no one paid his debts during this period, he was sold as a slave, and his wife and children were forced into servitude. If the debtor had no family, the creditor was allowed to make the debtor his slave.

Treason and murder were punishable by death preceded by torture. No man was allowed to be executed until he had confessed even though a dozen witnesses against him had already established his guilt. He was tortured until he did so, and torture thus became a method of examination. Fletcher gives this vivid account of the trial and execution of criminals:

"When any is taken for a matter of crime (as treason, murder, theft, and such like) he is first brought to the duke and diak [secretary in the chancery] that are for the province where the party is attached, by whom he is examined. The manner of examination in such cases is all by torture, as scourging with whips made of sinews or whiteleather (called the *pudkey*) as big as a man's finger, which gives a sore lash and enters into the flesh, or by tying to a spit and roasting at the fire; sometime by breaking and wresting one of their ribs with a pair of hot tongs, or cutting their flesh under the nails, and such like.

"The examination thus taken, with all the proofs and evidences that can be alleged against the party, it is sent up to Moscow to the lord of the chetfird or fourth-part under whom the province is, and by him is presented to the council table, to be read and sentenced there, where only judgment is given in matter of life and death, and that by evidence upon information, though they never saw nor heard the party. . . . If they find the party guilty, they give sentence of death according to the quality of the fact: which is sent down by the lord of the chetfird, to the duke and diak to be put in execution. The prisoner is carried to the place of execution with his hands bound, and a wax candle burning held betwixt his fingers.

"Their capital punishments are hanging, beheading, knocking on the head, drowning, putting under the ice, setting on a stake, and such like. But, for the most part, the prisoners that are condemned in summer are kept for the winter, to be knocked on the head and put under the ice."

Fletcher and other firsthand observers noted the fact that two standards of punishment existed—one for the common person, another for the noble. The trial and punishment Fletcher described above was for the former, but, as he pointed out, "if a man kills his own servant, little or nothing is said unto him . . . because he is accounted to be his *kolophey,* or bondslave, and so to have right over his very head. The most is some small mulct to the emperor if the party be rich: and so the quarrel is made rather against the purse than against the injustice."

This double standard—one for the rich and one for the poor—was accepted as the natural order of things. It was a system in which the question of right and wrong in a moral sense or just or unjust in a legal sense was not even considered. All relationships—servant to master, master to czar, wife to husband, children to parent, citizen to state—were based on the principle of service and position. And the fundamental idea of this service and position was that it was God's will that some are born slaves and others masters, that some are born to work like beasts and live in poverty and others are born to rule and live in luxury.

All this was accepted with a fatalism that is difficult in our times to understand. But the Russian of that time did not bother trying to understand; his problem was not understanding but survival. And to survive he had to obey, which he had learned to do without question.

Observations by Westerners of the time on the oppression and slavery that then existed in Russia were incomprehensible to the Russian. Not only did he not understand the Westerners' complaint, he could not understand why it was made, and from what strange philosophy it sprang. For instance, the Russian did not marvel as the Englishman Fletcher did in the following passage:

"The oppression and slavery is so open and so great that a man would marvel how the nobility and people should suffer themselves to be brought under it, while they had any means to avoid and repulse it: or being so strengthened as it is at this present, how the emperors themselves can be content to practice the same, with so open injustice and oppression of their subjects, being themselves of a Christian profession."

The Russian poet Lermontov in his "Song About Czar Ivan Vasilievich, His Young Body-Guard, and the Valiant Merchant Kalashnikov," has the bodyguard say after he has angered Ivan:

> I have angered thee—O lordly will;
> Prescribe thou punishment; cut off my head:
> My stalwart shoulders feel its weight;
> Toward the damp earth it droops.

Blind, unquestioning obedience made the Russian mass into a battering ram, which by sheer weight broke down those forces— natural and manmade—that stood in the way of Russia's destiny. Even in Ivan's time, keen foreign observers noted this phenomenon, giving it as one reason why a nation that by its very slave nature should have been supine and defeatist was showing an aggressiveness and energy that allowed it to overthrow the Tatar, challenge the West and expand its borders in every direction.

"They are so obedient to their prince in all things," Heberstein reported in his book, "that being summoned by him by never so mean a herald, they obey incontinent, as if it were to God, thinking nothing more glorious than to die in the quarrel of their prince. By reason of which obedience, they are able, in short time, to assemble an army of two or three hundred thousand men against their enemies, either the Tartars or the great Khan."

The inherently strong Russian nature that over two hundred years was strengthened by its contact and intermarriage with the Tatar—"Scratch the Muscovite and you will find the Tatar underneath"—gave them a stoic quality that allowed them to undergo the greatest privation and suffering without loss of the will to live. Thus, their outward docility was deceptive, for underneath there was a hard, tough core of determination, stalwartness, and contempt for suffering and pain. These were qualities that no slave condition or philosophy could completely submerge in the Russian people; rather, when given the opportunity, with these qualities they rose to heights of achievement that were second to none.

Russia of the sixteenth century was a joyless place. Its dark, brooding piety made the atmosphere of the country like a monk's cell. A heavy pall of gloom was everywhere; liberty nowhere. The very air seemed to be permeated with a depressing heaviness.

The Orthodox Church preached restraint and austerity. It told the Russian people that any activity that smacked of pleasure was sinful. Its outlook was dismal, foreboding, mirthless.

All amusements were forbidden, even the most innocent of them. Almost anything that departed from the trinity of work, prayer, and raising a family was interdicted. If the Church had its way—and it didn't completely, because even it could not altogether repress the spirit and glory of human beings—a smile would be a sin and a laugh a sure way of condemnation to Hell. The Church in large measure did not practice what it preached, and in many cases the monks themselves were the greatest violators of Church doctrines, and the monasteries the centers of the greatest profligacy. Still, in its preachings the Church insisted on austerity that was almost beyond belief. Sylvester, for instance, in his *Domostroy,* gave this admonition:

"If they give themselves up at table to filthy conversation; if they play the lute or the *gusli* [ancient zither]; if they dance, or jump, or clap their hands, then, as smoke chases the bees, the angels of God are made to fly from that table by those devilish words, and demons take their place. Those who give themselves up to diabolic songs; those who play the lute, the tambourine, or the trumpet; those who amuse themselves with bears, dogs, and falcons, with dice, chess, or backgammon, will together go to Hell, and together will be damned."

There was no source from which could flow an ameliorative counteraction to the brutality, ignorance, or disregard for life. There was no cultured class that could take the lead in setting an example or even criticizing the existing mores. Illiteracy was almost universal. There were few books—and these were mainly Church texts—and only a handful of people possessed them. No books were printed in Russia at all until Ivan's time, when the first printing press was set up. There were no schools, and, of course, no secular centers of higher learning.

The cultural life of the time consisted almost entirely of folk songs and tales on the one hand and Church music and art on the other. Except for Church theology, there was no intellectual life. Even intellectual conversation, unless it dealt with religious matters, was frowned upon. The few foreigners who were invited from time to time to come to Russia on matters other than diplomatic came to do specific jobs, not to instruct or to innovate. Maxim the Greek, for instance, was asked to come to Russia to translate certain Church texts, and when he attempted to spread his vast knowledge among the churchmen of the time he was imprisoned. Ridolfo Fieravanti Aristotele, architect, engineer, military expert, metal caster—a typical Renaissance man—was invited to come to Russia by the envoys of Ivan the Great to build various palaces and churches in the Kremlin as well as to rebuild its walls and towers. His workmanship was magnificent, yet he was discouraged from sharing his vast learning and knowledge, except in such mundane matters as the designing and building of a brick factory. His influence on the architecture of the Kremlin was profound; his influence as a man of learning was nought.

The cultural sterility of Russia at the very time when country after country in Europe was going through a renaissance was remarked upon by numerous foreigners. Bishop Paulus of Nuceria, for instance, in his report on his Russian mission to Pope Clement

VII, wrote that the Russians "have no manner of knowledge of philosophy, astronomy, or speculative physics, with other liberal sciences. But such are taken for physicians as profess that they have oftentimes observed the virtue and quality of some unknown herb." Fletcher wrote that though the Russian people have "some aptness to receive any art (as appears by the natural wit in the men, and very children), yet they excel in no kind of common art, much less in any learning or literal kind of knowledge: which they are kept from of purpose . . . that they may be fitter for the servile condition wherein now they are, and have neither reason nor valor to attempt innovation."

Russian architecture, because it was not, as Fletcher would have called it, a literal kind of knowledge, made an advance as an art form, although it did not succeed in achieving a truly national expression. After the initial influence of the Italo-Byzantine, the Russian churches, for instance, became imitative of the wooden Scandinavian churches, to which they added various Oriental features, such as the Eastern bulbed dome. Yet in their way, many of them were magnificent. For instance, the breathtaking St. Basil the Blessed on the Red Square in Moscow, which Ivan ordered built to commemorate his victory over the Kazan Tatars, is a monumental work that has excited comments throughout the centuries: "an immense dragon, with shining scales, crouching and sleeping"; "festive ensemble of Russian architecture"; "a many-colored monster [that] has the gift of stupefying the most blasé traveler"; "the most fantastic and astonishing of all earthly churches"; "a nightmare and a revelation."

It was the building of St. Basil the Blessed Cathedral, incidentally, which has occasioned the most persistent legend about Ivan. Although the Cathedral was quite definitely the work of two Pskov masters—Barma and Psnik Yakovlev—the legend insists that it was the work of an Italian. Upon completion of the Cathedral, Ivan was supposed to have called the unnamed Italian to the Kremlin and to have asked him if he could design another church as beautiful as St. Basil. The architect assured Ivan that he could. Upon hearing this, Ivan ordered his guards to seize the unlucky architect and blind him, so that he would never again be able to create for another ruler a church to rival the magnificence of St. Basil.

The Russian people, for the most part, reflected this stultifying, uncultured atmosphere. They were ignorant, superstitious, coarse, and brutal. They were expert dissemblers and cunning thieves. Children and adults, peasants and nobles drowned themselves in drink, and their drunkenness was a wonder to behold. Morality, in spite of the Church preachings and the constant admonitions of hellfire, was abysmally low, and abnormal sexual activity was so rampant that the Church constantly had to fulminate against sodomy. In lieu of any learning, the people put their confidence in magicians and faith healers. Bandit gangs terrorized the countryside and criminal elements infested the cities. Nowhere in the wide expanse of Rus were there individuals, groups, or organizations to counteract the evils. And worst of all it seemed that the people, miserable and oppressed, had no hope.

In Ivan's time, the great, wonderful, special qualities of the Russian people—their friendliness, their ingeniousness, their creativity, their compassion—remained, except in a few instances, submerged and unexpressed. Except for the few remarkable individuals who broke through the dark prison that was Russia and forced their way into the sunlight, the nation slumbered through a cold, dark winter that seemed to have no end.

If the people were, in effect, slumbering, it was a sleep that seemed like a nightmare to those who observed it. The poverty was so great and so extensive that it might be said that the periodic famines were merely the extension of the normal state of starvation. No observer of sixteenth-century Russian life could remain unimpressed by the poverty. For instance, the Englishman Best, who was in Russia at the time, wrote:

"There are a great number of poor people among them, which die daily for lack of sustenance, which is a pitiful case to behold . . . for a great many are forced in the winter to dry straw and stamp it, and to make bread thereof, or at least they eat it instead of bread. In the summer they make good shift with grass, herbs, and roots; barks of trees is good meat with them at all times. There is no people in the world, as I suppose, that live so miserably as do the poor in those parts: and the most part of them that have sufficiently for themselves, and also to relieve that need, are so unmerciful that they care not how many they see die of famine or hunger in the streets."

His countryman, Fletcher, observed that the "number of their vagrant and begging poor is almost infinite; that are so pinched with famine and extreme need, as that they beg after a violent and desperate manner, with *give me and cut me, give me and kill me,* and such like phrases . . . [they] are unnatural and cruel toward their own. And yet it may be doubted whether is the greater the cruelty or intemperance that is used in that country. I will not speak of it, because it is so foul and not to be named."

The drunkenness that Fletcher would not speak of—though he did elsewhere—was a national pastime, for there was no more efficient way of drowning one's misery than in drink. Moreover, drinking spirits was officially encouraged by Ivan. All taverns were a state monopoly, with the revenue going directly into the national treasury. It was a crime for spirits to be sold anywhere but in the state-controlled taverns, and an offense to urge a man to leave his kvass or wine or vodka, for he was depriving the Czar of revenue.

The extent—and results—of drunkenness were such, Fletcher noted, that "to drink drunk is an ordinary matter with them every day in the week," and "you shall have many there that have drunk all away to the very skin, and so walk naked."

Along these lines, the British envoy Jenkinson observed: "At my being there, I heard of men, and women, that drunk away their children, all their goods, at the Emperor's tavern, and not being able to pay, having impawned himself, the taverner brings him out to the highway, and beats him upon the legs; then they that pass by, knowing the cause, and having peradventure compassion upon him, give the money, and so he is ransomed." Another foreigner observed, at a later time, that he saw "a dozen [drunken] people brought upright on a sledge frozen to death. Some have their arms eaten off by dogs; others their faces, and of others nothing is left but bones. Two or three hundred have been brought after this manner in the time of Lent."

In spite of the horrible results of excessive drinking, the tavern performed the function of being the one place where, in his cups, the poor Russian could give free reign to a whole range of feelings he constantly tried to suppress—joy, sympathy, tenderness, friendship. The Church, unimpressed by this and even willing to incur the wrath of the Czar, preached that drinking was an evil. As one sober monk put it, it was a national sin.

"My brothers, what is worse than drunkenness?" appealed one monk. "You lose memory and reason, like a madman, who knows not what he does. Is this mirth, my friends, mirth according to the law and glory of God? The drunkard is senseless. He lies like a corpse. If you speak to him, he does not answer. He foams, he stinks, he grunts like a brute. Think of his poor soul which grows foul in his vile body, which is its prison. Drunkenness sends our guardian angels away, and makes the devil merry. To be drunk, is to perform sacrifices to Satan. . . . Fly, then, my brothers, the curse of drunkenness."

Drunkenness was not only the hallmark of the poor, but of the rich and much of the clergy as well. No party given by a noble or the Czar himself was considered festive unless the invited guests became roaring drunk, and one observer noted bluntly that "it was precisely in drunkenness that the gaiety consisted. The guests were never gay if they were not drunk." The priests making their daily rounds were often more drunk than sober, and Heberstein reported that it was not unusual to see priests lying in the streets dead drunk, and that sometimes they were beaten publicly because of it. Monks in the monasteries, which manufactured much of the liquor, became, as one critic observed, "theologically drunk."

Though the punishment for theft was most severe—flogging with the knout, imprisonment, and even death—the extreme poverty of the people, compounded by widespread drunkenness, encouraged it. However, theft was by no means a poor man's crime; all strata of society indulged in it from the Czar down to the starveling.

Ivan stole on a grand scale, but the name given for his taking of the property of others was not theft but expropriation. In addition to expropriating half the land of Russia for his Oprichnina, Ivan could claim for himself any booty that was taken by his generals in battle. His personal treasury was so immense that a paper in Queen Elizabeth's State Paper Office noted: "Touching the state of the Prince of Russia, Ivan Vasilievich, now reigning, it is said by creditable report of some which have seen much thereof, that he is the most rich prince of treasure that lives this day on earth, except the Turk."

As the supreme autocrat, with no laws to curtail him, Ivan extracted with the greatest ingenuity and imagination money and revenue from every section of the population. He once ordered the inhabitants of a city to deliver to him a calpac full of live fleas, declaring that the insects were needed so that medicine could be made from them for his royal highness. The inhabitants, after a great effort to satisfy the Czar, sent word that it was impossible: they couldn't collect that many, and the ones they did collect died or escaped. He fined the entire city seven thousand rubles for disobeying his command. On another occasion he instructed the inhabitants of a certain area to deliver a certain kind of cedar wood that he knew didn't grow there. When they informed the Czar that they could not meet his demand, he fined them twelve thousand rubles for concealing the wood.

The nobles were not exempt from this kind of extortion. Fletcher noted that "he extorted from his nobility thirty thousand rubles, because he missed of his game when he went a hunting for the hare; as if their hunting and murdering of hares had been the cause of it." The nobles paid their fine by charging the peasants with poaching, and levied a thirty thousand ruble fine upon them.

Ivan had no compunction about fleecing the people directly or through his nobles, for he believed that "his people were like his beard; the more often he shaved it, the thicker it will grow" and that "the people were like sheep that had to be shorn once a year at least to keep them from being overladen with their wool."

Ivan made a practice of looking the other way while the nobles, diaks, and various government officials through bribe-taking, fines, and levies became rich; he then stepped in and took their gains away from them. Fletcher, amusingly and colorfully, wrote that Ivan "suffered them to go on till their time be expired and to suck themselves full. Then to call them to the *praveush* (or whip) for their behavior, and to beat out of them all or the most part of the booty (as the honey from the bee), which they have wrung from the commons, and to turn it into the emperor's treasury; but never anything back again to the right owners, how great or evident soever the injury be."

Ivan was the largest trader in Russia, but it is doubtful if he could be called a merchant prince, for his business practices were so sharp that it is difficult to draw a line between what was legitimate commerce and what was outright theft. Ivan sent agents to markets in the provinces to buy up various commodities—honey, wax, hides, furs, hemp—at prices that were so ridiculously low that the sellers sustained a terrific loss. When they complained that they could not sell at such prices, they were informed that their refusal put them in opposition to the Czar and thus they were in jeopardy of being accused of treason. This argument cut short their objections.

Even the foreign traders in Russia were not exempt from Ivan's demands that he participate in their business. In granting rights to the Russia Company, Ivan insisted that it be written down that the Company shall "sell none of the fine wares before they be seen by our chancellors, except sorting clothes, and other wares not meet for our treasury." Interestingly enough, though Ivan demanded full participation in business affairs, he looked upon Englishmen as "boorish," because they seemed so completely concerned with commercial matters. He later attacked Queen Elizabeth as an unfit monarch because she was, he said, more interested in commerce than in her imperial dignity.

Ivan's hands dipped into everyone's pockets. Even the criminal helped to make the Czar's treasury grow. When a man was convicted of a felony, his goods were confiscated, and an interesting division then took place. The Czar took a half of the criminal's property and goods; the other half was equally divided between the officers and the informer or informers.

In addition to the monies that these various measures added to his treasury, Ivan received revenues from a multitude of other sources, including rents from his inheritance of crown lands, a yearly rent or imposition upon all grain that was grown in Russia, and customs duties that were imposed on goods transported within the country.

Since the basis of the economy was agriculture, and most of the country's wealth derived from the land, Ivan and the lords increased their economic power and personal wealth by squeezing as much revenue as possible from the peasants. What Ivan did not seize by all kinds of taxes, the lords took by the *obrok,* or rent, which the peasants paid them for using their land. This amounted to as much as one sheaf out of every three that the peasants produced. Payments of rent and taxes as well as commerce payments and trade were mainly made in goods and agricultural products, since silver and gold coins circulated in relatively small amounts.

This was so partly because only a limited amount was minted and partly because many of the lords and especially the Czar himself were notorious hoarders.

Ivan's immense wealth was stored in huge cavernous rooms underneath the Kremlin that were sealed with heavy iron doors. The labyrinthine passageways leading to these various treasure rooms were blocked at intervals by padlocked iron gates. These doors and gates were unlocked only when more treasure had to be deposited there or when Ivan requested that prized valuables, particularly his magnificent collection of precious gems, be brought to him so that he could gloat over them.

It is not difficult to understand why foreign dignitaries were so impressed by Ivan's wealth, for he made a point of conspicuously displaying it upon entertaining them. He himself escorted his guests to his treasure rooms, where they looked with wonder and disbelief at the huge mounds of pearls, emeralds, rubies, heavy gold plate, and exquisitely worked jewelry ablaze with precious stones that he and the grand dukes for generations preceding him had collected.

At table, the service was breathtaking. Jenkinson wrote that at one of the banquets he attended in the Kremlin, his table was "served all in gold and silver, and so likewise on other tables there were set bowls of gold, set with stone. . . . There was also a cupboard of plate, most sumptuous and rich, which was not used, among the which was a piece of gold two yards long, wrought in the top with towers and dragons' heads; also diverse barrels of gold and silver, with castles on the bungs, richly and artificially made."

At official receptions, Ivan had his retainers and attendants dress in the most sumptuous costumes of gold and silver tissue, velvet studded with pearls, headdresses that were adorned with ermine and other valuable furs. Jenkinson described his reception at the Kremlin in detail: "I came into the Emperor's presence and kissed his hand, who sat aloft in a goodly chair of estate, having on his head a crown most richly decked, and a staff of gold in his hand, all appareled with gold, and garnished with precious stones. There sat distant from him about two yards his brother [Yuri]. . . . Then sat his nobility round him, richly appareled with gold and stone."

However, what Jenkinson might not have known at the time was that the nobility who sat "round him, richly appareled with gold and stone" did not own these costumes; they belonged to the Czar. On official occasions, Ivan had them brought up from the treasure rooms and distributed to his nobles, who returned them when the reception was over. The nobles were proud of these fine costumes, and, as the visiting ambassador of Maximilian I, the emperor of the Holy Roman Empire, reported early in the sixteenth century, the nobles at one of these receptions—this one given by Vasili—insisted upon undressing before him and his companions to show off their rich undergarments, which, like their outer clothing, also belonged to the ruler.

As extreme as was the Czar's desire for wealth and possessions, there were those at the other extreme who scorned all possessions. These were the ascetics. In large numbers, these holy men roamed all over Russia, leading a vagabond existence. They claimed they had miraculous powers, and preyed upon the credulity of the ignorant masses of common people, who considered them partly as God-inspired and partly as seers and magicians. Some of these ascetics refused to wear clothing except for a small cloth around their middle, let their hair grow long so that it hung thick and wild around their shoulders. Many of them wore an iron collar or chains about their necks and waists. Even in the middle of the bitter cold Russian winters, they refused to put on clothes. They carried nothing with them, except in some cases a large cross, and depended upon the good will of the people to feed them. And the people did, for they considered them saintly. It was common practice for these ascetics to walk into a house or a shop, take food, and walk out without paying. The householder or shopkeeper did not object; in fact it was an honor to be so robbed by a holy man. In the case of the householder it meant he was being blessed and in the case of the shopkeeper he was not only being blessed but was receiving a sign that he would have a prosperous future.

These ascetics were considered to be endowed with unusual insights that were God-given. As divinely inspired prophets, their sayings and prophecies were listened to with respect and awe by lord and serf alike, and they were free to say anything they pleased, even to criticizing the Czar himself. Ivan was deeply impressed with their prophetic powers, and even named his famous church on the Red Square after one of these ascetics, St. Basil the Blessed, who is buried here. Ivan is said to have helped carry St. Basil's coffin when the holy man died.

The Church tolerated these unordained preachers, admitted them to monasteries, and, in spite of their unorthodox preachings and practices, did not deny Heaven to them.

Russia was not unique in having so many beggar holy men; other poverty-ridden countries had—and have—them. For in addition to those individuals who were sincerely and honestly inspired, many people took up outright vagabondage or vagabondage with spiritual overtones in order to escape, if they could, starvation. The very nature of village life drove the more restless souls to seek escape from the deadly monotony and boredom.

This monotony and boredom Maxim Gorky has described masterfully in the following passage:

"The boundless plain upon which the log-walled, thatch-roofed village huts stand huddled together, has the poisonous property of desolating a man's soul and draining him of all desire for action. The peasant may go beyond the limits of his village, take a look at the emptiness all about him, and after a while he will feel as if this desolation had entered into his own soul. Nowhere are lasting traces of toil to be seen. The estates of the landlords? But they are far away, and culturally not much more important than the village. As far as the eye can see stretches an endless plain, and in the midst of it stands an insignificant wretched little man, cast away upon this dreary earth to labor like a galley slave. And the man is overwhelmed by a feeling of indifference which kills his capacity to think, to remember past experience, and to draw inspiration from it."

The rural section of the population was divided into three groups: the *kholop,* or slave, who was usually a prisoner of war, or the offspring of such a man; the free farmer, who had the right to change his master, but lived off other people's land; and the peasant, who was legally free but fixed to the land. Eventually, the free farmer almost disappeared, and became amalgamated with the peasant, or serf. The serf was viewed by the state as a mere beast of burden, whose labor power was a productive force completely at the mercy of his lord and Czar. Organizationally, it was the *mir,* or commune, which possessed the land, not the individual, and, through its headman and elders, was responsible to the Czar for collecting the various taxes, and to the lord for various dues.

In all strata of society, family life was organized so that the father was lord and master over his wife and children. Within his family circle, he was as much the absolute autocrat as Ivan was of the nation as a whole, and just as tyrannical. The popular expression "Look on thy father as on God" was only too true, and the god the father aspired to be was a god of wrath. He demanded absolute obedience from his wife as well as his children, and the whip was always at hand to be used mercilessly if obedience was not forthcoming. Love played little or no part in the family relationship. The father did not want love; he demanded respect and obedience. The mother was a slave twice over—to her lord and to her husband. Concerning a woman's position in society, the Russians had a plethora of sayings, among them:

Beat your *shuba* [fur overcoat] and it will be warmer; beat your wife and she will be sweeter.

I love thee like my soul, and I dust thee like my jacket.

In ten women there is but one soul.

In woman there is no soul, but only a vapor.

Women have long hair but short intelligence.

Beat your wife with the butt end of the axe, then sniff; if she breathes, she is fooling you and wants more.

A wife is loved on two occasions: once, when you marry her, and again, when you take her to the grave.

There is no law for women or for cattle.

The more you beat your woman, the better the soup will taste.

A chicken is not a bird, and a woman is not a human being.

Women of the lower classes were workworn from long hours of labor in the fields, their household duties, and bearing children. A few years after marriage even the prettiest of them looked old and the gayest of them became dull-eyed.

Marriage for love was practically unknown; young people were matched, with the aid of a matchmaker, by their parents, without being consulted. The marriageable age was as low as twelve for girls and fourteen for boys. They were strangers when they married; in fact, the bridegroom was not even supposed to have seen his bride until the wedding. However, the bridegroom usually had some idea of his bride, for he would have a female relative observe his betrothed and then report to him. Sometimes this was pre-arranged; the girl was concealed behind a curtain when the "looker" entered the room, and then, for a brief moment, the curtain was pulled aside so that she could be seen.

In some instances, the boy was allowed to observe his chosen wife, and if what he saw displeased him, he could refuse to marry her. This, of course, was an unforgivable insult, and caused violent inter-family feuds. Usually, however, the stern father's pressure was sufficient to bring off the marriage, no matter what the boy thought of the girl. He would have his chance at ending the marriage in his own way after he became husband and master. If his wife was intolerable to him, he beat her mercilessly, and forced her to enter a convent.

Unfeeling as this method of arranging a marriage was, it was a great advance over the marriage methods of pre-Christian Russia, when the custom was marriage by rape. Then, kidnaping expeditions were carried out during sport or religious festivals arranged by various clans. At a given signal, the girls ran away, and the boys chased them. Then, as the Russian chronicles put it, "at their devilish sports he takes a woman to be his wife who first can seize upon her."

The preparations for marriage and the marriage ceremony were elaborate. Upon agreement that a marriage should be made, a dowry was paid by the bridegroom's family; subsequently, the bridegroom, through his betrothed's female relatives, received a few small gifts from her.

The night before the wedding the guests gathered at the house of the bridegroom's father. The hero of that occasion was congratulated on his coming marriage, and then, amidst a great deal of noise and joking, all became heroically drunk at a lavish banquet. Sometime during the evening the bridegroom sent his bride a parcel of presents consisting of some trinkets, cosmetics—and a whip.

The following morning, after various processions were held from both the bride and bridegroom's homes in which various symbolic objects were carried to signify the future wife's chastity, fertility, and docility and the future husband's manliness and dominance over his wife, the marriage ceremony itself was held. The bride and groom exchanged rings before the priest and the bridegroom's father gave a whip to the bridegroom, thus symbolizing the handing over of his responsibility to the husband of making sure the girl would be obedient. After the vows had been taken, the bride fell down at her husband's feet and knocked her head upon his shoe to signify her complete subjection and obedience. The bride-groom then covered her head with the bottom of his gown to show that it was his duty to protect and cherish her.

At the wedding feast that followed, there was again a great amount of noise, confusion, laughter, and tears. The bride was expected to weep copiously, while the guests sang sad songs about her girlhood that was behind her and her new role as a wife. The guests, by now in their cups, made lewd, suggestive remarks about the event that was soon to take place.

Finally, the bride and groom were escorted to the bedroom. There, the bride had to go through the ceremony of pulling off her husband's boots to show her subjection to him. One of the boots contained a coin, and if she pulled this one off first it was a good luck omen. On his part, the husband took the whip out of his belt, and playfully lashed his wife. Attendants helped them to undress, and then withdrew, leaving the couple alone. In about an hour or so, a young girl was sent to the bedroom door to ask if all was going well. If the husband answered that indeed all had gone well, the girl rushed back to the guests to tell them that the marriage had been successfully consummated. Shortly thereafter, food and drink were brought to the couple in the bedroom, with the all-important symbolic fowl as the main dish.

The morning after the wedding night the wife took a bath, and then had to show her shift to her mother-in-law to prove that she had been a virgin until the time of her marriage. More eating and drinking then took place, more suggestive remarks about what had taken place the night before, and finally the guests, loaded with drink and food, departed, leaving the couple to begin their new life together.

It was a life that soon became, especially for the women, mean, miserable, and boring. And out of boredom and desperation and ignorance, they indulged themselves in sexual adventures, in spite of the fact that if they were caught it might mean a severe beating from their husbands at best, or banishment to a convent at worst. The writings of foreign travelers are full of accounts of immorality. "The whole country overflows with sin," Fletcher, for instance, wrote, "and no marvel [for they] have no law to restrain whore-doms, adulteries, and like uncleanliness of life." Even the folk tales of the time constantly dealt with infidelity, and related how "the pitiless whip struck the white body of the wife," because she had broken her marriage vows.

The public baths that both men and women visited as often as twice a week were favorite places of, as one writer put it, "serious disorders. In them the sexes were nominally separated, but men and women came out of their respective hot rooms, stripped, streaming with sweat, and their blood heated by smart rubbing, met at the entrance, fell without any embarrassment into eager conversation, and cast themselves pellmell into the river, or rolled in the snow, amidst shouts and jests and jokes the nature of which will be easily divined."

The Russian's custom of taking hot, steaming baths followed by drenching himself with cold water amazed most Europeans, and even suggested to them that this was one reason why the Russians were able to bear greater pain and suffering than most people they had observed. "The Russe, because that he is used to both these extremities of heat and cold," one observer wrote, "can bear them both a great deal more patiently than strangers can do. You shall see them sometimes (to season their bodies) come out of their bathstoves all on a froth, and fuming as hot almost as a pig at a spit, and presently to leap into the river stark naked, or to pour cold water all over their bodies, and that in the coldest of all the winter time." More than one observer noticed that as soon as a Russian became depressed and in ill humor he would drink a glass of vodka or brandy spiced with pepper or garlic, eat a thick slice of onion, and then take a steaming hot bath.

Together with the climate that was far from benign—hot summers and brutally cold winters—the eating habits of the people contributed to making them sluggish and passive for the most part. Among the lower classes the diet consisted, to a large degree, of roots, onion, garlic, and cabbage, which Fletcher, for instance, insisted "bred gross humors." If food at the time happened to be plentiful, the Russian gorged himself with, among other things, pikes' heads dressed with garlic, fish soups spiced with saffron, hares' kidneys stewed in milk and ginger, and similar "gross meats and stinking fish," as Jenkinson, obviously accustomed to different fare, referred to the Russian dishes. They were preceded at table by a small cup of aqua vitae and followed at the end of the meal by various spirits. Then, as was the custom among all classes, he who had dined took a siesta.

In spite of the periodic fasts that were undertaken for religious reasons—even babies were forced to participate—the diet was such that it contributed to making the men portly and full-bellied and the women fat and fleshy. Paulus described the Muscovite of the time as being "universally of mean stature, yet very square set, and mightily brawned. They have all gray eyes, long beards, short legs, and big bellies."

Beards were worn by all men, and it was regarded as a sin for a man to shave his off. A Church council noted that "of all heretical practices, none was more reprehensible than that of shaving the beard, the delinquency being one which not even the blood of a martyr could wash away." As Peter the Great was to learn to his dismay more than a hundred years later, to deprive a man of his beard was a calamitous thing. The Church insisted that beardless men contributed to the sin of sodomy inasmuch as the shaven ones thus resembled women and stirred up sinful desires. The Russians themselves regarded a beardless man as a peculiar individual, and they insisted, for instance, that an oath given by a man without a beard was worthless.

Closely connected with the wearing of beards was the practice of having one's head shaven clean. A most disgraceful punishment was an order by the Czar forbidding someone who had displeased him to shave his head and compelling the offender to wear his hair long. The general physical appearance of the Russian of the sixteenth century was noted by Turberville in the following verse:

> The Rus men are round of bodies, fully fast,
> The greatest part with bellies big that overhang the waist,
> Flat-headed for the most, with faces nothing fair,
> But brown, by reason of the stove, and closeness of the air;
> It is their common use to shave or else to shear
> Their heads, for none in all the land long lolling locks do wear,
> Unless perhaps he have his sovereign prince displeased,
> For then he never cuts his hair until he be appeased.
> A certain sign to know who in displeasure be,
> For every man that views his head will say, Lo, this is he.

Although Paulus, Turberville, Fletcher, Heberstein, and other travelers in sixteenth-century Russia wrote sweeping generalizations about the physical appearance of the Russians, there were as in all peoples, a great number of persons who didn't fit the supposed popular mold. In dress, however, the peasant seemed to have a uniform. The man wore a loose gown that extended down to his calves and was tied together by a lace made of a coarse white or blue cloth. In the wintertime, underneath this gown he wore a long waistcoat made of fur or sheepskin, and a fur cap and buskins. In the summertime, he wore nothing except a long shirt that extended to his knees and buskins. As for the woman, she, too, in the wintertime wore a gown, usually of red or blue cloth, with a fur or sheepskin coat under it. In the summertime, she wore two gowns, one over another, both indoors and out-of-doors. A kerchief was almost always on her head, earrings on her ears, and a cross about her neck.

Except for the social life around the bath houses, festivities connected with marriages and christenings, and occasional community gatherings at which there was a certain amount of merrymaking and, of course, food and drink, the peasants lived a life that was dull, defeating, and dismal. Strangely enough—and most significantly—they did not blame their miserable life on the Czar. They considered their lot in life preordained, and if they did sometimes complain about individuals as the cause of their misery, the blame was placed upon the close-at-hand noble or government official. The attitude of the poor—and, in effect, all sections of society— towards the Czar was one of veneration.

The stories of loyalty and love of Czar, even under the most adverse conditions, are legend. For example, there was the occasion on which, while the Czar was dining, the Voivode of Slavitza, Boris Titov, presented himself to the Czar by kneeling and giving Ivan the usual greetings. "May God preserve you, my dear Voivode!" Ivan said. "You deserve a favor from me," and he took up a knife, approached the kneeling Titov, and cut off one of his ears. Titov, so the account goes, did not show the least sign of pain or resentment, and without changing expression thanked Ivan for his gracious punishment and wished him a long and happy reign. Another man, while being impaled and in terrible pain, shouted his praises of the Czar who had condemned him, even as he was dying.

Scores of similar stories dot the reign of Ivan and other czars. Even after a particularly horrible torture, the victim would fall at his oppressor's feet and say something to this effect: "May you reign long and happy, O illustrious prince, who honor your faithful subjects with such favors, and who condescend to punish them for the generous purpose of improving their conduct."

Foreigners could not understand such a response from the Russian to his oppressor. The Emperor Maximilian, who had heard from his envoys of the tyrannical practices of the Russian rulers, once asked the Russian ambassador how it was possible for Russians to serve and adulate their tyrannical sovereigns. The ambassador replied bluntly, "We Russians are devoted to our ruler whether he be merciful or cruel."

The veneration of the people for Ivan was unaffected by the brutality he unleashed. There was hatred of the Oprichniki, but it was not traced to the source, the Czar himself. The Czar was above and beyond criticism. Complaints and pleas and petitions could be directed to him as the omniscient one, but he was not to be blamed or condemned for those factors that caused his people to complain. And when he punished them, it was only right and just that he should do so, for he was God's avenger on earth. Even those who did not consider him so, at least looked upon the Czar's punishment of them as they would upon punishment given by their father. The autocracy of the father within the family made the Czar's autocratic ways understandable and bearable.

To a much smaller degree—and much of it was sham and much of it arose from fear—the noble and other high official received homage from his servant and serf. As Fletcher observed: "This may truly be said of them, that there is no servant nor bondslave more awed by his master, nor kept down in a more servile subjection, than the poor people are, and that universally, not only by the emperor, but by his nobility, chief officers, and soldiers. So that when a poor *mousick* meets with any of them upon a highway, he must turn himself about, as not daring to look him on the face, and fall down with knocking of his head to the very ground, as he does unto his idol."

Yet there were those in Russia at the time who refused to bow down and knock their foreheads on the ground in servile submission, and they—by the thousands—ran away to distant places, especially the virgin lands opening up in Siberia. The escapees included not only freedom-loving souls but those who had to flee because of debts, political persecution, or criminal acts they had committed. In some cases, the number of people fleeing beyond the immediate reach of the Czar's officials denuded entire towns of inhabitants. Fletcher reported that so many people left their homes that "in the way towards Moscow, betwixt Vologda and Yaroslavl"—a distance of a hundred miles or so—"there are in sight fifty *darieunes,* or villages, at the least, some half a mile, some a mile long, that stand vacant and desolate without any inhabitant. The like is in all places of the realm (as is said by those that have better traveled the country than myself had time or occasion to do)."

And it was these intrepid souls—together with criminals, adventurers, and vagabonds—who were among the relatively few hardy pioneer-soldiers who began the conquest of an area many times larger than European Russia itself and handed it over— willingly and graciously—to their oppressor. The area was Siberia; the czar was Ivan.

XVI

Background for Terror: The Boyars and the Clergy

OSTENSIBLY, it was the boyars, not the common people, that were the intended victims of the terror. Powerful, arrogant, a constant barrier to Ivan's insatiable drive for complete autocratic power, the boyars as individuals were destroyed; as a group they weren't because Ivan refused to take those measures that would abolish the function they served as a class in society. So the terror became senseless. And as it became more senseless it became more widespread, until both boyar and non-boyar suffered, while Ivan, almost forgetting, it seems, his purpose in instituting the terror, progressed from greater violence to greater violence and from a vicious persecution to one that was almost insane in its ferocity. The result: individuals, families, entire towns wiped out; social classes remaining the same and operating within the trappings of the dictatorial state, which included secret police, informers, torture chambers, the blackhooded executioners, the organization of Oprichniki above and beyond the law, dedicated to their leader.

The boyars reacted to Ivan's persecution by engaging in intrigues and factional alignments. The Czar, even though he was the central figure in the drama, remained the untouchable demi-God, immune from their intrigues and scandals. Open revolt was not even hinted at and impeding tactics were few, even though Ivan repeatedly insisted that the boyars were engaging in them. Thus, the resistance was ineffectual, and the intrigue centered on personalities other than the Czar himself.

At times it even seemed that the boyar-Czar conflict was some monstrous political charade, with the people involved going through tortuous movements that had no real meaning or substance. The Czar refused to consider actions that would go to the heart of the boyar-Czar conflict; many of the boyars refused to consider the Czar who claimed he was bent on destroying them as their enemy. The political pantomime would have been ludicrous if it had not been so deadly in its personal and human consequences.

Even during the terror, the boyars in the Zemschina continued, as they had for hundreds of years, as governors of towns and districts and as administrators of whatever justice existed in Russia at the time, and continued to provide leading officers for the army. They infiltrated into the select body of Oprichniki who were set up originally to destroy them. Ignorant, dull-witted, and degenerate as many of them were, the boyars still were the only group in Russia that could supply the necessary leadership to keep the state operating. Ivan knew this, and refused to oust them, en masse, from their posts and deprive them of their privileges. This being so, the class position of the boyars was secure, and to achieve security of person, they intrigued among themselves, implicating and informing on others in supposed schemes and scandals so as to appear indispensable to the Czar and state. It was a disgusting spectacle, and it resulted in the decline of whatever prestige and glory the boyars had achieved as the co-workers of their reigning princes in building up the Russian state, freeing it of the Tatar yoke, and making it a power to be reckoned with among other states of the time.

The decline of the aristocracy from its original role as a warrior group steeled in battle and powerful in personal qualities of courage, endurance, and loyalty had been going on for a long time, and was not a result of Ivan's pressure on the aristocracy. To a large extent, generations of easy living had made them fat, lazy, corrupt, and dull-witted. Many of them were little more than loafers, who spent their days hawking, drinking, carousing, and, in general, idling their lives away. Some nobles had lost their land and fortune for one reason or another and, though flaunting their title and family background, lived in mean circumstances. The poor, dispossessed nobleman was a well-known figure in Russian society, just as at the other extreme of the aristocratic spectrum there was the immensely wealthy nobleman with vast estates, thousands of serfs, and hundreds of servants. The former group, because poverty belied its pretensions, became a blemish on the prestige of the crown itself. The wealthy nobles, for their part, became a buffer for the Czar, the target of the people's resentment and hatred of their miserable conditions. Thus, on the one hand the rich boyars performed a vital function for the Czar, yet on the other hand their very power threatened him.

Ivan was not alone in casting a jaundiced eye at the profligate life and intrigues of the boyars. Previous rulers, especially Ivan the Great and Vasili III, looked upon them suspiciously. Ivan III, for instance, complained about their degenerate life and constant intrigues. On one occasion, upon dispatching some boyar envoys to the Polish court, he told them: "Look you that in all things you be forbearing—that you drink with caution, and not unto drunkenness, but rather do guard yourselves ever . . ." and then went on to caution them not to try any maneuvers concerning the succession to the throne.

The visitor to Russia was often amazed to find that nothing seemed to be as it actually was and nothing actually was as it seemed to be. They complained of this Russian deceptiveness, and traced it to Oriental influences, especially Byzantine and Tatar. They spoke of the Russians' cunning and shrewdness. They despaired at their inability to fathom the complex Russian character, and as a result condemned all Russians, as Jenkinson did, as "great talkers and liars, without any faith or trust in their words . . . flatterers and dissemblers." John Milton, the English poet, who never visited Russia but was intrigued enough with the country and the few Russians he had met in London to write "A Brief History of Moscovia," picked up Jenkinson's observation and wrote in his book that the Russians "have no learning . . . their greatest friendship is in drinking: they are great talkers, liars, flatterers, and dissemblers." Fletcher, who really got to know the Russians although he judged them in a distinctly British fashion, wrote: "As for the truth of his word, the Rus for the most part makes small regard of it, so he may gain by a lie, and breach of his promise. And it may be said truly (as they know best that have traded most with them) that from the great to the small (except some few that will scarcely be found) the Rus neither believes anything that another man speaks, nor speaks anything himself worthy to be believed."

The outward appearance and trappings of the Kremlin were such that they confounded even those envoys who had seen great wealth in other countries. Scarcely an ambassador who visited the Kremlin and who took the time and trouble to record his observations failed to write in the most glowing language of its display of fabulous riches. The same was true of the palaces of the rich, powerful boyars, whose wealth sometimes rivaled the Czar's. Still, the nature of the Czar-boyar relationship was such that the sons of the most powerful boyars competed vigorously for the opportunity to serve the Czar as a gentleman of the bedchamber or as waiters at his table.

It was not an uncommon sight to see the father of one of these noblemen-waiters in service of the Czar riding through the streets of Moscow toward the Kremlin from his estate in a style befitting a powerful monarch. There were long lines of carriages, or sleighs in wintertime, hundreds of attendants on horseback who waved their whips and sabers at the curious crowds to clear a way for their master, and a large number of armed men who formed the lord's personal guard. In the rear, running after the entourage, were the boyar's servants dressed in fine clothes but, if it were summertime, barefooted. The noise and bustle of the boyar's passage through the streets suggested a medieval army on the move.

The rich, influential boyar, whether on the move or in his manor, played the royal role to the hilt. As likely as not of the most noble stock himself, he insisted on the prerogatives of his royal bloodline. Everyone from lesser noble to slave was at his mercy. No female slave or serf on his manor could deny him if he wished to possess her. No male slave or serf could escape punishment if the lord decreed it. He was the "father" of all of them; they were his children, and he rewarded them or punished them as such. In return, they gave him their unswerving loyalty and, when the occasion demanded, willingly died for him. The lord's enemies were their enemies, and during the terror, when a boyar was banished to some remote province, they insisted on going with him.

A boyar often refused to pay his servants, causing them to steal from him where and when they could, or to go begging or robbing in the towns in order to get enough food to keep themselves alive. When they were caught, the boyar, stern father that he was, whipped them severely. Sometimes he whipped them for no particular reason except to rid himself of his own spleen, and the servant resignedly submitted, excusing the boyar's act with a loyal, "The master has a reason if he wishes to strike."

In dress, the rich boyar rivaled the magnificence of Ivan himself, and his wife, the boyarina, that of the Czaritsa. As described by Fletcher, the nobles "apparel themselves after the Greek manner. The nobleman's attire is on this fashion. First, a *taffia,* or little nightcap, on his head, that covers little more than his crown, commonly very rich wrought of silk and gold thread, and set with pearl and precious stone. . . . Over the *taffia* he wears a wide cape of black fox (which they account for the best fur) with a tiara or long bonnet put within it, standing up like a Persian or Babylonian hat. About his neck (which is seen all bare) is a collar set with pearl and precious stone, about three or four fingers broad. Next over his shirt (which is curiously wrought, because he strips himself into it in the summertime while he is within the house) is a *shepon,* or light garment of silk, made down to the knees, buttoned before; and then a *caftan,* or a close coat buttoned, and girt to him with a Persian girdle, whereat he hangs his knives and spoon. This commonly is of cloth of gold, and hangs down as low as his ankles. Over that he wears a loose garment of some rich silk, furred and faced about with some gold lace, called a *ferris.* Another over that of camlet or like stuff, called an *alkaben,* sleeved and hanging low, and the cape commonly brooched and set all with pearl.

"When he goes abroad he casts over all these (which are but slight, though they seem to be many) another garment, called an *honoratkey,* like to the *alkaben,* save that it is made without a collar for the neck. And this is commonly of fine cloth or camel's hair. His buskins (which he wears instead of hose, with linen folles under them instead of boot hose) are made of a Persian leather called *saphian,* embroidered with pearl. His upper stocks commonly are of cloth of gold. . . .

"The noblewoman . . . wears on her head, first, a caul of some soft silk (which is commonly red) and over it a frontlet called *obrosa,* of white color. Over that, her cap (made after the coif fashion of cloth of gold) called *shapka zempska,* edged with some rich fur, and set with pearl and stone. Though they have late began to disdain embroidering with pearl about their caps, because the diaks and some merchants' wives have taken up the fashion. In their ears they wear earrings (which they call *sargee*) of two inches or more compass, the matter of gold, set with rubies, or sapphires, or some like precious stone. In summer, they go often with kerchiefs of fine white lawn or cambric fastened under the chin, with two long tassels pendent. The kerchief spotted and set thick with rich pearl. When they ride or go abroad in rainy weather, they wear white hats with colored bands (called *stapa zemskoy*). About their necks they wear collars of three or four fingers broad, set with rich pearl and precious stone. Their upper garment is a loose gown, called *oposhen,* commonly of scarlet, with wide loose sleeves hanging down to the ground, buttoned before with great gold buttons, or, at least, silver and gilt, nigh as big as a walnut. Which has hanging over it, fastened under the cap, a large broad cape of some rich fur, that hangs down almost to the middle of their backs. Next under the *oposhen,* or upper garment, they wear another, called a *leitnick,* that is made close before with great wide sleeves, the cuff or half sleeve up to the elbows, commonly of cloth of gold; and under that a *ferris zemskoy,* which hangs loose, buttoned throughout to the very foot. On the hand wrists they wear very fair bracelets, about two fingers broad, of pearl and precious stone. They go all in buskins of white, yellow, blue, or some other colored leather, embroidered with pearl. This is the attire of the noblewoman of Russia, when she makes the best show of herself."

Though the lower classes were stout because of diet, the upper classes were stout because of diet and idleness. Among the women, stoutness was the ideal of beauty, and women even took drugs to become mountains of fat. The rich noblewomen, isolated in *terems,* would spend weeks on end in bed, eating constantly, drinking vodka, and moving as little as possible to achieve as much flesh as possible.

Both men and women of the upper classes had poor complexions, possibly because of their rich diet. The women, however, because of the bad state of their skin—and perhaps contributing to it—used cosmetics in profusion. Just as the well-rounded figure was the ideal of beauty for the body, the ideal of physiognomic beauty was "a face as white as snow, poppy-red cheeks, and black eyebrows, round as a cartwheel." As one observer put it, she strove to have "a face like a white hare, eyes like a hawk, and the gait of a swan."

One visitor to Moscow wrote that the women "paint themselves all colors—not only their faces, but their eyes, necks, and hands. They lay on white, red, blue, and black. Black eyelashes they tint white, and white ones black, or some dark color, but they put on the paint so badly that it is visible to everyone." Women insisted that white teeth were suitable "only for blackamoors and monkeys," and thus painted theirs black. Jenkinson complained that by using cosmetics so profusely, "a man might discern the colors hanging on the woman's face almost a flight shoot off," and they looked "as though they were beaten about the face with a bag of meal." Another foreigner, an Italian nobleman, noted that with their enormous figures, highly painted faces and necks, and black teeth, the noblewomen of the time "no longer retained any refined vestige of their sex."

The noblewoman, for all her efforts to make herself attractive according to the fashion of the times, was rarely seen by any man except her husband and male members of her family. She spent her time in the *terem,* together with other female members of the household. Here the women engaged in gossip and idleness, sometimes occupying themselves with weaving or needlework. She rarely left her house, and when she did she wore a *fata,* or veil. It was considered an outrage for a commoner to raise his eyes to a noblewoman; in the case of the Czaritsa it was a crime to do so.

Her seclusion was so great that she attended church services in a chapel within the manor; when she took some exercise, it was a walk within the manor's inner court. Only the lord had the key to her apartment, and the windows traditionally faced towards the court, not to the outside. In the Czar's court, foreign ambassadors, for instance, complained of spending months and even years at the Kremlin and of never having seen the Czaritsa. The rich boyar's wife was similarly secluded. Male servants sometimes never saw the boyar's wife during years of service. When the boyarina left the confines of the manor, she went in a carriage whose windows were completely covered with curtains, so that not only passersby could not see her but the boyar's men who escorted her could not either.

In less strict boyar homes, the wife was sometimes permitted to meet her husband's guests. At a given signal from her husband, the boyarina descended the staircase from her apartment or the *terem* on the upper floor. Her dress was sumptuous and her cosmetics lavish. She carried in her hand a golden cup, which she touched with her lips before offering it to every guest present. Then she walked over to a special place of honor and stood rigidly, and each guest was permitted to greet her with a very respectful kiss.

The noblewoman was under strict watch lest she engage in an immoral act. As a married woman, her charms were to be seen only by her husband, and even with her husband her hair at all times had to be concealed under some kind of hat or kerchief. A woman's hair was considered a source of evil, arousing lewd thoughts in a man. The Russian priests constantly fulminated against the devils that could be aroused in a man's breast upon seeing a woman's long, flowing tresses, and declared that women ensnared men for immoral purposes by exposing their hair.

Still, closely watched as she was, the noblewoman was not always faithful to her marriage vows, even though by infidelity she ran the risk of being banished to a nunnery by her husband. On occasion, unable to endure the boredom that resulted from her cloistered life, the noblewoman rebelled by taking a lover, which, under the strict conditions in which she lived, required the greatest skill in arranging. In extreme cases, she plotted the murder of her husband. The punishment for murder of a husband or attempts at it were most drastic. Death was preceded by extreme torture. The woman was buried alive, with only her head above the ground. And in this condition she lingered on until she died. Sometimes she was banished to a convent, but there she was forced to live in isolation and to wear heavy chains for the rest of her life.

The noblewoman, like the woman of the lower classes, was considered to be a child, and was treated as such. She was under the tutelage of her husband, or before marriage under the guidance of her father, brother, or uncle. But this tutelage or guidance had nothing to do with improving her mind; it was to instruct her how to behave properly and to make sure she was obedient. Women of the upper class were universally illiterate, ignorant, superstitious, and coarse. Even the softening influence of motherhood was denied them. Their children were raised from infancy on by servants and nursemaids, since the noblewoman was considered too childish to have the responsibility of attending to and caring for the heirs of her husband.

Except when they were called to military duties, the boyars spent their time hunting and hawking and, if they were extremely pious, like Ivan, in making pilgrimages to their favorate monasteries. Though some of them were literate, practically none of them was cultured. They used their minds only to further their practical interests, and they had no refinement to temper their usually coarse, vulgar, and brutal natures. They were more interested in preserving the form of life as they knew it than in investigating its content and meaning. They relied on their bloodline, not on their abilities. They were outwardly extremely religious, but followed few of the teachings of their Christ. They were servile to their superiors and overbearing to their inferiors. They bullied their wives and children and beat their heads on the ground before their Czar. They feared change and fought against it, viewing any form of social progress or enlightenment as a threat to their entrenched positions of privilege.

And when the terror came, they either cringed before their tyrant as their own slaves cringed before their tyranny, or they ran away, like Kurbsky, and from their sanctuaries condemned the Czar's actions, forgetting or refusing to remember their own torture, tyranny, and murdering. They appealed to the high clergy for protection in the name of Christ while at the same time placing their iron heels on the necks of the peasants in the name of privilege and tradition. They neither learned anything nor forgot anything and like bloated bloodsuckers drained the country of its vitality, wealth, and well-being.

The high clergy that the boyars appealed to for protection belonged to a Church that had a charmed life. From its very inception, the Church had understood its position in Russian society as the spiritual and moral guardian of the souls entrusted to it, had skilfully made its peace with the temporal rulers, and, though challenged from time to time by various schisms, had succeeded in keeping itself the national Church.

Even the introduction of Christianity into Russia had been less painless and bloodless than in other countries. Prince Vladimir, grand duke of Kiev and later called Vladimir the Saint, after investigating various religions—Mohammedanism, Judaism, and Christianity—had decided on the Christian faith, had become converted in the year 988, and then ordered his people to become converts, too. Most of the people obeyed, though some had to be taken by the scruff of the neck and forcibly baptized. In a few places, such as Novgorod, conversion was by the sword.

There were occasions through the years when the metropolitan, the most powerful figure in Russia next to the czar, defied his temporal leader. However, the defiances for the most part represented clashes between personalities; they were not the result of deep ideological differences. The Church, in effect, like other segments of Russian society, made its obeisance to the czar, and contributed its power and prestige to making Russia a country without light and a nation without hope.

Still, it had made its contribution, aside from its spiritual leadership, to the health of the state, for it was the one solid force existing unchanged and staunch in its actions and beliefs throughout the turbulent centuries of appanage feuds, Tatar dominance, and czar-boyar conflict. With the thongs of its spiritual whip, it had kept a bond around the nation during times when overwhelming adverse forces attempted to tear it asunder.

However, like the aristocracy, it was inflexible, ignorant, and a drug and a drain upon the social advancement of the nation. Side by side and together with the czar and the nobles it kept the people in ignorance, superstition, fear, and slavery. It contributed its share to the backward conditions existing in Russia, even though the conditions as such were not of the Church's making but a combination of forces of which it was only a part.

Still, the Church gave comfort to the people, tried in its peculiar and sometimes hypocritical way to uplift the moral standards, and provided an aesthetic glimpse of life through its elaborate and beautiful church ritual in an otherwise drab and dreary day-to-day existence that made Russia at the time appear a country of eternal night. It held up to an ignorant and coarse people in an otherwise inhumane and unbrotherly land, the vision of humaneness and brotherhood expressed by Christ and the saints. And if indeed it was an opiate of the mind, it was also an opiate that eased pain and suffering and made an otherwise unbearable life bearable and even at times spiritually glorious.

The Church had acted as a brake on the violent Czar. In the past, for thirteen years, the puritanical Sylvester had been at Ivan's side, quieting and restraining him. He was there no longer. Nor was Metropolitan Makary, that scholarly, moderate, pious, and intelligent ecclesiastic, who had inveighed against excess and had insisted that piety was the careful and conscientious performance of Church ritual. Yet for all his conservatism, Makary had supported the establishment of the first printing press in Russia, and had openly condemned those who advanced superstitious arguments against its establishment.

Makary had been followed as metropolitan by Ivan's confessor, the Archimandrite Athanasius. The gentle and timid Athanasius was no match for the Czar, who by now had set up the Oprichnina and was living in Alexandrov as a mock monk. Within a year after his appointment, Athanasius, in fear and confusion, retired, having neither the courage nor the will to contend with the violent storm now raging in Russia.

Ivan now proceeded to hand-pick his next metropolitan, and his choice was Germanus, the Archbishop of Kazan. Old, extremely pious, and with no desire to become involved in the confused and changing situation, Germanus tried to decline the appointment. Ivan ordered him to obey and to proceed to occupy the metropolitan's apartments until the public ceremony of consecration. After unsuccessfully trying to persuade Ivan in a personal interview that he was not the cleric for the post, he wrote a pastoral admonition on Ivan's actions. Infuriated, Ivan sent him back to his old post at Kazan. Within a year, Germanus was dead, quite probably murdered by one of Ivan's Oprichniki.

Ivan's next choice for metropolitan was Philip, the abbot of the distant Solovetsky Monastery by the White Sea. Philip's background was aristocratic. He came from an illustrious boyar family, the Kolichevs, who were now in disfavor. He had voluntarily retired from his estate and was leading an isolated life in the far north. Undoubtedly a very pious man, he was, nevertheless, a practical man, with remarkable administrative ability and intellectual stature. His activities at the Monastery were known, even to Ivan. The Monastery lands were well managed, with greater efficiency than most other monasteries and certainly better than a good number of the boyar holdings. He had drawn up a program for the reclamation of poor land, built roads, erected a salt factory, and established a fishing fleet. Philip's stature, intelligence, ability, and piety were such that many compared him to the famed Sylvester.

Informed of Ivan's intention of putting his name before the council of bishops for election as metropolitan, Philip refused the honor, stating that he was content to lead his life away from the affairs of state. He told Ivan that he could not serve a czar who had organized such a hated body as the Oprichnina. Philip's argument against the Oprichnina was based on his opposition not only to their brutal methods but to their persecution of the boyars, with whom, by blood and tradition, he aligned himself. Ivan persisted. Finally, the Czar's pressure was too great. Philip agreed to take the post, even agreeing not to abandon it as a protest against the Czar's policy and not to interfere in Ivan's personal or political life.

The choice was a most unusual one. For the most powerful position in the country next to his own, Ivan insisted on a man who strongly opposed his actions and policies, who had deep ties with his avowed enemies, and whose tremendous prestige and firmness of conviction would enable him to put up a battle again Ivan better than any other churchman in Russia. And from Philip's attitude, it was obvious that such a battle would take place.

Why did Ivan persist? Part of the answer was that Ivan, like many power-driven monarchs, did not flinch from a battle. The fawning lackeys of Alexandrov offered no challenge to his strength and no condemnation of his sins. Philip was a moral antagonist as well as a political one. The Czar missed the moral censure of Sylvester, who constantly had called him to a reckoning with his soul.

On the very day of Philip's consecration, the battle began. After Ivan gave the new metropolitan the customary speech of recognition, Philip, addressing the throne, said that in spite of his previous agreement to remain silent he would not do so. "For silence lays sin upon the soul, and brings death to the whole people." Then he called upon Ivan to become truly the Little Father to his people, to love, protect, and guide them, and to turn against the flatterers and murderers who now surrounded him.

Ivan listened attentively. He was intrigued by the new metropolitan's courage.

By and large, however, Philip was almost alone among the clergy in his opposition to Ivan. The overwhelming majority of the clergy were interested almost exclusively in saving souls, excoriating evil, and observing ritual. The enemy was sin and Satan, not the evils of society or the suppression of human dignity. The limit to which they went was a mild exhortation of the Czar and nobles to treat their subjects kindly by being indulgent of their crimes and sins and ignorance and not to punish them too harshly. They raised their voices only when their own interests were threatened—a drive against the power and wealth of the monasteries or an affront to their entrenched position as an arm of the State. Partly because of tradition, partly because of conviction, and partly because of self-preservation, the clergy wanted to keep aloof from the struggles for power. The only time its ire was aroused was during the occasional intra-Church battles over doctrine. It unqualifyingly supported its czar and indefatigably restrained his people. It was basically an indulgent Church, strict in its demands but permissive, in actuality, in its discipline. Its hands were much less red with the blood of Church dissidents, and its heart was much more humane and patient with its doctrinal antagonists, than the more intellectual and supposedly advanced Christian faiths of Western Europe, whose adherents at this time were fearfully persecuting and slaughtering each other over doctrinal differences.

In its way, the Church protected the soul but ignored the body of the people that in a hundred different ways was being violated by disease, poverty, filth, and whips. It chose not to look at the degradation of human spirit while it insisted on closely scrutinizing human sin. It inveighed against the base actions of its flock but refused to consider the social or political causes of them. Instead, it turned whatever wrath the depressed common people had against their masters to fear of demons, the Devil, and their own sinful passions. Through its preaching of docility and submission, it allowed aggressiveness to be a province almost exclusively of the Czar and nobles.

Except in a few instances, the Church not only did nothing to educate the people, but used its tremendous power to make sure that there were no printing presses, schools, or any form of intellectual or cultural activity. Unabashedly, the Church made no secret of this policy; it was proud of its role in serving the State as the keeper of darkness. Still, the clergy was in no position to lead its faithful flock away from ignorance, even should there have been those who desired to do so, for the overwhelming majority of the clergy was illiterate. Scarcely any ordained cleric could read or write, and even oral instruction was meager. There was little preaching worthy of the name; almost all was threat and admonition. The only exception came twice every year, on New Year's Day and St. John the Baptist's Day, when the members of the higher clergy made what amounted to the same plea, each in his particular church or cathedral: that the faithful should not have malice in their hearts; that they beware of having any thought of treason or rebellion against the Czar; and that they be sure to keep their vows and fasts.

This description of the hierarchy consciously keeping the people in ignorance springs from no latter-day analysis of the situation. Astute foreign travelers at the time commented on this state of affairs. Fletcher, for instance, wrote of the clergy: "As themselves are void of all manner of learning, so are they wary to keep out all means that might bring any in; as fearing to have their ignorance and ungodliness discovered. To that purpose they have persuaded the emperor that it would breed innovation, and so danger to their state, to have any novelty of learning come within the realm. Wherein they say but true, for that a man of spirit and understanding, helped by learning and liberal education, can hardly endure a tyrannical government."

Though the clergy was poor in learning, it was rich in vestments. The high clergy dressed in elaborately decorated cloth-of-gold robes embroidered with pearls. The mitre was set with pearls and precious stones, and the crosier was plated with gold. The black-robed low clergy, like the lower classes, dressed poorly. Both high and low clergy could, however, as one observer noted, "bless the people with their two forefingers with a marvelous grace."

Like the people, the clergy, in the main, were rough and vulgar. Drunkenness among them was widespread. Their personal lives were no more moral or uplifting than those of other Russians of the time. This was especially so among the lower clergy, who sprang from the same poverty-stricken, oppressive conditions as the common people. They treated their wives better, however, for if his wife died the priest was forbidden to remarry. In general, the clergy was neither better nor worse than other sections of the population in the extent of its sexual debauchery. "To speak of the life of their friars and nuns," Fletcher wrote, "it needs not to those that know the hypocrisy and uncleanness of that cloister brood. The Rus himself . . . speaks so foully of it, that it must needs gain silence of any modest man."

The churches were a far cry from the quiet, sedate places of worship one instinctively associates with religious edifices. The people who came to them talked and laughed during services, conducted their business affairs there, and substituted profane language for the chants they did not understand. To add to this confusion, the untrained choirs were noisy and discordant, and it was not unusual for the priests themselves to indulge in loud and abusive arguments during services, their angry voices from behind the iconostases audible to the worshipers themselves.

The outrages of the Oprichniki did not unduly disturb the Church, and except for the opposition of an advanced cleric such as Philip, there was no outcry against their violation of persons and property. The Church considered itself the guardian of personal morals but insisted that political morality was not its concern. The position was hypocritical, for in actuality the Church was deeply involved in politics as the staunchest ally of Ivan and his autocratic state. As the only highly organized group in all Russia, its power was enormous. But it was a power that was handed over willingly to the Czar. In return, the Czar interfered little in its shepherding of the flock. Even at those times when Ivan severely criticized the laxness and debauchery of the clerics in angry letters to the heads of monasteries or at various councils, these criticisms were given—and accepted—as fatherly chastisements and not as political polemics.

During the terror, the Church indicted itself by its silence. At the very time when its faithful in both high and low places were being sent by the thousands to meet their Maker, there was no rebuke except the usual plaintive cry of "Mercy! Mercy!" to restrain a bit Ivan's red-stained hand. Even when Philip, their metropolitan, took his unusual and courageous stand against Ivan, the rest of the Church stood aside, allowing, as it turned out, its leader to go down

to defeat, alone and unsupported. It was a sorry and tragic spectacle, and made a mockery of the incessant ringing of the bells in
thousands of churches throughout the land. For in truth no matter
what the occasion for their ringing, the glory to God that they
sang could not quiet the shrieks of pain in torture chambers or
still the weeping of bereaved widows and fatherless children or, for
that matter, wipe out with their mellifluous tones the shame of the
acquiescent ecclesiastics.

XVII

The Terror

IT WAS NOT the first time in world history that terror had been used as a political tool, and it was not to be the last. To one degree or another most countries have had their period of blood-letting, their cruel monarchs and dictators, their periods of revenge against political opponents, religious dissenters, and military foes. Tyranny has not been the province of the backward and uncivilized but has been used by both primitive tribes and highly civilized peoples. The road of time from the Mongols who built a pyramid with the skulls of their victims to the Nazi burial pits of Auschwitz is marked, among other terrors, by the fiery human torches of the Inquisition, mass slaughter by the conquistadors, and the dreary rumbling of tumbrils carrying condemned persons to the guillotine.

Even in Russian history Ivan is not alone as a mass murderer. Peter I, the greatest of the Romanov rulers, certainly shares this dubious distinction, as do others from early Russian history to modern times. However, Ivan's decade-long terror was carried on against foes who in reality were no foes, and as such was a perse-cution that went on not only for an excessively long time but was inexcusable in its fury and intensity. Whatever opposition the bo-yars gave Ivan—and there is reason to believe it has been exag-gerated—was disorganized, sporadic, and feeble. The ferocious measures he unleashed against them, and subsequently against other sections of the population, were highly organized, constant, and uncompromising, out of all proportion to the opposition they offered.

166

As expressed through the Oprichnina, Ivan's state was an early but highly instructive model for subsequent governments in Russia. Ivan initiated or advanced numerous methods and measures for totalitarian control that were to become standard practices at one time or another in Russian political life, under both czars and commissars—the secret police; the periodic purge of top government officials; the forced confession to any and all political crimes; the constant raising of the specter of treason; the mass exile and uprooting of peoples; the cry of encirclement by foreign states; the sealing and unsealing of the borders according to the political situation prevailing at a given time and the desire to keep the people isolated from contact with foreigners; the stifling of criticism as inimical to the interests and conception of an authoritarian state; the complete subservience of all sections of the population and all branches of the government to the will of the leader; and, finally, the creation of a mystique in which the leader is regarded as above and beyond the human condition, all-wise and all-powerful.

Around the time of Philip's inauguration as metropolitan, Ivan found a new excuse for stepping up the terror, one that could capture the imagination and support of the country as a whole—a plot, supported by a foreign power, to overthrow the government.

The circumstances and details of the plot, as is usual in such cases, are confused and contradictory. What can be pieced together, however, is that Kurbsky and other émigrés seem to have convinced King Sigismund that the boyars in the Zemschina were ready to take action against Ivan if they could be assured of Sigismund's support. The Polish king's own spies also told him that the division of the country into two parts had caused great dissatisfaction, and that the excesses of the Oprichnina were such that Ivan was unpopular. Sigismund sent a letter to the boyars in Moscow, urging them to rise against their czar, and promising them protection, sanctuary, arms, and even Polish troops. The letter came to the attention of Ivan, and at first he treated it lightly. In a roguish mood, he sent Sigismund several letters in answer to his urging, signing various boyars' names to them and demanding huge slices of Polish territory to supply the uprising. The tone of the letters was rude and insulting.

Soon afterward, Ivan seemed to realize that he had stumbled upon a most valuable incident that he could use to his advantage—

the safety of the country was at stake. His mood on the matter changed quickly; he ceased to treat the entire affair lightly and made political capital of it. All boyars now had to choose sides— for the Czar and the safety of Russia or for Sigismund and foreign intervention. Even Russian boyars living in various Western border areas that were in dispute between Russia and Poland-Lithuania were forced to declare themselves.

All the boyars were suspected of treason, even Metropolitan Philip, who intervened in the struggle by asking the Czar to have mercy. Ivan refused to be placated. His mood became uglier; the plot, which he had treated as little more than a childish folly of the émigrés at first, now became a matter of the life or death of Russia itself. Sigismund had given him, unwittingly, a rallying cry—the motherland is in danger! It was an excellent diversion of the anger caused by the Oprichnina excesses and the expropriation of boyars' land. Ivan lost no time now in making the most of Sigismund's blunder.

While to the foreign ambassadors in Moscow he let out only dark hints of a foreign conspiracy, Ivan staged a dramatic scene with his boyars to drive home his determination to wipe out any vestige of a conspiracy among them. He called them together, and then invited one boyar, a long-time confidant, to approach the throne. Ivan then stepped down, put his crown on the astonished boyar's head, saying that the old confidant must have seen himself in this role since he wanted to give Russia over to Poland. The boyar protested his innocence, but Ivan bowed low before him, and then wished him a long and happy reign as Czar. It was a huge joke, and the boyars laughed. Ivan mounted the platform where the old boyar stood with the crown on his head, and said, "Just as I have the power to place the crown on your head, I have the power to take it off again." Ivan then took out a dagger and plunged it into the boyar's heart, saying, "You were able to think of taking my place, but I am able to kill you." The joke was over.

Immediately thereafter, Oprichniki were sent all over the country to scour it for suspects. Boyars who were suspected of being in the conspiracy were either killed instantly or brought back to Moscow for execution. One of them, of the well-known Rostovsky family and a general in the army, was executed in Nizhny Novgorod, and his head brought back and placed at Ivan's feet to show him that the traitor had indeed been brought to justice. Ivan kicked the head from him in disgust. Others were burned to death. Some were drowned. Still others, together with their families, were hacked to pieces. The Oprichniki soon tired of hunting boyars, and began killing indiscriminately, looting, burning, and raping. Dead bodies of the victims lay in houses or fields or roads for weeks, the inhabitants too fearful to bury them lest they be charged with association with the traitors.

The Oprichnik Heinrich Staden claimed that as a result of the massacre the patience of the Zemschina gave out. The boyars plotted to put Prince Vladimir on the throne and kill Ivan and the Oprichniki. However, the Prince revealed the plot to Ivan, and demanded that he himself be given the task of killing the condemned Zemschina boyars, to prove his loyalty. Ivan obliged, Staden tells us, and had the condemned boyars brought before the leader of the plot, who "killed them as he thought fit—one one way, another a different way."

The extent of the murders was unknown to the people, for as Staden pointed out, "all the towns, highroads, and monasteries from Alexandrov to Livonia were occupied by pickets of Oprichniki on the pretext that it was a precaution against the plague, so that no town or monastery knew anything about what was going on in another."

The cruelty inflicted upon the victims was unbounded. Although many of the accounts were written by Ivan's enemies and by foreign ambassadors who got some of their information from dissidents, they cannot be discounted as malicious stories, for they are supported by local records of the time that are full of similar stories, and by Ivan's own plea in later life for the Church to pray for his victims. Though details may be conflicting and at times exaggerated, the substance of the cruelty cannot be denied.

From one account or another, there are such entries as, a certain boyar was "stripped naked, laid on a cart, whipped through the market with six whips of wire, which cut his back, belly, and bowels to death." Another "was hanged on a gibbet naked by the heels . . . the skin and flesh of his body from top to toe cut off." Many others were "knocked in the heads, cast into the pools and lakes . . . their flesh and carcasses fed upon by such huge overgrown pike, carps, and other fishes."

Jenkinson, in a letter to Sir William Cecil, Queen Elizabeth's principal minister who later was titled Lord Burghley, wrote that "this emperor of Moscovia has used lately great cruelty toward his nobility and gentlemen by putting to death, whipping, and banishing, above four hundred with confiscation of lands and goods for small offence, and specially toward four of them, viz., one worried with bears, of another he cut off his nose, his tongue, his ears, and his lips, the third was set upon a pole, and the fourth he commanded to be knocked in the head, and put under the ice of the river."

Edward Webbe, who accompanied Jenkinson on his later trips to Russia and also made subsequent journeys there, wrote: "I also noted that if any nobleman do offend the Emperor of Russia . . . there is a great hole made in the ice over some great river, and there the party principal is put in, and after him his wife, his children, and all other kinfolks."

Jerome Horsey wrote of a certain execution spot as "the valley compared to Gehenna or Tophet, where the faithless Egyptians did sacrifice their children to the hideous devils. Knez Berris Telupa, a great favorite of that time, being discovered to be a traitor against the emperor, and confederate with the discontented nobility, was drawn upon a long sharp made stake, shaped to enter so made as that it was thrust into his fundament through his body, which came out at his neck; upon which he languished in horrible pain for fifteen hours alive, and spake unto his mother, the Duchess, brought to behold that woeful sight. And she, a goodly matronly woman, upon like displeasure, given to a hundred gunners, who defiled her to death one after the other; her body, swollen and lying naked in the place, commanded his huntsmen to bring their hungry hounds to eat and devour her flesh and bones, dragged everywhere; the Emperor at that sight saying, 'Such as I favor I have honored, and such as be traitors will I have thus done unto.' "

Other accounts of this period and of the Livonia campaign spoke of further cruelties: a baby taken from its cradle by the Oprichniki and brought to Ivan, who first kissed it and then cut its throat; women brought to Ivan's court, violated, then murdered, and their corpses returned to their husbands; women stripped naked, and forced to stand in the snow exposed to public view; women flogged until blood flowed, and then when they prayed for mercy their tongues torn out; people killed by heated lance heads, murdered by hunting spears, and burned to death.

The accounts were almost without end, one exceeding the other in horror. However, the most damning indictment of this period was Ivan's own request, made near the end of his life to the Monastery of St. Cyril, for prayers to be said for the souls of his victims, and for his own soul as their murderer. The obituary notice of the Monastery enumerated thousands of the Czar's victims, which Ivan himself listed, many of them by name. The account book of the Monastery noted that Ivan gave the Monastery twenty-two hundred rubles for Masses for his victims' souls and his own. The request sometimes lists the victim by family name and sometimes by first name. The list includes individuals, entire families, and even entire populations that he ordered destroyed. A typical excerpt from the prayer book reads:

"In the year 7091 [1582 or 1583] the Czar, Gosudar, and Grand Duke Ivan Vasilievich of all Russia sent this memorial book to the Monastery of St. Cyril. And gave orders to remember and make daily intercession in the church of God at all liturgical offices and requiem Masses.

"For the only nun drowned by command of the Czar Ivan, Eudoxia, for the nun Maria, for Alexandra. . . .

"Be mindful, O Lord, of the souls of Thy servants who have died before their life had run its course, from the days of Adam down to our day. Be mindful, O Lord, of the men of Dubrov, Kazarin and his two sons, and of those ten persons who were willing to stand surety for him: Ishushka, Bogdan, Ivan, Ignati, Gregory.

"Of the men of Rostov: Feodor Istom, Prince Vasili. . . .

"Of the men of Novgorod! Be mindful, O Lord, of Thy servants and slaves, one thousand five hundred and five persons. Of Daniel, with his wife and children. . . .

"Be mindful of Ivan, Stefan, Burov, Ivan.

"Of Popov with his wife and two sons and daughters.

"Of Filippov, Suyev, Iskov, the son of Blagoveshchensky, Jacob, Ivan. . . .

"Of two Rumyantsevs. . . .

"Of the men of Pskov, with their wives and children, in all 700 persons. . . .

". . . of Kekludov with his wife. . . .

". . . of Krotkov with his sister and wife. . . ."

Other entries mention: "Twenty men belonging to the village of Kolomenskoe"; "Eighty belonging to Matvieche"; and so on.

The total number listed is 3,470 persons.

How many were killed will never be known, but they numbered many thousands. As a butcher of human beings, Ivan had few equals.

Ivan's epithet "terrible" was no misnomer, and even in his own time the qualities he was displaying were brought to his attention by a few intrepid souls. Among them was Metropolitan Philip, whose opposition to the Czar was uncompromising. From the day of his consecration, when he had broken his promise to remain silent and had attacked Ivan in public, Philip had continued the conflict, almost alone among the Church hierarchy. The Metropolitan's courage intrigued Ivan, and for a short time the Czar chose to ignore him. But Ivan's temperament was such that he could not brook opposition for any length of time. An incident would displease him, the Czar's anger would flare up, and then his violent temper and will would become master. Such an incident happened at the Cathedral of the Assumption one Sunday morning in the spring of 1568.

Dressed in their black costumes, Ivan and a number of his Oprichniki entered the Cathedral while Philip was celebrating the liturgy. They were noisy, boisterous, and drunk. Philip continued the service, keeping his eyes fixed on the Icon of the Saviour and pretending not to notice the Czar and his henchmen. Three times Ivan approached Philip to receive his blessing, and each time Philip ignored him. Finally, one of the Oprichniki told the Metropolitan in no uncertain terms that the Czar was present and that he was asking for the Metropolitan's blessing.

Philip interrupted the service, and, looking directly at Ivan, said, "I do not recognize the Czar in such a costume. Whom is he trying to imitate? I do not recognize him, either, in the acts of his government. What is this that you have done, O Czar, to put off from yourself the form of your honor? Fear the judgments of God. Here we are offering up the bloodless sacrifice to the Lord, while behind the altar there is flowing the innocent blood of Christian men."

Philip then accused Ivan of establishing a government without law and justice. He said that murder and robbery were being committed throughout Russia in the Czar's name. And finally he said, "But high as you are on the throne, there is yet another, our Judge and yours. How, think you, you will stand at His tribunal in the deafening chorus of the cries of the tormented, in the welter of the blood of the innocent? As the shepherd of souls, I beg you beware of the One God!"

Throughout the Metropolitan's speech, Ivan tried to stop him by shouting and pounding his iron-tipped staff on the floor. At last, when the Metropolitan finished, Ivan, livid with rage, yelled, "Until now I have been more than merciful with all of you who have rebelled against me. From now on I shall act according to the character you have given me!"

Philip calmly replied, "I am a stranger and a pilgrim upon earth, as all my fathers were, and I am ready to suffer for the truth. Where would my faith be if I kept silent?"

Ivan managed to control his anger, and instead of having Philip arrested or murdered on the spot, walked out of the Cathedral with his men trailing after him. However, from this moment on Philip was doomed. It was just a matter of method. Philip was no ordinary priest, but the highest prelate of the Church. An outright murder would have repercussions; there would have to be a show of legality and—as usual—the charges of treason.

Ivan now had the rumor spread that Philip was in league with the boyars in their plot, supported by King Sigismund, to overthrow him. The whispering campaign of slander soon gained momentum. Boyars and churchmen avoided the Metropolitan, afraid to be caught in the net that was rapidly tightening around him. Ivan never again allowed Philip into his presence, and the two of them met only at church ceremonies.

In July, 1568, another incident, this time during a religious observance at a monastery, gave Ivan the opportunity to abuse the prelate. At a procession which both the Metropolitan and Ivan attended, Philip noticed that one of Ivan's companions kept his head covered. The Metropolitan complained that by doing so he was following a Tatar custom. The Oprichnik complained to Ivan that Philip was calumniating him. Ivan supported his companion, and angrily accused Philip of being a troublemaker and a traitor.

The Czar's charges were made in a loud voice, and were heard by a number of people in the procession. The conflict was now made public. There was no turning back.

Ivan sent a commission, headed by the bishop of Suzdal, to the Solovetsky Monastery to dig up whatever damaging evidence it could concerning Philip's activities at the Monastery when he had been its abbot. The monks at the Monastery had only the most complimentary words for Philip. The commission's task seemed doomed to failure. However, by flattery, threats, and promises of reward, the commission finally managed to get the abbot himself, Paisius, to testify against Philip.

When the commission reported back to Ivan, he was overjoyed. He immediately ordered an indictment to be drawn up against the Metropolitan, citing Philip for the crime of sorcery. Before an ecclesiastical council, Philip stood trial, with the perjurer Paisius as the main witness against him. Under the circumstances only one verdict was possible—guilty.

Even so, Ivan was not satisfied. His victory and Philip's disgrace would have to be a public one. He ordered the Metropolitan to conduct for the last time a service of the liturgy. Philip pleaded with the Czar to send him immediately to prison, even though the council had not yet announced the verdict or the punishment. Ivan refused. The public disgrace he planned for the Metropolitan was too sweet to forgo.

At the Cathedral of the Assumption, where Philip held the services, a band of Oprichniki rushed into the Cathedral, presumably because they were outraged that a criminal should be allowed to conduct services, and assaulted Philip while he was standing at the altar. They ripped off his robes, leaving him in nothing but his shirt, and dragged him outside, where a sleigh was waiting to take him to prison. Philip did not resist. The people in the church cried, and prayed for his safety.

As he was being dragged out, he made the sign of the cross, gave his benediction to the people, and kept repeating over and over again the word "pray." At the doors of the Cathedral, he said, "I rejoice that I have received all this for the sake of the Church. Alas! the times of her widowhood are coming, when her shepherds will be despised as hirelings."

The prelate was then thrown into the sleigh, and as he was being driven away, the Oprichniki swept up the ground behind him and beat him with their brooms.

The next day Philip was brought to the Czar's quarters, and in Ivan's presence he was given the council's verdict: guilty. The punishment—life imprisonment. Philip received his sentence with apparent unconcern for his own safety, and quietly and firmly appealed to Ivan to remember the good example of his ancestors and to put an end to the terror. Ivan was unmoved.

Philip was taken to a monastery for temporary confinement, and heavy chains were put on him. With his typical macabre humor, the Czar then ordered Philip's nephew to be murdered, and had his severed head sent to Philip in his cell. Philip blessed it, and requested that it be returned to Ivan.

A few days later the chained Philip was sent to a monastery in Tver, where he spent his time in prayer. Ivan's victory, however, plagued him. He was about to embark on an expedition to Novgorod to punish its inhabitants, and he needed, he felt, his victim's blessings. He sent his head executioner, Skuratov, to Tver, with instructions to get them. Philip refused, saying he could not bless the evil Czar and his murderous undertaking. Skuratov insisted. Philip steadfastly refused. In anger at the Metropolitan's stubbornness and afraid of Ivan's wrath if he failed to fulfil his mission, Skuratov strangled the prelate. When the news of Philip's martyrdom reached the people of Moscow, they wept openly and unashamedly. A hundred years later Philip was canonized.

Philip's successors were Cyril, the Archimandrite of the Trinity Monastery, and then Anthony, the Archbishop of Polotsk, both of whom have been described, following their illustrious predecessor, as "mere shadows gliding through the gloom of the later dreadful years of Ivan's reign." They had neither prestige nor courage. But this was as Ivan wished it to be. He had had enough of intelligent and courageous metropolitans.

And so the terror claimed Philip for its victim, as it had so many other individuals and their families. In some cases the Czar had destroyed not only the boyar and his immediate family but also friends, distant relatives, servants, and even the boyar's serfs, so that there would be no one left to plan revenge for the boyar's murder. It was a method of breaking any personal and social ties and allegiances that stood between him and complete loyalty and adulation from every Russian.

The Oprichnina had already taken its toll of most of Ivan's former close associates. A few of them were in self-imposed exile, but most of the others had been executed for treason, and those who still remained alive lived in daily fear that black-robed and black-hooded Oprichniki would make a sudden raid upon their homes, murder them and their families, and burn their houses and lands.

The boyars in the greatest danger were those who at any time in the past had had dealings with the Czar's advisers. Guilt by association, not by act, was the order of the day, and it was almost impossible for any boyar who at one time or another had had contact with an already condemned boyar to escape suspicion. Even association with the Czar himself put a boyar in danger of losing his life, for this made him suspect of possessing secrets, worming himself into confidences, intriguing with others in the intimate confines of the court. The situation finally developed, as it did later during the time of Peter the Great, in which it became almost impossible for the Czar to recruit associates, since all but the most hardy and opportunistic were frightened away.

In his relations with his boyars was a certain familiar humor filled with proverbs and folk wisdom overlaying Ivan's cruelty. True wisdom, it was believed, sprang from the common people, from the mad, naked ascetics who roamed Russia, from long-bearded monks in their isolated cells, from village idiots; and Ivan, like other Russian leaders, insisted upon using this kind of approach rather than the more sophisticated wisdom of educated and cultured people. It placed Ivan with the people, and gave his intelligence the appearance of the wise man's sagacity rather than the educated man's knowledge. Even when an intimate was in danger of losing his life, Ivan loved to preach to him, to display the folk side of his nature, to parade as the Little Father chastising an errant child.

One of the best examples of Ivan's attitude toward one of his endangered associates is found in his correspondence with the Oprichnik Vasili Gryaznoy, who was captured by Devlet-Girai, the Crimean khan, in 1573 while engaged in a reconnoitering operation.

Vasili wrote to Ivan, begging that he be ransomed for Divai-Mirza, one of Devlet-Girai's leading generals, who was then being held prisoner in Moscow. Ivan answered his letter, and condemned him for his carelessness in allowing himself to be captured.

"You write that for your sins you have been taken captive," Ivan wrote. "You should not, Vasyushka, have gone lightheartedly among the Crimean heathens; but once having gone among them you should have kept your eyes open. You imagined that you had come with hounds and hares and the Crimeans caught and bound you. Did you think that being in the Crimea was the same as jesting at my table? Crimeans do not fall asleep as you do and can easily capture milksops like you. They do not say on reaching another land that it is time to go home. If the Crimeans were women, like you, they would never have crossed the river, let alone have reached Moscow."

Ivan then condemned his Vasyushka for thinking he was so important that he could be traded for a Tatar general. "Why do you pose as a great man?" Ivan wrote. Then, with typical self-pity, Ivan complained of his own problems. "I am afflicted for my sins, and how can I conceal it? Our princes and boyars have begun to betray us as they betrayed our father, and we drew your husbandmen [Oprichniki] close to our person, wanting from you service and truth."

After making sure that Vasyushka understood that the Czar had overwhelming problems and nothing but traitors all around him, Ivan wrote: "You command me to give two thousand [rubles] for you, whereas for an ordinary captive only fifty are given. How can you, a mere youth, be compared with Divai-Mirza? If you were freed you would not bring me, would not capture as many Tatars as Divai-Mirza can capture Christians. If I exchange Divai for you, it will not be a Christian for a Christian: you alone will be free, and on returning you will take to your bed with your wounds; but Divai, when he arrives home, will begin to fight, and how many hundreds of Christians, better than you, will he capture? What profit will that bring?"

Actually, Gryaznoy was no ordinary man brought into the Oprichnina from humble origins; he came from an old, though not influential, aristocratic background. He was part of Ivan's intimate group, a good conversationalist, a wit, and a boon companion that

Ivan found interesting and amusing. Even so, Ivan refused to ransom him. Gryaznoy sent Ivan two more letters during the next eighteen months. In them he stressed the many good times they had had together, that he had always shown zeal in Ivan's service, and that he was so loyal that he was ready to die for the Czar. In one passage, he wrote that the only ones who could help him were "God and the Czar," and in another passage wrote excitedly. "You, Czar, are like God. You create things great and small!" He pleaded with Ivan that even in captivity he was fighting treasonable activities against Ivan that other captives were engaging in, and that because of his vigilance almost all these traitors had perished. An exception was another Russian general, whom he would take care of very soon. In addition, he offered himself as a negotiator with the Crimean Tatars.

Ivan remained adamant, and even, there is some reason to believe, began to suspect Gryaznoy's own loyalty, especially since he had volunteered to treat in a diplomatic office with the Crimeans. Ivan's friend Vasyushka received the benefit of the Czar's shrewd humor but not his mercy. As for friendship, this was an extraneous matter that had no place in the autocrat's scheme of things.

And in this scheme of things everything was done under the shadow of the executioner. The entire country, like a bludgeoned ox, stared dumbly at the upraised hand of the black-hooded one, and waited resignedly and uncomprehendingly for the axe to fall.

XVIII

The Novgorod Massacre

B Y 1570, mass treason was to take a place in Ivan's reign beside
individual treason. All of a city's inhabitants—men, women,
children—were to be collectively guilty for treasonable activities
charged against any one of them.

The city Ivan selected for dire punishment was Novgorod. His
choice was not dictated by capriciousness or by, as Ivan claimed,
traitorous activities on the part of the city's inhabitants. The decision to destroy Novgorod had deep political, historical, and social
roots; the cry of treason was merely the excuse for the punitive
measures. Thus, though the method was madness, there was
method in the madness.

Proud, powerful, and democratic in comparison with the rest
of Russia, Novgorodians asserted aggressively, "Who can contend
against God and great Novgorod?" Founded in the fifth century,
according to the chronicler Nestor, it had been, together with Kiev,
the greatest of Russian cities until the ascendancy of Moscow. Even
during the time of Ivan, its territory was large and it dominated an
area embracing hundreds of square miles that was rich in valuable
furs, timber, raw materials, and numerous settlements. Its people,
mainly of Finnish origin, were adventuresome, fearless, fun-loving,
and fiercely jealous of their democratic rights and their independent
spirit. It had a higher cultural level than any city in Russia, and its
outlook, because of its long-time contact with the West, was more
worldly. The Tatar conquest had never reached Novgorod, and

thus it had been spared the more than two centuries of shame and servitude that had been the lot of other Russian territories.

It was the city that appealed most to foreigners, and, like St. Petersburg in later years, was the most West-Europeanized city in Russia. It was no wonder that Chancellor, when he visited Novgorod in 1554, wrote glowingly and sympathetically about it: "Next to Moscow, [Novgorod is] the chiefest in Russia, for though it be in majesty inferior to it, yet in greatness it goes beyond it. It is the chiefest and greatest mart town of all Muscovy; and albeit the emperor's seat is not there but at Moscow, yet the commodiousness of the river falling into that gulf which is called Sinus Finnicus, whereby it is well frequented by merchants, makes it more famous than Moscow itself."

For centuries the Novgorodians had fought, schemed, and made alliances in order to keep their independence. Through battle and trade they had had dealings with the Teutonic Order, Swedes, Lithuanians, and even the Papal envoys from Rome. They had been fierce in battle and clever in trade. Domestically, they had had their feuds and tensions, but from each they had emerged stronger. In their particular, and peculiar, brand of democratic life, the majority ruled, even though the lot of the minority was often drowning in the Volkhov River, which flowed through the city. The citizens were assured many rights that were not even hinted at in other parts of Russia. Many of the nobles spent their time in trade and business enterprises, and indolence among them was as uncommon as it was common among the nobles of Moscow. Even in religion they were less given to gloom and superstition, and many religious reformers and Church leaders, such as Makary and Sylvester, came from the great city in the north to influence the religious life of the country centered in Moscow.

Because of its unique position in Russia, Novgorod was always suspected by the grand dukes of Moscow of plotting with its Western neighbors, with whom it had many ties, against the ever-growing power of Moscow, and of severing its ties with Russia and placing itself under the protection of another power, such as Poland.

By the time of Ivan the Great, these suspicions became so great that measures were taken to prevent such an occurrence. Furthermore, the commercial rivalry between Moscow and Novgorod was

such that the grand dukes of Moscow tried to limit the trade dominance of Novgorod. Ivan the Great, who had already begun the
unification of Russia, had marched on Novgorod, had removed
hundreds of nobles and merchants from the city, forcing them to
live in and around Moscow. In addition, he had taken from them
a vast amount of gold, silver, gems, and stores, and their symbolic
great bell that had been used for summoning the council to decide
in a quasi-democratic way issues confronting the Novgorodians
such as the election of their prince and archbishops, declarations of
war, and even the judging of individuals accused of crimes against
the state. Ivan the Great had destroyed Novgorod's political independence by annexing it and its surrounding territory, but even
under Moscow's hegemony it had continued to maintain its trade
advantages and to carry on its non-Muscovite type of life.

Ivan the Terrible's drive to eliminate from Russian life any and
all opposition to his super-autocratic state was anathema to Novgorod, for it threatened whatever measure of freedom and self-rule
was still left in the city. Conversely, the independent spirit of
Novgorod was anathema to Ivan, threatening as it did the content
and spirit of his totalitarian state.

It was just a question of time until Novgorod would be forced
into line. However, the ferocity of Ivan's vengeance on the city was
unexpected, even considering the brutality of his acts until that
time.

The immediate reason given for the punitive expedition was that
leaders of the city, including Pimen, the Archbishop of Novgorod,
were plotting with Poland. Rumors to this effect had been circulating for some time, and the Russian émigrés in such centers as Warsaw, Cracow, and Kovno had given credence to these rumors by
using their places of refuge as distributing centers for propaganda
against Ivan. They had succeeded to some extent in convincing the
Poles that the boyar dissatisfaction was deep-rooted, affecting the
common people as well, and that the unusual kind of state Ivan
had organized was weak, corrupt, and ready to fall if given the
slightest push. Novgorod, as a major trading town, became a center
for the supply of information and misinformation that was emanat-
ing from the anti-Ivan propagandists in Poland. The Polish king
and nobles, who kept their country in almost as great oppression,
poverty, and ignorance as their Slav neighbor, were only too eager

to accept the half-truths and outright lies of the Russian émigré nobles.

The first sign that Ivan was planning violent action on Novgorod was the forcible removal of five hundred families from Novgorod and a hundred and fifty families from its sister city, Pskov, as hostages for the continued loyalty of the cities. Pskov had been included in the action against Novgorod, for it had been the last of the independent city-states to be annexed by Moscow, and by tradition and history had much in common with the larger and more powerful Novgorod. The forcible removal of citizens took place in the spring of 1569.

In the late fall of that year, a vagabond by the name of Peter asked—and received—an audience with the Czar's advisers. He claimed that he had just come from Novgorod and had definite information that the Archbishop and other leading citizens were plotting to turn the area over to Sigismund. To buttress his story, he insisted that proof of his allegations could be found in a written agreement signed by the Archbishop and other important Novgorodians. However, the letter had not yet been sent, but it could be found behind an icon of the Virgin in the Church of St. Sophia in Novgorod. When Ivan was informed of this plot, he sent an agent to the church to get the letter. The letter was where Peter had said it was, and the document was promptly returned to Moscow so that Ivan could see it for himself. The Archbishop's signature—forged or authentic—and others, too, were indeed on the letter, and the letter itself—forged or authentic—contained damning information of the intention of the Novgorodian leaders, together with others from Pskov, to turn these areas over to Poland, and called on Sigismund's help in deposing Ivan as Czar.

Using the letter as a pretext—and it was only a pretext, for the destruction of Novgorod had been planned for some time—Ivan gave orders for a large military force, composed principally of Oprichniki, to march on the city. Ivan announced that he would himself lead the avengers, and insisted on taking along his eldest son, the Czarevich Ivan, so that he could be properly instructed in such affairs of state. Also in the party were his head Oprichniki—Skuratov, Viazemsky, and Feodor Basmanov, the latter by now having become his closest adviser and companion.

In December, 1569, the military expedition set out from Alexandrov as though it were going forth to meet a foreign invader, not the peaceful inhabitants of the motherland. An army regiment was sent ahead to surround quickly the city of Novgorod, and the generals were admonished not to allow anyone in or out of the city. Ivan and his party of Oprichniki warriors set out at a slower pace.

The army arrived in Novgorod on the first days of January, 1570, and immediately occupied the city. One of its first accomplishments was the closing down of the monasteries in and around Novgorod and the seizure of all the priests. To defray the cost of the army and the expedition, the clerics were ordered to pay twenty rubles apiece. Those who gave the money—a huge sum for those days—were released; those who could not were flogged, many of them to death. In addition, the army seized numerous hostages among the nobility, all commercial establishments were put under guard, all warehouses with their rich stores of supplies were sealed, and the houses of the nobles were padlocked, their inhabitants warned not to leave their homes under penalty of death. Then the city—its commerce shut off, its church bells stilled, its streets deserted, its prisons filled—waited in fearful apprehension for the arrival of its executioner, the Czar.

Ivan and his party, however, dallied along the way; they were in no hurry to reach the city, for the situation there was well in hand and part of the torture consisted in allowing the Novgorodians to wait in terrified expectation of their fate.

Ivan and his Oprichniki were having great adventures on the road to Novgorod. They burned the city of Tver and killed a large number of its inhabitants because, as the Czar explained, they were friendly with the traitorous Novgorodians. Similar acts took place in other cities and towns along the way not only to satisfy imperial vengeance but, Ivan insisted, because the campaign was secret and no one should be left alive to speak of it. On the road from the town of Klin to Novgorod, for instance, as far as the eye could see there were burned houses and fields. Hundreds of corpses lay in the snow.

Ivan did not insist that his Oprichniki stay close by his side, but allowed them freedom to roam the countryside. The Oprichnik Staden, who took part in this adventure, wrote: "I undertook campaigns of my own and led my men back into the interior by another road. For this my men remained faithful to me. Every time they took a captive they questioned him honestly where—in monasteries, churches, or hostels—it was possible to obtain money and valuables, and particularly good horses. If the captive refused to answer voluntarily they tortured him until he did. In this way they obtained money and valuables for me."

A week or so after the army had entered Novgorod, Ivan and his force of about fifteen hundred Oprichniki reached the city. Archbishop Pimen, the supposed leader of the plot, together with a large number of the clergy, met Ivan on a bridge in the city, and offered the Czar his blessing. Ivan refused to accept it, and called the Archbishop a "ravenous wolf." Nevertheless, Ivan ordered Pimen to conduct services at the Church of St. Sophia, which he attended and where he prayed most fervently. After the services were over, Ivan accepted the Archbishop's invitation to have dinner with him at his house.

If the Archbishop was surprised at Ivan's sudden reversal in accepting his hospitality, he did not have to wait long to learn the reason why the Czar had become so gracious. In the middle of the banquet, Ivan let out a loud cry—a prepared signal—and his Oprichnik bodyguard rushed in, seized the Archbishop, bound him, and carried him off to a dungeon. Ivan continued his dinner without the company of his host.

The next day the punishment of Novgorod began in earnest. A thousand or more inhabitants each day were executed, many of them in full view of Ivan and his son, who sat on a platform especially erected for the occasion. Before them were various diabolical instruments of torture and death, many of them ingenious inventions. The barbarity was almost unbelievable. Wives were forced to witness the quartering of their husbands; husbands were forced to see their wives roasted alive; babes in arms were put on execution blocks together with their mothers.

However, the formal executions proved too slow, and soon they were supplemented by mass drownings in the Volkhov River. The method was to tie a number of people to sleighs, and then run them into the river. Oprichniki equipped with long poles stood on bridges or were deployed in boats to push under the water any victim who managed to break his fetters. Other Oprichniki and the famed *Streltsy* stood on the banks farther downriver and shot those who tried, by taking advantage of the current, to make an escape.

Sadly, the chroniclers of the time wrote: "And so great was the disaster and our agony of fear before the untamable savagery of the Czar, so terrible was the wrath of God at our sins that for five weeks, or even more, a thousand persons a day, and at times even fifteen hundred, were cast into the water; but we were thankful for every day on which no more than five or six hundred persons were thrown into the river."

Another account, by Horsey, noted that "without any respect [they] ravished all the women and maids, ransacked, robbed and spoiled all that were within it [Novgorod] of their household stuff, merchandise, and warehouses, of wax, flax, tallow, hides, salt, wines, cloth, and silks, set all on fire . . . together with the blood of 700 thousand [sic] men, women, and children, slain and murdered; so that with the blood that ran into the river, and of all other living creatures and cattle, their dead carcasses did stop as it were the stream of the river Volkhov, being cast therein."

Finally, Ivan became weary of the mass slaughter. He ordered his followers to stop the carnage, and to round up all male survivors and have them brought before him. Only a handful could be found. Then Ivan spoke to them, without shame, without pity, without remorse, in what must be one of the most amazing speeches of all times by an annihilator of an entire city to its few miserable survivors.

"Men of Novgorod, surviving through the grace of the Almighty Lord God and the spotless Mother of God and all the saints, pray for our God-fearing rule as Czar, for our sons Ivan and Feodor, and for our Christian army, that God may grant us victory over all our enemies and adversaries, visible and invisible. But may God judge him who had betrayed us and you. . . . May all the blood that has been shed fall upon them, and may the traitors be held accountable for it. But as for you, lament no more over all this, but live thankfully in this city."

But it was impossible to "live thankfully" in Novgorod; it had been so thoroughly destroyed and depopulated that never since has it had even a semblance of its former power and glory. For hundreds of years it had successfully withstood the onslaughts of its powerful neighbors—the Teutonic Knights, the Swedes; in a few weeks it was destroyed by its own Czar. From this time on,

Novgorod has been a small, unimportant town, undistinguished from hundreds of other provincial towns throughout Russia.

Accounts of the number of people killed in Novgorod and the surrounding area vary considerably. Horsey's figure of seven hundred thousand cannot be credited. The Pskov Chronicle stated that the number was sixty thousand. Kurbsky insisted that fifteen thousand people died. Some modern historians place the number as low as two thousand.

Whatever the number, the destruction of Novgorod made a lasting impression. Folk songs still speak of the famous bridge across the Volkhov where the Oprichniki speared the victims of the Czar's fury, and of the waters of the river that are forever disturbed because of the tortured, writhing spirits of those who were drowned there.

Leaving Novgorod behind him, that city with "infected and noisome air," as Horsey described it, Ivan and his victorious troops marched on Pskov. The inhabitants had heard of the destruction of Novgorod, and waited fearfully for a similar fate to strike them. Church bells rang incessantly, calling the faithful to prayer. The Pskovians needed no prodding; they flocked to the churches, and there prayed for mercy and deliverance from the rage of their Little Father.

Encamped at the suburbs of Pskov, Ivan hesitated to give orders for the sacking of the city. His hesitancy was not based on the possibility of resistance by the inhabitants. In fear and resignation, they waited for death. Nor was he hesitant because his Oprichniki were tired of slaughtering and looting. They were, apparently, insatiable. Their horses were loaded with booty, and more was to be had in Pskov. Perhaps he hesitated because he had spent his wrath. Or perhaps it was a flash of fear that as God's scourge on earth he was exceeding his duties. Or perhaps, too, it was, as the story of the time suggests, the warnings of one of those holy men who periodically crossed Ivan's path, and whose words seemed to have a strong influence upon him.

The incessant ringing of the church bells to call people to prayer might have warmed his heart, mellowing for a brief moment his violent nature, giving him a desire to speak with one of those peculiar, outspoken hermits that so intrigued him with their bluntness on the one hand and their parabolical wisdom on the other. Whatever his reason, Ivan visited the cell of the hermit Salos, described as a mad, holy man. Exactly what happened in the cell is lost in legend. But the hermit is supposed to have spoken bluntly to Ivan, and, as Horsey's account put it, "by imprecations and exorcisms, railings and threats, terming him the Emperor a bloodsucker, the devourer and eater of Christian flesh, swore by his angel that he should not escape death of a present thunderbolt, if he or any of his army did touch a hair in displeasure of the least child's head in that city, which God, by his good angel, did preserve for better purpose than his rapine; therefore to get him thence before the fiery cloud, God's wrath were raised, hanging over his head as he might behold, being in a very great and dark storm at that instant. These words made the Emperor to tremble, so as he desired prayers for his deliverance and forgiveness of his cruel thoughts."

Other accounts state that it was a fast day when Ivan visited Salos, and that the hermit offered the Czar raw meat. Ivan replied haughtily, "I am a Christian, and do not eat flesh on a fast day." The hermit answered, "How is that, since you drink human blood?" Taken aback by Salos' answer, Ivan immediately left the hermit's cell, and, deep in thought, returned to his tent on the outskirts of Pskov.

In his tent, Ivan is supposed to have spent the night in meditation and prayer. The next morning he gave orders that Pskov should be spared. When the news reached the inhabitants, they came by the thousands to his tent, and in the snow they kneeled before him, and gave him their blessings.

Ivan now commanded that his troops return to Moscow. There, the Oprichniki, in their full regalia of black robes and black hoods, and with their dogs' heads and brooms, marched in a triumphal procession.

XIX

All Moscow Trembles

WHEN Ivan finally returned to Alexandrov, he spent long hours trying to convince himself that his annihilation of the Novgorodians was just. Point by point he went over the evidence of the purported treason. He blew up small details to gigantic proportions. Where there were no details, his imagination and suspicions supplied them. He tied tenuous threads together, and where he could not tie them he crossed them, so that obscure contacts between people and idle remarks assumed the proportions of treacherous activities. Finally, by devious reasoning he connected the treason of Novgorod with the Oprichnina itself. Archbishop Pimen and others were in league with his own Oprichnik leaders. Everyone, even his most trusted advisers, were traitors. He vowed that their day of reckoning would come, too.

The more Ivan brooded on the Oprichnik traitors the more embittered he became, and soon it was almost impossible for any of his onetime close companions to approach him. He lashed out at them with his iron-pointed staff, called them traitors, and frequently isolated himself for hours in his rooms, where at times he raved wildly and at other times devoted hour upon hour to prayer. He felt betrayed and deserted.

A few months before, in September, 1569, Maria, his wild Circassian, had died. He had not loved her, but she had been able to divert him from his troubles with her unbridled passion. He insisted that she had been poisoned, like Anastasia, by his enemies. It is possible that if she was poisoned, Ivan himsel´ had ordered it in a fit of despair or anger. Certainly, his behavior at her funeral indicated that he cared little that she was dead; at her last rites he seemed unconcerned and unmoved. He took no steps to implicate anyone in the murder, even though he insisted she had been poisoned.

Now forty years of age, he began to look more and more as a visitor to the Kremlin described him during his later years, "sinister and ferocious to the last degree." In addition, he was prematurely aged, with lines of care and anxiety deeply creasing his face. His somewhat stooped carriage, which had characterized him even as a young man, became more pronounced, and he scarcely ever held his head high, allowing it to droop upon his chest. Only his eyes, which had always been bright and darting, retained their brilliance, and they seemed to bore through the very soul of the person to whom he was talking. However, they took on a more wild look, reflecting the smoldering anger that seemed always to be burning within him. And the wild, piercing eyes, together with his high forehead and beaked nose that seemed to become sharper with the years, gave him the look of a hawk, or an eagle, or some other kind of ferocious bird of prey.

The years had not mellowed him; rather, they accentuated those qualities that distinguished him: his unbridled temper, his moodiness, his self-pity, his maddening suspiciousness, his impulsiveness, and his lack of patience. His appetites, too, grew with the years, and now at Alexandrov he indulged them to the limit. He ate to the bursting point, drank himself into insensibility, watched scenes of torture and cruelty with insatiable curiosity, and wallowed in sexual excesses of all kinds.

During the early months of 1570, Ivan's agents were busy rounding up new suspects and torturing confessions from them. In July, Ivan announced that on the twenty-fifth of that month the public execution of the confessed traitors would take place at the *Lebnoye Meso,* or Place of Skulls, in the Red Square, just outside the Kremlin walls and near the present-day Lenin Mausoleum.

Workmen labored day and night to erect the various intricate instruments of torture and execution—huge caldrons of water suspended over faggots, large pans for frying the victims, furnaces, ropes that when tightened would cut a body in half, bear cages, chopping blocks, iron claws, pincers, gallows.

However, on the day set for execution the Square was empty of spectators. The inhabitants of Moscow had become frightened at the sight of such elaborate death-dealing instruments, and, fearing for their own necks, stayed in their homes. Spectacles such as this had usually drawn large crowds, but this time the inhabitants had a premonition that the executioners' long arms might reach out for them as well as the announced traitors. Ivan, accompanied by his son and guards, rode into the Square. The only spectator was a naked holy man, who ran alongside the Czar and hurled insults at him. Enraged at the lack of curiosity and patriotism of Moscow's citizens, Ivan, accompanied by his guards, rode through the city in an attempt to round up spectators.

"Come, good people!" Ivan cried. "There is nothing to be afraid of. No harm shall overtake you. I will protect you."

Thus assured of their safety by the Czar himself, the people came out of their homes, and soon the Square was filled with onlookers. When they had gathered together, the Czar made a speech, and then asked them if he was justified in condemning these traitors to torture and death. The crowd gave a thunderous shout of approval, and cries of "Long live the Czar!" and "God bless the Czar!" rang through the Square.

Three hundred miserable-looking prisoners, their chains clanking eerily on the stones of the Square, were then led to the place of execution. Most of them were half-dead from the torture they had undergone. In a dramatic show of mercy, Ivan spared a number of Novogorodians, including Pimen, the Archbishop of Novgorod, who was banished to a monastery in the province of Riazan.

He showed no mercy to the Oprichnina leaders; they were the new-found scapegoats. As highly placed advisers of the Czar, their disgrace was the greatest, and the most extreme torture was reserved for the new enemies of the state. Prince Ivan Viskovaty, the Chancellor, was hung up by his feet and cut into pieces. Skuratov, to show his loyalty to the Czar, dismounted from his horse and cut off one of Viskovaty's ears as he was dying. Founikov, the Treasurer, was placed repeatedly first in iced water and then in boiling water "till his skin came off him like an eel's." Basmanov, the Czar's favorite, was executed.

Other Oprichnina leaders met their death in other ways, and at other times. Viazemsky missed the Red Square fete; he died of torture while in prison. The elder Basmanov died at the hands of his son, Feodor Basmanov; the Czar had forced the younger Basmanov to kill his own father before he himself faced the executioner, so that he would meet his Maker with this sin upon him.

The executions continued all day long. At the end of the day, Ivan and his son went to the home of Viskovaty, where Ivan had his widow tortured until she told him where the family treasure was hidden. Then he ravished her. The executed man's fifteen-year-old daughter was given to the Czarevich. From Viskovaty's home, Ivan and his son paid similar visits to the homes of others who had been executed. Men were also sent to other homes to seize treasure, and they, too, violated the wives and daughters of the dead Oprichniki. As a climax to the day's events, Ivan ordered eighty widows of executed Oprichniki to be drowned.

To add to the traitors' disgrace, the mutilated bodies were not buried immediately; they were allowed to remain in the Square for days, rotting and stinking in the heat of the midsummer sun. Dogs ate their flesh, and Moscow citizens spat on them to show their contempt for traitors to the motherland. Finally, Ivan ordered the foul-smelling bodies to be carted away. Oprichniki with long knives and axes were sent to hack the bodies into small pieces, to facilitate their removal. Skuratov, in another display of loyalty, volunteered to head the ghoulish party.

The mass executions temporarily at an end, Ivan now proceeded to adorn various churches and monasteries. He gave large sums to the Trinity Monastery and to the Monastery of St. Cyril. He ordered two cathedrals—the Assumption, and the Descent of the Holy Ghost—to be built in the former. He directed that the Monastery of Bieloozero should be fortified with strong walls, so that it could be a repository for some of the treasure he had collected at Novgorod and from his Oprichnina victims.

Ivan then retired to Alexandrov, where he spent many days in fervent prayer.

XX

Famine, Plague, Fire

As IF in punishment for the sins of their Czar, for a year or so after the massacre at Novgorod and the mass executions in Moscow the people of Russia were afflicted by a series of calamities.

Adverse climatic conditions during the summer of 1570 destroyed a large number of crops, and in the autumn of that year the harvest was the worst in decades. The tragedy was the worse because many peasants had limited the amount of their planting, hoping by doing so to escape the heavy taxation that Ivan had imposed upon them for the upkeep of the Oprichnina. In addition, the Oprichniki had cut down the amount of acreage under cultivation by driving large numbers of landowners and their peasants into exile, and burning the fields of boyars suspected or implicated in treasonable activities. Still others, both nobles and commoners, had fled to faraway places to escape the terror, leaving large, fertile areas unplanted or, in some cases, already planted to crops that rotted in the fields.

By the time winter came, the full effect of the crop shortage was realized; throughout a large section of Russia people were starving to death. The measures they took to keep alive were extreme; even cannibalism was resorted to. Jenkinson, who was in Russia at the time, wrote to Lord Burghley that "God hath plagued it [Russia] in many ways: first by famine, that the people have been enforced to eat bread made of bark of trees, besides many unclean things, yea, and it is reported for certain, that in some places they have eaten one another."

Other accounts speak of the people eating dogs, cats, and rats. The cannibalism that was resorted to included the eating of corpses by the starving survivors, and parents killing their own children, and eating them.

In addition to the famine—or because of it—the plague struck. In Moscow alone, thousands died, and a Dutch merchant, whose affairs had taken him to Russia's capital, reported that upwards of 250,000 people perished. Jenkinson gave the figure of 300,000, and wrote that the "plague continued so fiercely that in the end everyone wondered when he met an acquaintance."

In May, 1571, the Crimean Tatars, who had been threatening for some time to take advantage of Ivan's involvement in Livonia to regain for themselves and for their allies the Turks the lost Tatar areas of Kazan and Astrakhan, began marching northward toward Moscow. An immense army, consisting of two hundred thousand men, went as far as the Oka River without meeting any Russian resistance. At the river, a force of Russians faced them. But the commander, having received no orders from Ivan and afraid that if he used his own initiative he would incur the Czar's wrath, put up only a token resistance, and then fled, leaving the road to Moscow wide open.

Ivan, who had twice visited his troops for a short period, now fled, too, as the Tatar khan, Devlet-Girai, and his troops approached Moscow. Collecting his treasure, his family, his personal servants, and the elite of his troops, said to number almost twenty thousand men, he went to the Trinity Monastery. Then, realizing that this was too near the onrushing Tatars, he fled farther north to a place of safety more than three hundred and fifty miles from Moscow.

Moscow was defenseless—and leaderless. As at Kazan and elsewhere, Ivan refused to take chances with his own person when faced with danger. His humiliation now, however, was increased by the insulting messages that Devlet-Girai continually sent him by his messengers. In one of them, the Khan challenged Ivan to personal combat, threatening that he would kill him, cut off his ears, and send them to the Sultan.

The Tatars in their march on Moscow burned, looted, and killed at every town they entered. Refugees flocked into defenseless Moscow, adding to the confusion that already was reigning there. Together with the inhabitants of Moscow, they sought safety behind the stout walls of the Kremlin, but the gates were locked tight, the dignitaries within declaring that if they allowed such a horde of people to enter the fortress everyone would starve to death.

Thus denied sanctuary in the fortress, the inhabitants tried to flee the city, but the Tatar forces had already blocked some avenues of escape with their troops, and other avenues were blocked by a raging fire that was spreading toward the city from the suburbs, which the Tatars had put to the torch. Whipped by a fierce wind, the flames spread quickly over all Moscow. The inhabitants were panicked. At the gates farthest away from the Tatar invaders, the crush of people trying to escape the enemy and the fire was the greatest. Fletcher wrote that the inhabitants there were so wedged between the gates and in some of the streets leading to them that "three ranks walked one upon the other's head, the uppermost treading down those that were lower: so that there perished at the time (as was said) by the fire and the press, the number of 800,000 [sic] people or more."

Fletcher's figure was obviously exaggerated, but the number burned or crushed to death was enormous. The huge city, composed almost entirely of wood structures, "kindled so quickly" as Fletcher put it, "and went on with such rage, as that consumed the greatest part of the city almost within the space of four hours, being of thirty miles or more of compass." Some of the inhabitants tried to save themselves by jumping into the Moscow River and other waters, but the crush and the fire caught up with them and, as Horsey wrote, "the river and ditches about Moscow stopped and filled with the multitude of people laden with gold, silver, jewels, chains, earrings, bracelets and treasure, that went for succor even to save their heads above water."

Several Englishmen of the Russia Company, who saw thirty of their countrymen burned to death in the fire, reported that the city was reduced to ashes. One of them, identified only as T.G. in Elizabeth I's State Papers, wrote to Sir William Gerard, a knight and alderman, that "assuredly I think Sodom and Gomorrha was not in so short time consumed. I believe it was a plague sent by God, for the wickedness of the people. . . . I pray God I never see the like."

Jenkinson in a letter to Lord Burghley stated that the fire set by the Tatars did "not leave one house standing, and few people are now escaped." He estimated that the total of Russians captured for slaves and burned to death was 300,000, and added that it was "a just punishment of God for such a wicked nation."

The Tatars did not stay in Moscow among the ruins and death. They took as much loot as they could, a hundred thousand prisoners, mostly women and girls, to be sold in the slave markets of Kaffa, and retired towards the Crimea, burning everything they could on their way home.

The extent of the tragedy was unbelievable. The city was leveled, except for the Kremlin, which was relatively untouched; in the citadel only the Belfry of Ivan the Great was damaged. The city's survivors had no shelter of any kind. Tens of thousands of corpses were in the streets and burned-out houses. The lucky few who escaped were too few to bury the dead.

The Moscow River was polluted by the corpses. Horsey reported that "so many thousands were there burned and drowned, as the river could not be rid nor cleansed of the dead carcasses, with all the means and industry [that] could be used in twelve months after; but those alive, and many from other towns and places, every day were occupied within a great circuit to search, dreg, and fish, as it were, for rings, jewels, plate, bags of gold and silver, by which many were enriched ever after. The streets of the city, churches, cellars, and vaults, lay so thick and full of dead and smothered carcasses, as no man could pass for the noisome smells and putrefaction of the air long after."

As soon as the Tatars were a good distance from Moscow, Ivan returned from his place of refuge. He was both contrite and angry, not at the Tatars but at his own cowardice and the cowardice of his leaders. As for the dispossessed, hungry, distraught inhabitants, he offered them no compensation or assistance. To the Khan's ambassador who had come to press Ivan for concessions, he expressed the lament that the calamity that had befallen Moscow was because of "my sins and the sins of my people against my God and Christ," and that the Khan was merely "the instrument of God's anger!"

Ivan's anger fell upon the army and various government administrators. He accused them of failing to do their duty, and scores were executed and their goods and possessions confiscated. He then ordered that the city be cleared of the corpses, and the rebuilding of Moscow undertaken immediately.

The Khan had not finished with Ivan. The ambassador that he sent to Ivan demanded that the Czar give up Kazan and Astrakhan. To emphasize Ivan's desperate situation, the ambassador gave him a way out—a knife with which to cut his throat. Ordinarily, Ivan would have had the ambassador killed on the spot for such an insult, but he was in no position to avenge insult. He restrained his anger, treated the ambassador well, even outfitting him in a golden robe and rich fur cap in place of his sheepskin clothing, and gained time by endless negotiations. By the time the Khan realized that Ivan had no intention of giving in to his demands, the momentum of his victory was gone. Infuriated at the Czar's wile, the Khan organized another expedition in 1572, but it failed miserably; his forces were dispersed long before they reached the capital. This time the repulse of the Tatars was undertaken by the Zemschina boyars, not by the Oprichnina.

Meanwhile, in the capital itself thousands of people from the provinces, who had been pressed into service, were rebuilding the gutted city. Within a year, a new city was erected on the ashes of the old.

XXI

"Czar" Simeon

THE DESTRUCTION of Moscow by the Tatars and their defeat the following year by an army led by the Zemschina boyars had an unforeseen effect—the abolishment of the Oprichnina. Just as in previous centuries the Tatars inadvertently contributed to the unification of Russia by rallying the Russian people around the Moscow grand dukes, this mid-sixteenth-century struggle had the effect of pulling together the state that Ivan had rent asunder. The Oprichnina leaders had fled during the first Tatar expedition; the old, traditional warrior group, the Zemschina voivodes, had resolutely stood their ground in defense of the motherland during the second expedition. Ivan's confidence in his Oprichnina was destroyed.

The aftermath of the massacre at Novgorod, in which hundreds of Oprichnina leaders were executed in Moscow for treachery, was the beginning of the end for the elite corps that proved itself somewhat less than elite. Their inability to stop the relatively weak Tatar forces was their final disgrace.

Ivan now proceeded to disband his hated organization. The army service lists were revised and the manors of the Oprichniki were confiscated and returned to their former owners who had been banished or, if they had been executed, to their heirs. The Oprichniki were now hunted down as ruthlessly as the boyars had been previously. Few of them were spared, and, together with their servants and followers, they were either exiled or executed.

The very word Oprichnina was, so to speak, abolished from the language, and nobody dared mention it under penalty of severe punishment. Russian ambassadors in foreign courts who had insisted during the heyday of the Oprichnina that the charge of cruelty against the organization was slander against Russia and the Czar, now flatly denied, straightfacedly, as the Russian ambassador to Poland had done a few years previously, that such an organization ever existed. In effect, it was not a rewriting of history; it was a denial of it.

Russia now returned to the condition that had existed almost a decade before, with one important exception. Ivan's struggle against the boyars had impressed upon them the absolute power of the Czar, and their claim of parallel, though not equal, rights with the monarch was weakened. Yet in an over-all sense, Ivan had lost his battle. He had not broken the boyar power, and the aristocracy remained the foundation upon which the elaborate monarchial superstructure rested. Henceforth, the crown and the aristocracy would go down the road together, their fate and fortune inextricably tied, until the downfall of both Czar and aristocrats three hundred and fifty years later.

Ivan's personal life, too, at this time underwent a change. For two years or so, the Czar had been a widower, and though there had been no lack of women in his life he now felt the need of having a czaritsa at his side. The dozens of virgins that Basmanov and other Oprichnik intimates had brought to his Alexandrov retreat had satisfied him only for the moment. The harem of fifty or sixty women that he had maintained there like some Eastern potentate was an affectation of imperial rights that had never really pleased him. He yearned for the comfort and companionship that he had had with Anastasia. Besides, a pious man in his fashion, he was disturbed by what he considered his living in sin. He decided to marry again.

At the same time that the Czar made up his mind to take a wife, the young Czarevich Ivan also decided to do so. The usual call for virgins from good families from all over Russia was sent out, and hundreds of candidates were brought to Alexandrov to be inspected by the Czar and the Czarevich. Father and son had done much in company lately, from joining together at Novgorod to watching the executions on Red Square. Now they observed the young women, compared notes as to their virtues and faults, and helped each other in making a final choice. Doctors and midwives were kept busy giving examinations to the young women. At last the choices were made: for the Czar a daughter of a merchant from Novgorod by the name of Martha Sobakin; for the Czarevich a commoner's daughter named Eudoxia Saburov.

After father and son each had dropped a handkerchief into his future bride's lap, to announce in the traditional way their choice, the father of each girl was elevated to the rank of boyar. About the same time, Prince Michael Temgryuk, the brother of the late Czaritsa Maria, was executed, ostensibly because he had not fought against the Tatars; actually because Ivan wished to destroy the influence of Maria's family in court circles. To have the members of the families of three wives in positions of influence was both complicated and confusing.

Ivan's marriage took place on October 28, 1571; the Czarevich's a few days later, on November third. Two weeks after the Czar's marriage, his bride Martha died under mysterious circumstances. Ivan hurled the usual charge that Martha had been poisoned, and insisted that because she had been ill from the day he married her until the time of her death he had never consummated the marriage. He made this claim for an obvious reason; the Church forbade a fourth marriage.

As it was supposed to do, the Church did indeed object, but feebly. Metropolitan Cyril had just died, and the metropolitanate was vacant. The bishops were in no position to have a serious battle with the Czar. They listened to Ivan plead that his marriage was no marriage because Martha had died a virgin, and that he had to have their dispensation to marry again so that he would not be forced into sin with women because he lacked a wife. The Church first imposed a penance upon him, and then granted the Czar his wish. Ivan was free to marry again.

He waited until the following year, and then chose for his bride Anna Koltovsky, the daughter of one of his government officials. Anna lasted for three years, and then Ivan sent her to a nunnery. Ivan had tired of Anna, but gave as his excuse for banishing her that she had involved herself in a plot against him. Her entire family was murdered, but Anna, under the name of Daria, lived the life of a nun for many years, dying a natural death in 1626.

Little is known about Anna, but she obviously did not have the necessary charms to intrigue Ivan. In addition, she had not borne him any heirs, and this put her in double jeopardy. Anna had entered quietly into his life, and just as quietly left it. From the moment he sent her to the nunnery, he never seemed to think of her again, except to send the convent a sum of money each year. It was a cheap—and easy—way to ease his conscience.

Within a space of three years or so, Ivan had tried two marriages; neither of them had proven successful. He now decided to take a mistress. His decision was dictated in part by the fact that he had used up the number of marriages the Church allowed, and, though he could have used his power to force the Metropolitan to waive or overlook this Church rule, he was in no mood to do so. Instead, he asked his confessor's permission to live with a mistress. His confessor reproved him mildly, but made no strong objection.

In fact, his mistress, or his two mistresses, for he took a second a few years after the first, and for a time had both together, were looked upon as his wives, and he treated them as such, allowing them many of the prerogatives of authentic czaritsas. The first mistress was Anna Vasilchikov; the second was Vasilissa Melentiev.

As of his other wives, little is known of Anna or Vasilissa. Anna became his mistress in the early part of 1575; Vasilissa probably around 1578. Both were his mistresses for a short period in that year, when Anna suddenly died, probably by violent means. Vasilissa was sent away the following year to a nunnery in Novgorod. Ivan accused her of having an affair with a Prince Ivan Devtelev, who was executed for daring to share the Czar's mistress.

The lack of knowledge about Ivan's wives and mistresses is understandable, since they were kept isolated in the *terem,* where few Russians and almost no foreigners ever saw them. Except for Anastasia, Ivan never mentioned them in his writings, and the few scattered references to his other wives come mainly from legend and later-day suppositions.

One of the most intriguing stories of the two mistress-wives was woven by Ostrovsky, who made them rival heroines in a play. In his version, Anna, after being the Czar's mistress for a while, has

lost Ivan's favor, and has been supplanted by Vasilissa. Now little
more than a servant, Anna bemoans her sad fate:

> I am terrified here, I cannot breathe; my heart
> Is not at rest: the Czar is no longer kind to me:
> The servants look at me askance. From far away
> I hear the echoes of the master's pleasures,
> The noise of his gaiety. . . . This dreary place, for an instant
> Is full of singing and laughter.
> Then the silence of the grave falls on it again, as though
> Death were everywhere. Only in the recesses
> Of the *terem* I hear low whispers—of executions!
> Nothing to warm my heart! I am the Czar's wife in the flesh,
> But in my heart I am a stranger to him! He frightens me. . . .
> He terrifies me when he is angry, and quite as much when he is
>   merry.
> I do not know his love. . . .
> Like a beast he seeks my caresses. . . . Never a tender word!
> He never asks what I feel in my heart!

To explain Vasilissa's downfall, there is the hint of her affair
with Prince Devtelev. Of the reason for Anna's, there is not even
a hint. Ostrovsky's guess is as good as any; in his play he has Ivan
say: "You are growing thin. . . . I do not like thin women!"

In a broad sense, however, the brevity of Ivan's marriages, with
the exception of the one with Anastasia, and the relatively short
period of his attachment to his two mistress-wives, was a result
of the essential restlessness and impulsiveness of his nature.

It was this restlessness and impulsiveness, among other causes,
that moved him in 1575 to take a most unusual step. He relin-
quished his crown, and conferred it upon a former Tatar khan,
Sain Bulat of Kasimov, who had been christened Simeon Bek-
bulatovich and who had married a daughter of the well-known
boyar Mstislavsky.

The action was taken, apparently, quite impulsively, for there
seems to be nothing immediately preceding the unusual step to
foreshadow such a move. True, Ivan had conferred his crown before, when he had, in jest, placed it upon an old boyar's head, and
then had snatched it back with one hand while with the other he
had plunged a dagger into the old man's heart.

This time, however, Ivan did not snatch back his crown. In the
presence of his court, he called the Tatar khan before him, took

off his crown, placed it on the astonished Simeon's head, declared him by the full title Czar and Autocrat of All Russia, and then kneeled down before him as his faithful subject. The court was stunned, although many thought the act another of the Czar's practical jokes. It was no joke, however. The crown stayed on Simeon's head for more than a year.

Politically and practically, Ivan had much to gain by such a move. It was a dramatic expression of faith and friendship to the large Tatar population in Russia, and a conciliatory move to the Crimean khan. It was an expression of faith, too, in the boyars that assisted "Czar" Simeon in governing—a backhanded way of smoothing the path for their return to their traditional position in government circles and Ivan's way of admitting his mistake in giving the Oprichnina its former position of power. It relieved Ivan to an extent of the responsibility of piecing together the shambles he had made of the state structure when he had created the Oprichnina.

The Englishmen who were in Russia at the time or shortly thereafter viewed Ivan's move as an attempt to free himself of debt and to gain other economic advantages. Horsey stated that Ivan gave up his crown so that henceforth he could "take no notice of any debts owing in his time; letters patent, privileges to towns and monasteries all void." And when after a year or so Ivan took back his crown, Horsey noted that Ivan demanded—and received—large gifts, "amounting and valued to be a great treasure," for doing so from boyars and monasteries, and that he was "freed of all old debts and former charge whatever."

Fletcher went into some detail on the economic advantages the Czar gained by his move, and stated that "towards the end of the year, he caused this new king to call in all charters granted to bishoprics and monasteries, which they had enjoyed many hundred years before. Which were all cancelled. This done (as in dislike of the fact and of the misgovernment of the new king) he resumed his scepter, and so was content (as in favor to the Church and religious men) that they should renew their charters and take them of himself: reserving and annexing to the crown so much of their lands as himself thought good.

"By this practice he wrung from the bishoprics and monasteries (besides the lands which he annexed to the crown) a huge mass of money. From some forty, from some fifty, from some a hundred thousand rubles. And this as well for the increase of his treasury, as to abate the ill opinion of his hard government, by a show of worse in another man."

Still, the economic and political advantages could have been achieved by other means, and not by the extreme measure of giving up his crown. Moreover, there was the possibility that the crown might not have been returned to him when he wanted it back. As Fletcher neatly put it, there was the danger that by setting "another in his saddle, that might have ridden away with his horse while himself walked by on foot."

Ivan was a master political strategist, especially on the domestic scene, and there was the possibility that this strange move was a piece of diplomacy, in the Eastern manner, to save face and at the same time confuse, disturb, and throw off balance his domestic antagonists. And there were many. For scarcely a Zemschina or Oprichnina family in Russia had escaped the torture or murder of at least one of its members. The abolition of the Oprichnina and the ascendancy once again of the boyars of the Zemschina did not, after all, bring back the numerous dead from their graves. Always fearful for his life, and even at this time planning to take refuge in England should the situation demand it, Ivan did not wish to share the fate of his murdered opponents. The times called for a stepping away from power for a while, not the pursuit of it. Moreover, should his plans for finding refuge in England fall through, he did not want a powerful rival on the throne. Simeon had no one's support or loyalty. He was alone and unimportant. Ivan had made him, and Ivan could break him.

Yet, valid as any or all of these reasons might be, there was a certain amount of masquerading, a too impressive display of obeisance to the new Czar on Ivan's part to discount completely the elements of buffoonery, caprice, and practical joking that were so much a part of Ivan's character. He exaggeratedly bowed down before the new ruler and referred to him as Czar. He palmed himself off as an ordinary boyar, and used the titles of Lord and Prince, and Prince of Moscow, avoiding the more exalted titles of Grand Duke or Prince of Russia. Whenever he visited Simeon, he bowed as low as any boyar, introduced himself as "Ivan Vasilievich, Prince of Moscow, who has come hither, with these my sons, to do you homage."

"Czar" Simeon, on his part, fulfilled the role of Czar. He lived in monarchial style in the Kremlin, signed state documents "Simeon, Czar and Autocrat of All Russia," answered petitions, and delegated responsibility. He was not particularly bright; in fact, some observers considered him somewhat on the doltish side. Yet he managed to carry on as Czar without any disastrous mistakes, and to put on a somewhat regal bearing, even on the most difficult occasions, when the dread Czar Ivan himself kneeled down in homage to him.

Ivan never revealed his reason or reasons for making Simeon the Czar. He played his part in the drama—or farce—straight through to the end, only on rare occasions revealing what his future plans were for the khan now become Czar. One such occasion was a conversation with Queen Elizabeth's agent, Daniel Sylvester, to whom he had just admitted that it was true that Simeon was crowned. "There was nothing final about that, however," Ivan remarked. "I can take up my czardom again. Czar Simeon has my crown, but I have seven more."

In 1576, Ivan did take back his crown with the same lack of formality with which he had given it away. For his year or so of employment as Czar, Simeon was given the Duchy of Tver to govern, and henceforth in his correspondence with Ivan signed himself "your slave." Later, he commanded an army group in Livonia. He was one of the few people ever to come into close contact with Ivan who survived the Czar's fury. He even survived the Czar himself. His fortunes, however, which were indeed great under Ivan, changed under Ivan's successors. Czar Feodor deprived him of his duchy, and Boris Godunov, who feared him as a possible rival for the throne, blinded him. Simeon died around 1611, according to some accounts, in the monastery to which he had been exiled and where he spent the last few years of his life, or, according to other accounts, in 1616 in Moscow under the reign of Michael Romanov.

Back on the throne once again, Ivan found much to keep him busy, not the least being the conquest of Livonia, which he had begun twenty years before, and which, though thousands of men had died on both sides and dozens of town and cities had been laid waste, was still not resolved.

XXII

War and—at Last—Peace

SINCE 1557 when Ivan first sent his troops into Livonia, the Czar had been engaged in war—interrupted occasionally by short periods of peace—over the Baltic provinces with various combinations of foreign powers. By 1572, the year in which his arch enemy King Sigismund II of Poland died, Ivan still had not achieved his objective of expanding the territory of Russia "to its natural borders"—the Baltic Sea. His armies had achieved some notable victories, but there had also been severe defeats. Poland-Lithuania, Sweden, the remnants of the Teutonic Order, and even the Pope in distant Rome were determined that the banners of the Orthodox Czar should not wave over non-Orthodox ramparts, that Russia, the restless bear, should be prevented from stretching its barbarous paws into civilized Europe, and, if possible, that the bear's claws should be trimmed by consolidating and expanding Polish domination of south Russia.

Through the years there had been much maneuvering, many alliances, and intricate schemes by both Russia and her enemies as they attempted to gather additional strength to break the long and bloody stalemate. Political and personal intrigues were rife. And through it all Ivan revealed himself as a master strategist who had a keen intelligence and a wily nature. In his contacts and negotiations with the countries of Western Europe, he was largely unaware of the main issues of conflict that were raging there at the time, but when it came to protecting and advancing Russian aims he pursued them stolidly and, at times, adroitly. As the first Russian Czar to plunge deeply into the intricate web of European politics, he was just as often the spider as the fly.

The very fact that he had even limited successes is a tribute to his intelligence. For centuries, Russia had isolated itself and had been forced into isolation by her Western neighbors. Even on the few occasions when Russia tried to import scholars, technicians, engineers, and craftsmen of various kinds to learn of the advances that were then being made in Europe, the efforts had been blocked. The most striking case occurred early in Ivan's reign, when Hans Schlitte, a Saxon adventurer, had received the Czar's permission to recruit artisans and scholars in Germany and send them to Russia. The Emperor Charles V in Augsburg had agreed to co-operate with Schlitte's endeavors, and more than a hundred "doctors, masters of arts, and men of learning, bell-founders, printers, and similar craftsmen" were engaged. But when the group reached Lubeck, the members of the group were sent home and Schlitte was imprisoned on charges of debt. The Hanseatic merchants in Revel, much keener than Charles V on the dangers of possible Russian advances, were determined to keep Russia as isolated as possible, and prevailed upon the city fathers of Lubeck not to let the group proceed to Moscow.

Ivan's limited knowledge of European affairs and customs, coupled with his own arrogance, sometimes involved him in outrageous situations with the crowned heads of Europe. Ivan had never forgotten his rebuff by King Sigismund when, after Anastasia's death, he had attempted to marry the Polish monarch's sister, the noted beauty Catherine. Subsequently, Catherine had married John, Duke of Finland and the brother of the mad King Eric of Sweden. Even though she was now married, Ivan demanded that John should give up his wife so that Ivan could marry her. Ivan even went so far as to send a delegation to King Eric to press his claim to Catherine. The delegation was empowered to offer the Swedish king, who by now had imprisoned John, rights to Revel and Estonia and assistance in a struggle against Poland in return for John's giving up his wife. King Eric was intrigued by the offer. However, he soon thereafter was deposed, and John, the new king of Sweden, would have nothing to do with the fantastic offer, and ordered the Russian delegation home.

During the three-year peace that Ivan had agreed to with

Sigismund in 1570, the Czar tried desperately to achieve an alliance with Denmark for the future pursuit of his Livonian campaign. For a while Ivan entertained the thought that the annexation of Livonia to Russia was almost impossible, and that the best he could hope for was the establishment of a Russian protectorate over the area. He had previously tried to get the Teutonic Order's Grand Masters Kettler and Furstenberg to agree to head a protectorate, but had been unsuccessful. Now, through the efforts of two Livonian renegades, Taube and Kruse, he negotiated with the Danes, and succeeded in having Magnus, the brother of King Frederick II of Denmark, agree to the undertaking. Magnus, who has been described by an unsympathetic observer, as "misshapen, one-eyed, and club-footed," was an arch opportunist, and was pleased at the thought of being head of a strong principality.

In 1570, Magnus arrived in Moscow, accompanied by a large retinue of four hundred persons. He was treated with elaborate pomp and circumstance and, as it turned out, was offered more than he hoped for. Ivan, playing his own wily game, offered the Danish prince all of Livonia, even though Ivan had not yet conquered it, and announced that henceforth Magnus was King of Livonia. The Czar promised not to interfere with the religion or institutions of Livonia, and assured Magnus of Russia's unswerving support for his kingdom, and that all territory in the area captured by efforts of the Russians and Magnus would be under the Dane's suzerainty. To underscore the new alliance, Ivan offered Magnus his cousin, Euphemia, in marriage. Euphemia was the daughter of Prince Vladimir of Staritsa, whom Ivan had murdered during the purge of the boyars. As a wedding present, Ivan promised the Danish prince five barrels of gold. Magnus accepted. However, before the marriage could be consummated, Euphemia died, and a marriage was arranged between Magnus and her thirteen-year-old younger sister, Maria.

Magnus' fortunes in battle were varied. The help expected from the King of Denmark never materialized, and Magnus was left with troops composed mainly of mercenaries and Russian auxiliaries. In name, Magnus was a king, but the nature of his kingdom, to say the least, was ill-defined and unstable. The Livonians were no more ready to accept bondage under a Danish king than under a Russian Czar, and they continued to resist. At Revel, for instance, which

Magnus besieged for weeks, the inhabitants made a stout defense, and repelled their announced liberators. Not long afterwards, the town of Paide was taken, and there the murderous Oprichnik leader Skuratov, who had miraculously managed to escape the execution-er's axe during the purge of the Oprichnina, was killed in battle.

Meanwhile, the death of Sigismund of Poland, who left no heirs, had thrown a good part of Europe into a contest for choosing an heir to Sigismund's throne. Some Polish and Lithuanian nobles, fired by the idea of a great empire that would ally their lands with Russia, favored Ivan's second son, Feodor, for the throne. The idea did not appeal to the Czar, who already had visions of himself on the Polish-Lithuanian throne. He offered no encouragement to the idea, turned down his son's candidacy, and instead proposed him-self, even writing a letter expressing his unbounded grief over the death of his "brother" Sigismund, the same brother for whom he had previously ordered a coffin to be made. Other candidates in-cluded King John of Sweden; Henry of Valois, the son of Catherine de Medici and the brother of Charles IX, King of France; and Prince Stephen Batory of Hungary. Emissaries representing the various candidates flocked to Warsaw, and the bargaining and maneuvering that took place there was a mixture of high drama and low comedy. Other interested groups sent their representa-tives—the Teutonic Order, the Jesuits, Protestants, the Emperor of the Holy Roman Empire, the Pope.

Ivan sent no emissaries, or at least no formal ones. Haughtily he insisted that the representatives of the joint kingdom of Poland and Lithuania should come to Moscow if they wanted him to consider seriously putting on the vacant crown. Ivan's haughtiness at such a time was not as arrogant as it would first appear. His chances for the Polish throne were actually quite good. The idea of a power-ful empire appealed to many Poles and Lithuanians who had seen their joint kingdom become so impoverished and weak that it could scarcely, so it was exaggeratedly said, raise a full regiment of soldiers or enough money to bury its king in proper style.

However, in actuality the animosity that had developed over the centuries between Poland and Russia was too difficult to heal so quickly. Deep religious and cultural differences separated the two peoples. Specifically, Polish lords feared the intrusion of Russian mores and religion upon their way of life; Ivan feared the effect of

Catholic and Westernized Poland on his obedient and loyal Orthodox subjects. Both the Polish-Lithuanian aristocrats and Ivan
played with the tempting idea of uniting the two kingdoms, but in
the long run it came to nothing.

While Ivan temporized, arrogantly demanding more and more
concessions and raising one objection after another to the Polish-
Lithuanian emissaries who did indeed come to Moscow as he insisted they should, the choice was made in Warsaw in April, 1573:
the new king of Poland was to be the weak-minded, weak-kneed
fop, Henry of Valois.

Henry was made king in a ceremony, not in Warsaw, but in
Paris, at Notre Dame. Soon, Henry was as disgusted with the
Polish nobles who surrounded him as they were with their effemi-
nate king. In May, 1754, his brother Charles IX died, and the new
king secretly made plans to return to France, to claim his brother's
throne. Yet, as dissatisfied as the Poles were with him, they did not
want to see him leave, and watched him carefully. One night, however, he stole out of the palace, and, with the Polish nobles in
pursuit, dashed successfully across the border. Shortly thereafter,
he was installed as Henry III, King of France, and as such had no
intention of ever returning to what he considered a barbarous
country, or even, as some Poles insisted, ruling Poland from Ver-
sailles. The choice was now between Emperor Maximilian and the
Sultan of Turkey's vassal, Stephen Batory of Hungary. Although
Maximilian won the election in the Polish senate, the Polish gentry,
through force of arms, finally succeeded in installing Batory as
king.

In Batory, Ivan had a strong, intelligent, determined opponent.
The battle for the Baltic area continued, both against the new
Polish king and against Sweden, who throughout the Livonian war
took full advantage of the complicated and unresolved situation.
For a while, the fortunes of battle favored the Russians, and they
captured town after town. But then the tide of battle turned. Faced
by Swedes, Lithuanians, Poles, Livonians, and even by Tatar
troops sent by the Crimean khan, the Russians fell back. In 1580,
military defeats were numerous. In addition, the treacherous Magnus, after servilely working with Ivan, threw in his lot with the
Poles. Batory's troops made deep incursions into Russian territory
and even laid siege to Pskov. But here the Russians, always more

powerful in defense, especially on their own land, than in offense, put up a sturdy and determined fight. Batory's dream of annexing Russia, or at least part of it, to Poland, ended in the defeat of his army in Russia. However, the Russians had been cleared out of most of the Baltic area. Batory taunted Ivan over his losses. The Czar, after more than two decades of trying to gain access to the sea, was ready to admit defeat.

The end of the war was drawing near. Ivan's troops had been bled white. His treasury had been drained. The enemies he faced had increased in power and number. His soldiers, as the defense of Pskov proved, were willing to fight and die for the defense of Russia, but they had no more heart for conquering lands that were alien to them or being stationed among foreign people who hated their presence and who rebelled each time their conqueror's guard was down.

Ivan had constantly refused to allow negotiations to take place in Lithuania or Poland, insisting that they should be held in Moscow. Now he was quite willing to negotiate anywhere in order to end the war. He had allowed the Livonian war to go on much too long, but it had been the dream of his life to see the standards of Russia waved by the breezes from the Baltic, and he could not abandon this dream so easily. But now that it seemed—and was— impossible to achieve, he capitulated. He wrote to Batory that he was willing to sue for peace. His letter was a mixture of humility and arrogance. He began meekly, "We by the grace of God, and not by the rebellious judgment of men, Ivan, humble Czar and Grand Duke of All Russia," and then went on for many pages praising the wonderful government of Russia, and finished the letter by saying he was prepared to negotiate, but if that was impossible he would decide the issue on the battlefield. This last statement was to save face. Ivan had had enough of battles. Batory refused the offer to negotiate, and with a flourish of bravado challenged Ivan to a personal duel.

Batory, too, was less secure than he seemed, and he was not as adamant as he appeared. The Czar pursued the question of negotiations for peace, even instructing his emissaries to humble themselves before Batory if necessary. "If the King does not inquire about the Czar's health," Ivan told his envoys, "and does not rise when the Czar's greetings are conveyed, pay no attention to it. If he begins to dishonor, persecute, annoy, or scold, enter a mild complaint to his attendant, but make no quick retort. Be patient." To his commanders in the field, he did not even bother sending instructions, merely the message to "carry on as God shall guide you. My hope now is based on God's help and your zeal."

This tone was a far cry from Ivan's previous anger when speaking of Batory or when he sent him notes. Then, Ivan had compared Batory to Amalek and Sennacherib. Batory's contempt for Ivan was just as violent. He called Ivan a Cain, the Moscow Pharaoh, Herod, Phalaris, a wolf, and a bad protector of his people. "Why did you yourself not come out against us with your troops," Batory wrote, "why did you not protect your subjects? Even a poor hen protects her chicks from the hawk with her wings; but you, a double-headed eagle, hide yourself."

In August, 1580, Ivan took a momentous step. He called together his council and told it that he was determined to seek peace, and would try to have the Emperor of the Holy Roman Empire and the Pope as mediators. Meekly, the council agreed, even though Ivan would have proceeded without its consent. The Russian Shevrigin, the Livonian Poper, and the Italian Pallavicino were entrusted with the mission of going to the two courts.

The Emperor was not interested in acting as a mediator, and received the emissaries cooly. Pallavicino insisted that the Doge of Venice should be approached. This, too, proved fruitless. Finally, the delegation arrived in Rome, and presented its credentials and papers to Pope Gregory XIII. To Gregory's disappointment, there was not a word in the documents about Church matters, especially the long-sought-after unity of the two Churches. Still, it was a great concession that Ivan had made, approaching the Catholic Pope to mediate a dispute involving Orthodox Russia. The Pope hoped to take advantage of the opportunity of having his emissary raise Church matters, even though Ivan's request for assistance was limited to Polish-Russian affairs.

In March, 1581, the Pope appointed as his emissary the Jesuit Antonio Possevino, who had recently conducted negotiations with King John III of Sweden. After visiting Batory, Possevino arrived in Moscow in August. The presents that Possevino brought from the Pope for the Czar were, according to an item in Queen Elizabeth I's State Papers, "a hallowed rose, twelve 'pair' of beads, valued at a hundred crowns apiece, the image of our Lady esteemed at seven hundred crowns, and many *Agnos Dei.*"

Following the Pope's instructions, Possevino tried at every interview to interest Ivan in Church unity. Ivan, however, was adamant. He insisted that Possevino's task was to effect a peace treaty between Russia and Poland. Reluctantly, the Jesuit had to admit his failure in this area. Even his task of getting the two sides to agree was a most difficult one, but here he had more success. After repeated negotiations with Batory and Ivan, a peace treaty was finally agreed upon in 1582. By the treaty, Russia gave up its claims to Livonia and ceded certain territory.

Possevino lingered on in Moscow for several months, still trying to interest Ivan in Church matters. Ivan was quite willing to talk about religious doctrine and philosophy, but resolutely refused to be enticed into the subject of the amalgamation of the two Churches. In spite of his particular brand of erudition, the wily Jesuit was no match for Ivan, who not only had his own brand of religious knowledge but a much quicker mind and a sharper tongue. Towards the end of their talks, the atmosphere between them cooled. Ivan not only insulted Possevino by washing his hands each time he came into contact with him so that he wouldn't be contaminated by a non-believer, but even began insulting the smooth-faced Jesuit by mocking him because of his lack of a beard. On one occasion, after Possevino had angered him, the Czar cried, "Your Roman Pope is not a shepherd at all: he is a wolf!"

In May, 1582, Possevino left Moscow to return to Rome, accompanied by a Russian ambassador, Molvianiov. Contrary to Ivan's usual openhandedness with gifts to foreign dignitaries, the presents he sent to the Pope with his ambassador were miserly—merely a few sable skins—and indicative of the lack of progress Possevino had made in bringing the Czar of Russia closer to the Pope of Rome.

Ivan was in no mood to be gracious. The end of his dream of securing for Russia the Baltic area was a crushing blow. He felt his reign had been a failure, and that his time had run out and he would never again be able to take up such a battle. His vision of Russia expanding westward would not be realized for over a hundred years more, until the reign of Peter the Great, who in many ways was the pupil of Ivan and whose plans and methods were later-day copies of his illustrious teacher's. The fact that during the last years of his reign, his imperialistic ambitions were being realized, without his help and encouragement, at the other end of his empire—in Siberia—did little to cheer him. There, a few Cossacks and vagabond adventurers under amazing leaders such as Ermak, and entrepreneurs such as the Stroganovs, were carving out an addition to the Russian empire many times larger than the Russia Ivan had inherited when he became Czar.

At the bottom of defeat, Ivan was in no temper to think of the long-range achievements his disastrous campaign had yielded. For Russia had now become a power to be reckoned with, and no longer would sovereigns throughout Europe look at maps and wonder what manner of government operated in those vast expanses. Foreigners by the hundreds were now in Russia—adventurers, merchants, fugitives, deserters, rebels, Protestants, Knights of the Order—and at last Russia was to be introduced, even against its will, to outside influences. The German colony in the suburbs of Moscow, for instance, was to play a considerable role in the future of Russia. Moreover, the struggle had in many ways united the Russian people, and had helped to heal the split caused by the Oprichnina. And even Ivan himself had achieved one of his ambitions—he was now considered a great Czar, even though he was universally considered a terrible one.

XXIII

Ivan-Kurbsky Correspondence

A T THE TIME when Ivan was reaching a decision to sue for peace in Livonia, the Czar received his fifth—and last—letter from Kurbsky. Since 1564, when Kurbsky fled Russia and sought sanctuary in Poland, he had written Ivan a total of five letters. Ivan, in return, had written two to Kurbsky. In these two letters, the first one running to sixty pages, Ivan revealed himself as both a person and a Czar as no other Russian ruler, with the exception of Catherine the Great, has ever done in the history of Russian czardom. As a source of enlightenment on the attitudes and goals of Ivan the Terrible, the correspondence is invaluable.

Kurbsky's decision to go into exile was a most difficult one to make, and only a man with a profound grievance against his ruler and a deep-seated fear for his personal safety would have taken such a step. When he fled to Poland from his military post in Dorpat, leaving behind him his wife and son, who later were put to death by Ivan, he knew he was cutting off any possibility of ever again returning to Russia. For the rest of his life, Kurbsky carried on a campaign against the Czar and his policies to justify his running away.

As for Ivan, there was no one he hated more than Kurbsky after his self-imposed exile. He attacked him on every front, and called him every conceivable name from "vicious dog" to "cowardly traitor," even sneering at Kurbsky's complexion and the color of his eyes. "You value your face dearly!" Ivan wrote. "Who indeed wishes to see such an Ethiopian face? Where will one find a just

214

man who has pale-blue eyes? For your countenance betrays your wicked disposition."

In 1564, when their correspondence began, Ivan was thirty-four, Kurbsky was thirty-six. Both men were at the height of their intellectual powers; their passions were strong, their ambitions great, and their hatreds deep. Both men had great pride, and their letters reflect the profound hurt each felt at the other's betrayal of his person and belittlement of his stature.

Kurbsky was highly conscious of his illustrious family, and traced it back to his paternal grandfather to the ninth degree, Feodor Rostislavich, prince of Yaraslavl, who ruled in Mozhaisk at the end of the thirteenth century. Feodor died in 1299 and was canonized in 1463. Throughout the centuries, the Kurbskys had been one of the most powerful boyar families; Prince Andrei Kurbsky, at the time of his defection, was Ivan's leading general and, next to Adashev and Sylvester, his most trusted adviser. Kurbsky had been a leading general in the battle for Kazan and in the early Livonian campaigns. It is no wonder, therefore, that when he applied for sanctuary to King Sigismund of Poland, the Polish king welcomed him as the most important political exile who had ever left Russia under Ivan's regime, and gave him not only political sanctuary but immense holdings of land and many peasants so that he could live in his exile as well as he had lived in Russia. The Polish town of Kowell, situated east of Lublin, became his, as well as the magnificent castle that was there.

When Ivan heard of Kurbsky's flight, he was enraged. He compelled all the important boyars to renounce their right of departure, and made them take an oath that they would not go abroad for any purpose whatsoever, unless as diplomatic emissaries under Ivan's specific permission and direction.

Ivan's action, however, was no particular departure from Russian policy, except that it was formalized by an oath. For centuries, Russian grand dukes had frowned upon—and at times had expressly forbidden—travel out of Russia. Except during the period of Tatar vassalage when Russian grand dukes traveled to Mongolia to grovel at the feet of the Great Khans, Russian rulers had not crossed the Russian border, the last reigning prince to do so was the Grand Duke of Kiev, Izaslav, who paid a visit to Emperor Henry IV at Mayence in 1075. The next ruler of Russia to travel outside Russia was Peter the Great, in 1697. Thus, for a period of six hundred years, except for visits to the Great Khan, as noted before, no Russian ruler ever set foot on foreign soil; his personal contact with the outside world was limited to the foreigners who came to Russia.

Kurbsky, in his third letter to Ivan, seized upon the Czar's strict interdiction on foreign travel, and accused him of putting Russia within prison walls. He claimed that he was unable to send Ivan a reply to his previous letter in a reasonable length of time because of the "unpraiseworthy habit" existing in Russia; "for you shut up the kingdom of Russia—in other words, free human nature—as in a fortress in hell; and whoever . . . goes from your land to strange countries . . . you call a traitor; and if he is caught on the frontier, you punish him with various forms of death."

The immediate causes of Kurbsky's flight were his recent defeat in an important battle in Livonia, for which he feared Ivan's wrath, and the punishment of Sylvester and Adashev, which had just taken place and which Kurbsky feared would be his fate, too, since he was closely allied with them. However, his opposition to Ivan had deep roots; namely, Ivan's determination to break the power of the boyars. Kurbsky, as it developed, became their outstanding spokesman, reiterating over and over their belief that the state did not rest upon the will and power of the Czar alone, but jointly upon the Czar and the boyars, as expressed through boyar advisers and the boyar council. The Czar had to be firmly and unalterably attached to his boyars and to cherish them "as he would his own limbs." Kurbsky's program, in essence, was the maintenance of the status quo in the relation of Czar and boyars; he offered no new program or modification of the existing order of things.

Kurbsky's first letter to Ivan was dated July 5, 1564, and was probably delivered by his servant Vaska Shibanov. This is the same Vaska that Ivan was supposed to have maltreated. As a seventeenth-century source relates the incident, "Vaska Shibanov handed to the Czar . . . the letter from his prince. And the Czar asked him: 'Who are you and whence have you brought this writing?' And he answered the Czar, saying: 'I am the servant of your traitor, Prince Andrei Kurbsky, and this letter which I have given you is from him.' Then the Czar was filled with wrath, and calling this servant unto him, transfixed his foot with the sharp end of his staff. Then he leaned upon his staff and ordered him to read the letter. . . ." The authenticity of the story is in doubt because an earlier source in the sixteenth century reports that Vaska was not Kurbsky's emissary but was arrested by Ivan's voivodes and delivered to the Czar.

However, there is little doubt that Ivan was "filled with wrath." Kurbsky wrote Ivan in angry accusation that he "subjected to death" many boyars and that he murdered them even during "sacerdotal ceremonies" and thus "stained the thresholds of the churches with the blood of martyrs." Furthermore, he insisted that Ivan falsely accused the boyars of "treachery and magic and other abuses," and that Ivan rewarded his boyars who were personally faithful to the Czar and who expressed this loyalty by being zealous in battle and conquest, "by destroying whole families."

Kurbsky's tone in his letter was one not of anger but of pain. Almost hysterically Kurbsky wrote that his letter "soaked in my tears, will I order to be put into my grave with me, when I shall be about to come with you before the Judgment of my God, Jesus Christ." From the very first sentence of his letter, its tone was bitter, and he immediately charged Ivan with sins, declaring that his actions were contrary to his former illustriousness, "particularly in the Orthodox faith," and that "if you have understanding, may you understand this with your leprous conscience—such a conscience as cannot be found even amongst the godless people."

Kurbsky then went on, as a friend who had been betrayed, to list his personal grievances against the Czar. "What evil and persecutions have I not suffered from you!" Kurbsky wrote. "What ills and misfortunes have you not brought upon me! And what iniquitous tissues of lies have you not woven against me! . . . You have recompensed me with evil for good and for my love with implacable hatred. My blood, spilt like water for you, cries out against you to my Lord. . . . Throughout many years have I toiled with much sweat and patience; and always have I been separated from my fatherland, and little have I seen my parents, and my wife have I not known; but always in far-distant towns have I stood in arms against your foes and I have suffered many wants and natural illness, of which my Lord Jesus Christ is witness. Still more, I was visited with wounds inflicted by barbarian hands in various battles and all my body is already afflicted with sores. But to you, O Czar, was all this as nought; rather do you show us your intolerable wrath and bitterest hatred, and, furthermore, burning stoves."

Near the end of his letter, Kurbsky vowed that he would be an implacable enemy of Ivan's because of the Czar's crimes and that he would never "remain silent before the Czar, but to my end will I incessantly cry out with tears against you to the everlasting Trinity, in which I believe. . . ." And in truth he did so, not only "with tears" but, though in exile, as the leader of the boyars against Ivan's policies, even to co-operating with Ivan's foreign enemies. Kurbsky, in effect, became the boyars' organizational and intellectual leader, and his place of exile in Poland became the center for propaganda against Ivan.

Kurbsky's first letter was comparatively brief, running only a few pages. Ivan's reply, which he wrote shortly after receiving Kurbsky's letter, was extremely long; it makes up more than sixty per cent of the whole correspondence. The length of Ivan's letter and the manner in which it was written gives some credibility to the idea that not only were he and Kurbsky engaging in a personal debate but that their letters were intended for public consumption. This conjecture is further strengthened by the fact that even though Kurbsky had the earlier letters published in Poland and widely distributed, Ivan was still willing to carry on the correspondence, and wrote his second letter to Kurbsky as late as 1577.

In essence, Ivan's lengthy reply was his political treatise on the right—and duty—of the Czar to be an absolute monarch, free of any interference from any group and immune from criticism from any quarter, and a polemic against the boyars and their political claims to any position, except that which the absolute monarch deigned to assign them, in the government. In this regard, Ivan's letters are the first written expression in Russia until that time— and for years later, the fullest expression—of the divine origin of the Czar's supreme and absolute power. Thus, Ivan was the father of the theory of czardom as it existed in Russia in later centuries and, as the most extreme practitioner of that theory, the original model of the autocratic monarchs who ruled in Russia until 1917, as well as the traditional national model for the supreme leader of the Russian state, best exemplified by Stalin, that existed after the Revolution.

Ivan was so convinced that a Czar was divinely appointed, and that for him to rule was a natural order of things, that in his letters he scarcely bothers to justify his theory but asks the following rhetorical questions: "To turn light into darkness, I do not endeavor," he wrote, "and that which is bitter I do not call sweet. Is this then light or sweetness for servants to rule? And is this darkness or bitterness for a divinely ordained sovereign to rule?"

As a divinely appointed ruler, Ivan was convinced that a Czar was answerable for his actions only to God. In replying to Kurbsky's charges of his cruelty and punishment of boyars, Ivan wrote: "Concerning our subjects' guilt before us and our wrath towards them; hitherto the Russian masters were questioned by no man, but they were free to reward and punish their subjects; and they did not litigate with them before any judge. . . ." In other words, Ivan conceived the Czar as having a God role much like that of a rewarding and punishing Jehovah, who was—and should be—wrathful and, at times, merciful.

Ivan believed that resistance to the Czar was also resistance to God. "Let every soul be subject unto the higher powers," Ivan wrote. "For there is no power ordained that is not of God. . . . Whosoever, therefore, resisteth the power, resisteth the ordinance of God. . . . And these words were said concerning all power, even when power is obtained by blood and strife. . . . If you then resist power, all the more so do you resist God."

A confusion existed in Ivan's mind whether his power, as he stated in his first letter to Kurbsky, was "handed down to me by God from our forefathers," or, as he stated in his second letter thirteen years or so later, was handed to him directly by God. He preferred to have got the power both ways, for there were others in the complicated royal line in Russia whose forefathers had been rulers. He constantly referred to his direct royal lineage as opposed to other boyars', and made clear that he did not "ascend the throne by robbery or armed force of blood," but that he was "born to rule by the grace of God; and I do not even remember my father bequeathing the kingdom to me and blessing me—I grew up upon the throne."

Ivan did not believe that the sovereign was merely the first person, so to speak, in the empire, but that he was apart and above the empire. As the only one appointed by God and the only one responsible to God, the Czar's responsibility was only to Him, and it was a crime and sinful for him to accept any control from human beings. In a letter to Batory, Ivan underlined this thought when he wrote: "We know what is due to the majesty of Princes. But the Empire is majesty, and above that majesty stands the Sovereign in his Empire, and the Sovereign is above the Empire." Earlier, when King Sigismund of Poland had refused to recognize the long title that indicated Ivan considered himself ruler over lands that were in dispute, Ivan protested that this title had been given to him by God, and that he didn't need the Polish king's confirmation of it or care whether he had it. In his letters to Kurbsky, this idea that the sovereign is not first in the state but above the state is confirmed.

Ivan believed that he was the guardian of the state, too—so much the guardian that he accepted anything that happened in the state as his personal responsibility, for he was ultimately responsible to God for his subjects' actions. Thus, it was his lot to be the object of their hatred as well as their love. He wanted—practically demanded—their love, but it was his particular cross, which he had to bear as God's appointed one, to bear their hatred, too. This was his fate and his destiny, and it was his sin if he allowed human emotions to interfere with those actions he had to undertake to fulfill his destiny.

Ivan did not delude himself that he was a demi-god or of a different stamp than other human beings. He considered himself to be like other men, except that he had a special appointment directly from God as His personal servant on earth. Ivan constantly referred to his human weaknesses and failings, his human passions and desires, his mortality. The right to rule was divine, but he, as a person, was not divine. He did not confuse royalty with godliness, and stated bluntly in his first letter to Kurbsky that "I do not consider myself to be immortal, for death is the debt that all must pay for the sin of Adam. For even if I wear the purple, none the less I know this, that, like unto all men, I am altogether clothed with frailty by nature."

Ivan refused to recognize that any of his subjects had a right to determine how they should be governed. This was a right he denied even to the great nobles. Speaking of monarchs under whom there existed some form of democracy, Ivan noted that they are "godless people . . . for none of these rule their own kingdoms. As their servants order them, so too do they rule. But as for the Russian autocracy, they themselves [i.e. the autocrats] from the beginning have ruled all their dominions, and not the boyars and not the grandees." Here, Ivan either forgot his history or chose to ignore it, for the Russian princes for hundreds of years had shared their rule with the boyars.

This supreme power, even though he protested he was only a human being, made him feel—and act—as though he were, indeed, different from the human herd. He felt close to such great Biblical leaders as Moses, David, or Solomon, about whom he constantly read in religious works of all kinds. He believed he was the Lord's Anointed, and as such wanted—and demanded—the kind of worship reserved for holy ones. If he did not consider himself divine, he did at least consider himself to be, and acted as though, he were a high priest. Under Ivan, the Little Father figure became a reality. In a sense, from the time of Ivan on, the Russian people worshipped and adulated two figures—their supreme leader on earth and their heavenly Father. The Russian's mystical awe of his supreme political leader, his sense of him as a man of transcendental powers, stems from Ivan's insistence that the Czar of Russia was appointed by God and God alone. For Ivan, there was not a question of one role or another; it was how to play all roles —the human being with frailties, the high priest, the all-wise and all-powerful political leader—simultaneously.

It was this almost impossibly difficult task that nearly drove Ivan mad, though he was not mad by nature nor, as some have claimed, by the effects of syphilis. Even Kurbsky, who knew Ivan so well, could not fathom Ivan's strange role, or roles, and through the pen of Cicero, wrote: " 'All foolish men are mad'; but I will prove by true facts that you are not being foolish, as you often are, not wicked, as you always are, but out of your mind and mad."

Whatever caused Ivan sometimes to appear a madman was not his cruelty and murders, for this was an age of cruelty and murder, but his violent efforts to live up to the almost impossible position he had made for himself. Later Russian leaders had their way paved for them by Ivan in the performance of their triple role. As an extremely religious man, Ivan was conscience-stricken that he was betraying his God by assuming for himself more than God had given him. Though he proclaimed to Kurbsky and others that the

Czar was divinely inspired and divinely ordained, he had little to go on except his own belief that this was so. And since he proclaimed to others and acted as though he were God's scourge on earth, he could not express his doubts to anyone. To himself, and no doubt in his prayers, he was maddeningly aware of the great moral burden he had placed upon himself. And as he grew older, he feared the day of reckoning with his Lord. His crimes to his subjects and his crimes to his God destroyed him spiritually and physically.

Ivan was a complex man, and inconsistent. There are times when it is possible to believe that he was emotionless about his crimes against persons. Even his petition made to the Church shortly before he died, to have prayers said for the souls of his victims may have been simply a safeguard against his meeting with his Maker, a reaction to Kurbsky's frightening threat that "those massacred by you, standing at the throne of Our Lord, ask vengeance against you." He vacillated between feeling remorse for his cruelty and feeling nothing. He could at times justify himself by saying that when he punished those who had transgressed against the earthly Czar, he was only doing what the heavenly Czar had asked him to do. He could, and did, ease his conscience by believing, as he wrote to Kurbsky, that "as for our subjects, we recompense the good with good, and to the evil are meted out evil punishments, not because we wish it, not because we desire it, but of necessity, because of their evil crime is there punishment." And then in another passage, comparing himself with others commissioned by the Lord, he wrote: "Will you remind me of the lament of David? Was he not a just ruler, even though he committed murder?"

Ivan's letters to Kurbsky are filled with vainglory. Ivan cannot refrain from parading before Kurbsky as the greatest sovereign on earth. Even the pompous titles that other Russian Czars gave themselves pale a bit before the grandiloquent title Ivan used for himself in his second letter to Kurbsky. As if to further the great distance that separated him from Kurbsky, who responded sneeringly by addressing himself to Ivan as "the lowly Andrei Kurbsky, Prince of Kowell," Ivan began his letter:

"By the all-powerful and almighty right hand of Him who holds the ends of the earth, our Lord God and Saviour Jesus Christ, who, with the Father and the Holy Ghost in unity worshiped and glorified, by his mercy had permitted us, his humble and unworthy servants, to hold the scepters of the Russian kingdom, and from his almighty right hand has given us the Christ-bearing banners—so do we write, the great sovereign, Czar and Grand Prince Ivan Vasilievich of All Russia, of Vladimir, Moscow, Novgorod, Czar of Kazan, Czar of Astrakhan, Sovereign of Pskov and Grand Prince of Smolensk, Tver, Yugra [the north Ural district between the Pechora and Ob Rivers], Perm, Vyatka, Bolgar, [old capital of Voga Bulgars, south of Kazan], and others, Sovereign and Grand Prince of Novgorod of the Lower Land [i.e., Nizhny Novgorod], Chernigov, Riazan, Polotsk, Rostov, Yaroslavl, Bieloozero, hereditary Sovereign and Master of the Livonian land of the German Order, of Udora [roughly, the area bounded by the Mezen, Vychegda, and Northern Dvina Rivers], of Obdoria [area at the mouth of the Ob River], Kondia [area along the Konda River], and all the Siberian land and ruler of the Northern land—to our former boyar and voivode, Prince Andrei Mikhailovich Kurbsky."

When it suited his purpose, Ivan forgot his vainglory and had no hesitation in craftily seeking out a scapegoat upon whom to blame his shortcomings. For instance, he wrote to Kurbsky, who accused him of backsliding in spiritual matters, that "if there is any question of small sins to be imputed to me, then this is only because of your corruption and treachery. . . ." And then as if he realized he had been too blunt and direct in using Kurbsky for a scapegoat, he softened his accusation by adding this remark: ". . . still more so because I am only human; for there is no man without sin, only God alone."

Yet at another place he does not even bother to soften the accusation, and puts the burden of his lapses in religious matters squarely on others. Ivan wrote: "But if you consider that my observance of church ritual has been at fault and that games have been encouraged, then this is only the result of your cunning plans, for you tore me from a spiritual and a quiet life, and put upon me, in your pharisaical manner, a scarcely bearable burden and yourselves have not touched the burden with one of your fingers."

This self-pity that is so obvious here Ivan could not contain at any time in his life. He constantly answered attacks on himself by bemoaning his sad lot in life, the troubles he had to bear, the ill luck that was his, and the lack of appreciation everyone had for his noble and sincere efforts. To Kurbsky's charge that Ivan persecuted him, Ivan wrote: "You lay before us the charge of persecuting men—yet have not you together with the priest [Sylvester] and Alexei [Adashev] persecuted me?" Even when the Metropolitan Philip, duty-bound by custom, had approached him in the Uspensky Cathedral to save the lives of several men condemned to death, Ivan ignored his pleas for the condemned but, when the Metropolitan persisted, shouted, "Silence, you! I have but one word to say to you—and that is 'silence,' holy father, and accord me your blessing!" The Metropolitan replied, "Verily, shall my silence be laid upon your soul for a sin, and shall one day bring you to death." Ivan raised his hands beseechingly, and turned to those in the Cathedral, and said, "See how my friends and neighbors do rise against me, and conspire me evil!" Ivan's pity was for himself, not for the men about to be executed.

Throughout the correspondence, Kurbsky raked up as much evil as he could about Ivan's personal life. For years, Feodor Basmanov had slept in the same room with Ivan, ostensibly to protect him against assassins, but Kurbsky, probably referring to Basmanov and others, wrote that "they defiled the temple of your body with various forms of uncleanliness, and furthermore practiced their wantonness with pederastic atrocities and other countless and unutterable wicked deeds." Previously, Ivan had executed an old boyar for telling Basmanov that "you serve the Czar for the infamous vice of sodomy, but I, descended from a noble family, serve the Czar, like my forefathers before me, for the glory and profit of the fatherland."

But if Kurbsky resorted to personal defamation, so could Ivan. In fact, the Czar in his letters was not content to accuse Kurbsky of treason and crimes but insisted on including his family, and even his ancestors, as state criminals. He wrote that Kurbsky's grandfather was guilty of plotting against Ivan the Great, and that Kurbsky's father plotted against his father, Vasili. He then began on Kurbsky's maternal side and made similar accusations against these ancestors, and finally concluded that Kurbsky was "born from a generation of vipers."

It was for Kurbsky himself, however, that Ivan saved his harshest language. The Czar was a master of invective, and some of his choicest abuse was used on Kurbsky. A random sampling of the invective, occurring throughout Ivan's letters, includes the statement that Kurbsky wrote his first letter "in an unseemly manner, barking like a dog or belching forth serpent's venom." In another passage, Ivan accuses Kurbsky of acting "in your houndish, treacherous manner," and in still another passage calls him "a stinking hound and evil, unjust traitor." To Kurbsky's charge that he is a sodomist, Ivan first sneers at Kurbsky for his assertion, and then labels him and others "traitors and fornicators." To Kurbsky's advice to Ivan to mend his evil ways, Ivan retorts that Kurbsky is a "cur," and that his counsel "stinks worse than dung."

Yet, brutal as Ivan's words could be, he had a gift for language that could reach poetic heights at times. In his second letter, Ivan spoke of the coming of Orthodoxy to Russia, and then noted, "And as the words of God encircle the whole world like an eagle in flight, so a spark of piety reached even the Russian kingdom."

Still, the most notable aspect of Ivan's epistolary style is not his invective or his occasional poetic phrases, but his use of innumerable quotations and passages from the historical and religious works that he had read. His memory was indeed prodigious, if inaccurate, and literally scores of quotations and short passages —many of them obviously from memory—were interpolated into the correspondence. The main source was the Bible, especially the Old Testament prophets and the Epistles of St. Paul. His use of facts left much to be desired, and he either twisted them because of faulty memory or distorted them to prove a point. Even in such a matter as the number of times Chancellor visited Russia, Ivan stated in a letter to Queen Elizabeth that Chancellor had visited his kingdom three times, when in fact it had been only twice. Most of his allusions to history were to the Byzantine Empire and the East, only rarely to the West. His knowledge of the Roman Empire was extensive for the period, and he seemed to have some knowledge of France, Poland, Lithuania, and Greece. As for the rest of Europe, he knew little, though his knowledge was certainly greater than that of some later-day Russian rulers. Of Elizabeth, for instance, who ruled in the eighteenth century, it was said that to her dying day she believed that England could be reached by land from the European continent.

For a sixteenth-century Muscovite, Ivan was extremely well

read. His contemporaries referred to him as a "rhetorician of lettered cunning." Books were his favorite pursuit, and he had the best library in Russia. His interest in ancient manuscripts amounted to a passion, and, even though he was miserly, he spent a fortune in sending emissaries to all parts of Russia, especially the old intellectual center of Kiev, and to various countries in the Balkans and in Asia Minor to buy manuscripts. Besides the old manuscripts from Kiev, he inherited the manuscripts that his grandmother, Zoe Paleologus, had inherited from her uncle, John Paleologus, the last emperor in Constantinople before it fell to the Turks in 1453, and from her father, Thomas, as well as from his father, Vasili.

At one time, he engaged six German scholars, headed by the Dorpat pastor Vetterman, who were knowledgeable in ancient languages as well as Slavonic, to translate a number of these manuscripts. However, suspicious as ever, he insisted that they work in the underground Kremlin and that they be guarded by Russian soldiers. After some work on the manuscripts under such conditions, the Germans quit in disgust. Ivan was furious at their lack of co-operation and dedication, and, in anger, had the manuscripts buried deep in a vault under the Kremlin, to protect them from fire, theft, or destruction by invaders. They have never been recovered, and are probably the source from which has come the legend of a Secret Library of Ivan the Terrible.*

Although in his younger days Ivan read because he was intellectually curious, it appears that in his later days he read only those works that were pertinent to his own task of ruling and that he concentrated on remembering only those things that were applicable to himself, his position as Czar, and what could be of benefit to him in advancing his own ideas of czardom and the relation of ruler to ruled. His mind, to judge from the letters to Kurbsky at least, appeared to have retained from his reading an unsorted clutter of disconnected passages, phrases, and ideas from religious and historical works.

It is this clutter of information that Kurbsky could not refrain from commenting upon. Kurbsky in his third letter, written around 1578, wrote disparagingly of Ivan's writing ability and erudition.

---

* For an account of the efforts made in later centuries to recover the Secret Library of Ivan the Terrible, see Chapter 12, "The Kremlin," by Jules Koslow, New York, 1958.

About Ivan's letters, he wrote that they were "astonishing and worthy of amazement and limping strongly on both hips and betraying the unseemly movements of the inner man. . . . Now you humiliate yourself exceedingly, now you raise yourself up without limit and beyond measure!"

Kurbsky's belittling of Ivan's knowledge and literary style was the result not only of Ivan's frequent lapses of recall and his habit of raking over his memory and throwing in quotations and passages whether they applied or not but also of Kurbsky's desire to preen himself before Ivan now that he was in a land of civilized men, not in the intellectual desert that Russia was at that time. Kurbsky was overwhelmed by the learning he found outside Russia and tried to fit himself into the role of the learned man. He undertook some translations and wrote "A History of the Czar of Moscow," in which he gave full rein to his main thesis that the boyars must share in government with the czar. Considering the almost complete lack of intellectual creativeness in Russia at the time, Kurbsky's literary efforts were outstanding, and he represented to the Western world of the time the highest type of intellectual then produced by Russia.

However, Kurbsky is unjust in sneering at Ivan's literary style, which, though extremely rough and disjointed, had a vigorous, satiric ring that was extremely effective at times. The fact that his historical references, as well as his religious ones, were often inaccurate is understandable, since he quoted mainly from memory; the remarkable thing is that he was acquainted with history at all, considering the almost complete lack of books or intellectual curiosity that then prevailed in Russia. In his intellectual interests Ivan was in advance of his times. He did not share the superstitious belief that books, except for religious works, were evil, and would lead people away from the true faith. And to evidence his disbelief, Ivan insisted that a printing press be established in Moscow. In 1553, this was done, under the direction of Ivan Fedorov and Peter Mstislavets, and shortly afterward the first book printed on a printing press in Russia was completed. It was the Acts of the Apostles and the Epistles of St. Paul. For years, the only books printed were religious ones.

Ivan's intellectual curiosity was great, and though he expressed it mainly by seeking out illustrious opponents for debates on religious topics, he also wrote many letters and briefs in which he expressed his views on Protestants, Jews, the Catholic Church, and other subjects. His support was asked by the few monks interested in doing translations of old manuscripts, and he usually gave it. In Ivan, Russia had for the first time a ruler who gave some thought and effort to affairs of the intellect and assistance in the dissemination of knowledge. He did this, however, not as a political or social move, for he was opposed as much as other Russian rulers to educating and uplifting the ignorant mass; he did so because of his great intellectual drive and curiosity.

He was a masterful orator, and he carried people away with his passionate delivery. He had the ability to speak from the very depths of his feeling, and the ring of sincerity and heartfelt emotion moved his audiences to anger or tears. In the deeply religious atmosphere of Russia, speeches and writings heavily weighted with Biblical allusions did not appear stilted, but full of meaning to every man. Some of his power can be felt in the following passage:

"With what sins have I not offended against God between then and now! With what chastenings did He not visit us, that He might lead us to repentance! Over and over again we tried to avenge ourselves upon our enemies. Our efforts were in vain. We were not aware that our misfortune was a punishment of God and not a triumph for the heathen. These severe chastisements did not lead us to repentance; of our own accord we conjured up the horrors of a civil war, and the unhappy Christians were abandoned to every violence. And God in His mercy chastened our countless sins by floods, pestilence, and a thousand diseases. But even these punishments were in vain. Then the Lord sent us terrible fires. The treasure of my forefathers went up in flames. Fire destroyed God's holy churches, people without number were destroyed. Then terror entered into my soul, and fear seized upon my bones. My spirit humbled itself and was appeased, and I confessed my sins."

Ivan's emotionalism in his writing, to which he brought little restraint or organization, was sharply criticized by the more sophisticated Kurbsky. Sarcastically, he called Ivan's writings the gossip of a crazy old woman and said that Ivan was so unlearned that people in foreign lands would laugh at such an ignorant presentation. Kurbsky's words in the opening of his second letter read:

"I have received your grandiloquent and big-sounding screed, and I have understood it and realized that it was belched forth in untamable wrath with poisonous words, such as is unbecoming not only to a Czar, so great and glorified throughout the universe, but even to a simple lowly soldier; and all the more so, as it was of many sacred words—and those were used with much wrath and fierceness, not in measured lines or verses, as is the custom for skilled and learned men, should it occur to anyone to write about anything, enclosing much wisdom in short words; but beyond measure diffusely and noisily, in whole books and paroemias and epistles! And here too there are passages about beds, about body-warmers, and countless other things, in truth, as it were the tales of crazy women; and so barbarically did you write that not only learned and skilled men, but also simple people and children would read your letter with astonishment and laughter, all the more so as it was sent to a foreign land, where there are certain people who are learned not only in grammatical and rhetorical matters, but in dialectical and philosophical matters as well."

Still, Kurbsky with his finish and polish could not measure up to Ivan in the power of phrase that Ivan could deliver so tellingly. In his first letter to Kurbsky, Ivan wrote: "How much more does our blood cry out against you to God, our blood spilt by you your-selves, not in wounds nor in bloody streams, but in much sweat and a profusion of toil and senseless oppression caused by you, for in all too much were we oppressed by you beyond the limit of our strength! And because of your animosity and provocation and coercion, instead of blood there flowed many a tear of ours and there was much sighing and groaning of the heart."

In one area after another, Ivan wrote tellingly, and at times brilliantly.

On pride: "But I boast of nought in my pride, and indeed I have no need of pride, for I perform my kingly task and consider no man higher than myself."

On sin: "For a sin is not evil when it is committed; but when a man, after committing sin, has no perception and no repentance, then is the sin more evil, for transgression of the law is confirmed as law."

On piety: "I thank my God that I know how to maintain—at least partially—my piety, in as far as, thanks to the grace of God, I have strength."

On the hereafter: "I believe in the last judgment of our Saviour, when the souls of men together with the bodies with which they were united will be received together in one choir and will be separated into two, each man according to his deeds."

On each man keeping his station in life: "Rank shall not be turned against rank, but let each be in his rank and in his own service."

On war: "Now this is praiseworthy—to wage war willingly, of one's own accord."

On the qualities of Czars: "And it is ever befitting for Czars to be perspicacious, now most gentle, now fierce; mercy and gentleness for the good; for the evil—fierceness and torment. If a Czar does not possess this quality, then he is no Czar, for the Czar is not a terror to good works, but to the evil."

On obedience: "If a Czar's subjects do not obey him, then never will they cease from internecine strife."

On the role of the autocrat: "I endeavor with zeal to guide people to the truth and to the light in order that they may know the one true God, who is glorified in the Trinity, and the sovereign given to them by God; and in order that they may cease from internecine strife and a forward life, which things cause kingdoms to crumble."

The Ivan-Kurbsky correspondence, which lasted from 1564 to 1579, took place during a period of profound changes and of ambitious imperial designs. For all the petty personal backbiting and animosity, the correspondence reveals the temper of the times and the deep cleavage that existed within Russia between the Czar and his boyars. It reveals Ivan's ideas on the role of the autocracy and the relationship between the ruler and the ruled. And most important for an understanding of the terrible Czar, the correspondence reveals Ivan as a man as well as a Czar, a man who, though arrogant and cruel in the extreme, had a brilliant mind and a dynamic, forceful character. The correspondence helps to lay to rest the canard that Ivan was nothing but a vicious madman, and helps to restore him to his rightful place in Russian history as the originator of the ideology of Russian autocracy, the architect of the methodology of the totalitarian state, and the prototype of the all-wise, all-powerful leader.

XXIV

Ivan and Elizabeth I of England

WHEN Richard Chancellor dropped anchor in Russian waters in 1554, he began a chain of events that led not only to the formation of the Russia Company and important commercial relations between England and Russia but also to significant personal ones between Ivan and Queen Elizabeth. Their relationship reached the point where, though the two rulers never met, Ivan asked Elizabeth's help in getting him an English wife, as well as to guarantee him refuge in England in case he should have to seek sanctuary in a foreign country.

Of all the foreigners making their appearance in Russia for commercial or diplomatic reasons, none impressed Ivan as much as the English. Though there were relatively few foreigners in Russia, there were representatives from many countries. The Italians had helped to build the Kremlin, and relations with them had continued. The Dutch had a trade group in Russia before Chancellor stumbled into the far north. The Germans had supplied the few artisans and scholars who trickled into Russia. A Danish engineer had led the blowing up of the fortifications of Kazan, and the Danish king had sent the first printer, Hans Missenheim, into Russia. The Austrians had a diplomatic mission in Moscow, and Heberstein, the envoy, wrote the most lucid account of Muscovy by any foreigner who visited Russia in the sixteenth century. There were, in addition, traders from many Eastern countries, Greek scholars and merchants, and vagabonds and exiles from various Slavic-speaking countries.

Though Ivan as Czar to a large extent isolated himself and his people from the West, he personally welcomed the opportunity of meeting foreigners, hearing about their rulers and customs, and engaging them in debates over religious matters. As the largest trader in Russia, Ivan asked sharp questions dealing with commerce, and insisted upon scrutinizing all trade agreements himself. Though the course of English-Russian relations was not always smooth, yet no foreign representatives received such favored treatment as the English officials and commercial agents stationed in Russia. In the agreement that Ivan signed giving the Russia Company a virtual trade monopoly in Russia, the Czar agreed to provide the Company's agents, unreservedly, with passports and safe-conduct guarantees. Ivan proclaimed that his new-found English friends were not to be molested in any way, under pain of imprisonment or death. He sent out notices to all provincial governors to co-operate with the English in all possible ways, and to respect their customs and their liberty. He even took the unprecedented step of allowing the Company itself to have special jurisdiction over the Englishmen working in Russia and the right to settle differences and disputes that arose among English nationals.

It is no exaggeration to state that Ivan was an Anglophile, so much, in fact, that in intimate court circles he was called the English Czar. Throughout his regime, Ivan looked upon England as a possible ally in his war to conquer Livonia. Completely at a loss to understand England's far-flung commitments throughout the world, and specifically her political role in Europe, Ivan took offense when England did not rush to welcome an alliance with such a great power as Russia. The Czar had to be content with a few shiploads of military supplies that England sent by way of Russia's northern ports, among them the important port of Archangel, founded by the English in 1583.

When Napeia, the Russian envoy who went to England with Chancellor in 1556, returned to Russia the following year, he was accompanied by Anthony Jenkinson, who was to head the Russia Company in Moscow. His wages: forty pounds a year, payable in two half-yearly installments.

Jenkinson was admirably suited for the job; he was bold but not arrogant, tireless, curious, ready to undertake any adventure, diplomatic, a good administrator, knowledgeable in commercial matters, and had already traveled widely. His expansive character and extensive knowledge made him a most attractive person to Ivan, and in time the Czar became extremely fond of the English merchant-explorer, and so well-disposed toward him he even granted him permission to cross Russia to explore trade routes and trade possibilities with Eastern countries. Over the next few years, Jenkinson's explorations took him to such places as Bokhara and Persia, though he never succeeded in his grand plan of reaching India. Jenkinson was always mindful to return with gifts for Ivan as well as for his own monarch. He gave Ivan, among other presents, the tail of a white buffalo and a Tatar drum, and he introduced into Elizabeth's court a young Asiatic beauty, the Sultana Aura.

Once commercial relations were well under way between Russia and England, Ivan hoped to expand these relations to state matters as well. He specifically wanted to enlist England's aid in his battle for Livonia. Elizabeth, however, was primarily interested in advancing English trade in Russia, and had no desire to become involved in Russian plans of conquest. By 1567, Ivan lost patience with Elizabeth's ambiguity on matters other than mercantile ones. He rescinded certain English trade privileges in Russia, and through Jenkinson sent Elizabeth a message expressing his hurt and his grievances.

Ivan proposed that between Elizabeth and himself there be established "a perpetual friendship and kindred." He offered the English Queen an offensive and defensive alliance against all enemies, an agreement to insure that "England and Russia might be in all matters as one." He requested that Elizabeth treat Poland as an enemy nation and "not to suffer her people to have trade of merchandise with the subjects of the King of Poland." He asked for shipwrights and mariners, "masters who can make ships and sail them," and for various kinds of artillery and war munition. He requested that "assurance be made by oath and faith betwixt the Queen's Majesty and the Czar, that if any misfortune might fall or chance upon either of them to go out of their country, that it might be lawful to either of them to come into the other's country for the safeguard of themselves and their lives. And there to live and have relief without any fear or danger until such time as such misfortune be past, and that God has otherwise provided, and that the one may be received of the other with honor. And this to be kept most secret." Finally, Ivan asked that Elizabeth answer him on all these matters not later than June of the following year.

It is known that Jenkinson received secret instructions from Ivan, and there has been speculation that one of his tasks was to sound out the Queen about her plans for marriage, and to convey to her Ivan's offer of himself as a husband.

If indeed Ivan did propose marriage to Elizabeth, the Queen neatly sidestepped the offer, without offending her Russian suitor. Her instructions to Thomas Randolph, the English envoy she sent to Ivan to replace Jenkinson, were confined to a general expression of good will. As for the secret treaty, she told Randolph to convey to the Czar the thought that the Queen must have misunderstood the message brought by Jenkinson, for she understood that the Czar's state was powerful and that Ivan was a wise Czar. Randolph, who had been Elizabeth's confidential agent for several years at the Court of Mary of Scotland and had the reputation as a skillful diplomat, was further instructed that if Elizabeth's diplomatic temporizing aroused the Czar's anger, he was to question Ivan further on the subject and get more details.

Randolph and his party arrived in Russia at the end of September, 1568, but the ambassador had to cool his heels for five months, until February the twentieth, before Ivan deigned to receive him. There were several reasons for Ivan's rebuff of the ambassador. He had expected Jenkinson to come back to Russia, and when he discovered that it was not his friend, but another, he took it as a personal rebuff. The Czar was angry with Elizabeth for her long delays, and decided to respond in kind. Further, Moscow at the time was the scene of numerous executions, and Ivan did not wish the English ambassador to be a witness to them, and give a report of them to Elizabeth.

The Englishmen were lodged in a house that had been specially reserved for visitors, and strict orders were given that they were not to leave the house or to receive visitors. Russian soldiers guarded the house day and night. No amount of pleading by Randolph could persuade the Czar to relax the severe restrictions. In effect, the Englishmen were imprisoned, although everything was provided for their material comfort. Randolph was fearful that an attempt would be made on his life, and during the months of his virtual imprisonment built up a dislike of Russia that later found expression in his unfavorable report on conditions there.

Later, when Elizabeth protested the Czar's shabby treatment of her ambassador, Ivan laid the blame for his conduct on Randolph; he had stubbornly refused to meet with Ivan's counselors before being presented to the Czar.

When Ivan finally decided to give Randolph an audience, he sent two splendidly attired officers to escort him to the palace. The officers had two extravagantly caparisoned horses, but brought none with them for the envoy. Randolph suffered the humiliation of having to rent a horse for his trip to the palace, and his retinue had to follow along on foot.

At the palace, Randolph suffered further indignities. As he passed through a large hall on his way to the Czar's room, he saluted a number of impressive-looking, richly attired boyars, who, possibly instructed beforehand by the Czar, ignored the envoy's greeting and stared solemnly in front of them. Randolph took his own revenge for the insult; when he was ushered into Ivan's presence he did not remove his hat. Instead of taking the envoy's audacious discourtesy as insult, Ivan chose to overlook it. Ivan's reaction was quite different on another occasion, so legend has it, when the French ambassador refused to take off his hat. Ivan, enraged, ordered that it be nailed to his head.

The meeting itself was pleasant. Ivan reassured Randolph of his kindly feelings towards Elizabeth, while Randolph diplomatically assured Ivan that the Queen had the greatest respect for "her brother," the Czar. Trade matters were discussed at this and subsequent sessions in a friendly manner. Randolph told Ivan, as Elizabeth had requested, that if ever the time should come when he would want to seek refuge in England, the Queen would readily allow him to do so, and that he would be "friendly received into our dominions, and shall find assured friendship in us toward the maintenance of all his just causes." Randolph, however, assured Ivan that Elizabeth had "no manner of doubt of the continuance of our peaceable government without danger either of our subjects or of any foreign enemies."

Randolph was treated courteously from this time on, and after his first audience wrote glowingly that shortly after arriving at his quarters "comes a duke richly apparaled, accompanied with fifty persons, each of them carrying a silver dish with meat, and covered with silver. The duke first delivered twenty loaves of bread of the Emperor's own eating, having tasted the same, and delivered every dish into my hands, and tasted of every kind of drink that he brought."

By the summer of 1569, Randolph had managed to get Ivan to agree to give back the various privileges he had taken away from the Russia Company. The Company's monopoly was restored; it was granted the right to trade in all parts of Russia, and to pass through Russian territory in carrying out trade with Persia and other countries without paying custom fees, tolls, or other impositions. The Company received other privileges, including the right to coin money. The English merchants were obliged, however, to bring their best wares to the Czar before offering them elsewhere, so that he could make a selection for his own use. They further had to agree to undertake the sale or barter of the Czar's goods in their trade with other countries.

In the fall of that year, Randolph left Russia, accompanied by Andrei Savin, Ivan's new ambassador to England. Savin was entrusted with a message to Elizabeth in which Ivan gave his reasons for refusing to see Randolph when he first arrived in Russia. Savin was given specific instructions, too, to insist that a treaty be drawn up in Russian, and that it follow word for word the copy that he carried with him. Savin was to insist that no changes be made, and that the Queen should kiss the cross in the ambassador's presence and put her seal on the document. Furthermore, Ivan requested that Jenkinson be sent back to Russia.

For almost a year, from July, 1569, to May, 1570, Savin conferred with various lords of Elizabeth's Privy Council. The English negotiators insisted that before Elizabeth could become involved with Russia in its war, all efforts would have to be made to negotiate a settlement of it, and that the Queen would have to be convinced of the justice of Russia's position. Savin insisted that the treaty be signed as it was presented, and that there should be no discussion of the merits or justice of Ivan's military undertakings. The negotiations became deadlocked.

In May, 1570, Savin departed for Russia, accompanied by Daniel Sylvester, his interpreter in England. The Queen had instructed that Jenkinson should not be present in London at the time, so that an excuse could be made not to send him back to Russia. Sylvester brought with him a secret letter that verified what Randolph had told the Czar when they discussed Ivan's desire to seek sanctuary in England should the need arise. An excerpt from the letter stated:

". . . we offer that if at any time it so mishappens that you, Lord, our brother Emperor and great Duke, be by any casual chance, either of secret conspiracy or outward hostility, driven to change your country, and shall like to repair into our Kingdom and Dominions, with the noble empress, your wife, and your dear children, the Princes, we shall with such honors and courtesies receive and treat your highness and them, as shall become so great a Prince. And shall earnestly endeavor to make all things fall out according to your majesty's desire, to the free and quiet breeding of your highness' life, with all those whom you shall bring with you. And that it may be lawful for you, the Emperor and great Duke, to use your Christian religion in such sort as it shall like you, for neither mean we to attempt any thing to offend either your majesty or any of your people, nor intermeddle any ways with your highness' faith and religion, nor yet to sever your highness' household from you, or to suffer any of yours to be taken from you by violence.

"Besides, we shall appoint you, the Emperor and great Duke, a place in our Kingdom fit upon your own charges, as long as you shall like to remain with us.

"And if it shall seem good unto you, the Emperor and great Duke, to depart from our countries, we shall suffer you with all yours quietly to depart, either into your Empire of Muscovy, or else whither it shall best like you to pass through our dominions and countries. Neither shall we any wise let or stay you, but with all offices and courtesies let you, our dear brother Emperor and great Duke, pass into your country or elsewhere at your pleasure.

"This we promise by virtue of these our letters, and by the word of a Christian prince, in witness whereof, and for the further testification of this our letter, we, Queen Elizabeth, do subscribe this with our own hand, in the presence of these our nobles and counselors. . . .

"And have also thereto hanged our privy seal, promising that we, against our common enemies, shall, with one accord, fight with our common forces and do every and singular things mentioned in this writing, as long as God shall lend us life, and that by the word and faith of a Prince.

"Given at our honor of Hampton court, the xvii day of the month of May, in the xiith year of our Reign, and in the year of our Lord one thousand five hundred threescore and ten."

Elizabeth's promise to fight "against our common enemies" was loose and meaningless, and Savin's mission was a failure; he had not been able to get Elizabeth's signature on a treaty according to the wording he brought with him from Ivan. Back in Russia, Savin, to save himself from Ivan's wrath, wrote a long memorandum to the Czar complaining about the evasions and equivocations he had had to endure from the English.

In October, Ivan sent Elizabeth a wrathful letter. After stating all the advantages he had given England and her merchants, he took her to task for the way Savin had been treated by the lords of the Privy Council, who had insisted that the talks should be about commercial matters instead of political and military ones. Ivan upbraided her for having set "aside those great affairs, and your Council did deal with our Ambassador about merchants' affairs. And your merchants did rule all our business. And we had thought that you had been ruler over your land and had sought honor to yourself and profit to your country and therefore we did pretend those weighty affairs between you and us. But now we perceive there be other men that do rule, and not men, but bowers and merchants, the which seek not the wealth and honor of our majesties, but they seek their own profit of merchandise. And you flow in your maidenly estate like a maid. . . ."

Ivan concluded his harsh letter by canceling "all those privileges which we have given aforetime."

The letter was delivered to Elizabeth by Sylvester in the winter of 1570. The following January Elizabeth sent her reply through Robert Best, who journeyed to Russia by way of Sweden. In her letter, Elizabeth assured Ivan that Savin had been treated honorably, and appealed to the Czar to restore trade privileges to the Russia Company. She promised to send Jenkinson back to Russia, and then, showing that she could be as firm as the Russian Czar, she wrote that Jenkinson when he arrived in Russia "will tell you most truly that no merchants govern our country, but we rule it ourselves, in manner befitting a Virgin Queen, appointed by the great and good God; nor was ever better obedience shown to any Prince than to us by our people. And since this is the gift of God, to Him give we our most humble and best thanks."

Relations between England and Russia were deteriorating, and Elizabeth and the heads of the Russia Company in London had long discussions over the situation. When word reached the Queen that Russia was affected by famine in 1571, she directed that shiploads of food should be sent from England, to relieve the suffering of the inhabitants. This gesture, together with the impending departure of Jenkinson for Russia, was designed to mollify the Czar. Jenkinson would have preferred to go into retirement, but agreed to undertake another mission to Moscow, and in a letter to Ivan in the late spring Elizabeth again noted that she was immediately sending "her Orator and servant, dear to and beloved by us, Anthony Jenkinson," to Russia.

In July, 1571, Jenkinson and two ships, the *Swallow* and the *Harry,* arrived at the mouth of the Dvina. He was met there by Nicholas Proctor, of the Russia Company, who informed him that the Czar was greatly displeased with the English, and that Jenkinson's life might be endangered if he proceeded to Moscow. Jenkinson insisted on carrying out his mission, and started for the capital. However, when he got as far as Kholmogory, he was stopped by guards, who insisted that he could go no further because of the plague. Jenkinson tried to send a messenger to the Czar, but was unsuccessful and almost lost his life in the attempt.

Ivan's attitude toward Jenkinson was inexplicable, since the Czar had insisted that Jenkinson was the envoy he specifically wanted. The troubles of the time had completely upset the Czar. Famine was rife, the plague had broken out, the Tatars had just burned Moscow, and he was in the process of breaking up the Oprichnina. He was in no mood to treat English envoys, even Jenkinson, with respect and courtesy.

Jenkinson remained in Kholmogory for several weeks, where he was treated shabbily. No one was assigned to look after him, and even the customary financial allowance granted to foreign envoys was denied him. The people of the town were warned not to have anything to do with the foreigner, and they refused to supply him with provisions. Finally, he was advised that the plague had diminished enough to allow him to proceed. With typical change of attitude, Ivan now ordered that Jenkinson should be supplied with post horses for the journey. However, he no sooner started out than orders were received that he should turn back. Finally, after several rounds of contradictory orders he was allowed to go on and arrived in Pereslavl in February. Here he met the same fate that Randolph had met previously, and for five weeks was held a virtual prisoner. Then, as if nothing untoward had happened, he was informed that Ivan's representative would call for him and take him to the Czar. While they were on their way, counter orders were given for them to return to Pereslavl. Jenkinson in his account remarked candidly, "wherewith I was much dismayed and marveled what that sudden change meant."

At last, at the end of March, Jenkinson reached Moscow and was granted an audience with the Czar. Jenkinson bowed low before Ivan, presented him with Elizabeth's letters and gifts, as well as personal presents that included a silver basin and ewer, a mirror, and a bunch of ostrich feathers. Jenkinson then proceeded to try to heal the differences and misunderstandings between the English and the Russians—the failure to sign a treaty, Savin's treatment in England, Randolph's complaints of his treatment in Russia, and the loss of trade rights the Russia Company had suffered. Subsequently, other meetings between Jenkinson and the Czar were held, and in May, Ivan promised he would give Jenkinson his reply shortly on the various matters that he had raised. Soon thereafter, Ivan told Jenkinson, who had a particular genius for negotiating with the Czar, that Savin himself was to blame for failing to carry out the Czar's wishes, that he was willing to consider that the troubles of the Russia Company were the result of misconduct by certain employees and would not hold the Company itself responsible, and that as far as "princely and secret affairs" were at issue, he was willing to set them aside for the time being. Moreover, he promised to restore the Russia Company's trade privileges, and that he would make a proclamation to that effect. He concluded with a personal tribute to Jenkinson by saying that "if the Queen had not sent you, Anthony, unto us at this present time, God knows what we should have done to the merchants, or whether we would have called back our indignation."

His mission accomplished, Jenkinson left Russia on July the twenty-third. He never returned.

Upon his arrival in London, Jenkinson presented Elizabeth with the following letter from Ivan:

"You have sent to us your ambassador, Anthony Jenkinson, with your letters. And in those letters you wrote to us that you wish our favor and our love, and you wrote to us on other matters. And Anthony told us some speeches on his embassage; the which letters and speeches of your ambassador, Anthony, we did hear. And this you do wisely, that you wish for our favor and our love. And the business about which you wrote to us in your secret letter, the time for this business is past, because such business among princes cannot be done without confirmation by oath, and furthermore, this business has tarried too long. And when we sent to you our ambassador, Andrei Savin, about this business, and you did not write anything to our Imperial Majesty about this matter of the oath, but wrote only about trade. And whereas you wrote in your letter with your ambassador, Anthony, that you do not so much desire to be in such brotherly love with any as with our Imperial Majesty, you do wisely that you seek our favor and brotherly love. And our Imperial Majesty wishes to keep you in our love. And whereas you wrote to us about your merchants, that we should grant them in our dominions liberty of trade according to our former privileges, and give to your merchants our charter for their trade. And for your sake we have granted to your merchants, and ordered them in all our realms to trade freely, and have given orders to let them pass out of our dominions into any other dominions, according to their wish, without let or hindrance. And we have ordered for your sake to give them a charter of privileges such as is most convenient to them. And we have lovingly received your letters which you sent to our Imperial Majesty, brought by your ambassador, Anthony. And therefore our Imperial Majesty wishes to keep love unto you. Given in our dominion of the grand dukedom of Tver, in Staritsa, in the year 7080, May."

Elizabeth was pleased to receive the letter, and wrote him a letter in return the following October in which she told him that she had always been his "loving sister" and thanked him for his consideration to the merchants and for restoring their trade privileges. She requested that Ivan send any merchants who did wrong back to England, where they would be dealt with by her. However, she could not refrain from giving the Russian Czar a lesson in government, and concluded by writing:

"Lastly, we beg you, our Brother, that if any Englishman offend against your laws and justice, the offender may alone suffer the penalty, but that the whole Company, being innocent of the offense, may not be punished; for this is equitable, that everyone should answer for himself and not be responsible for others. And by complying with this, your sister's demand, Your Highness will indeed confer benefit, both on your own subjects as well as on ours. And we shall continue to enjoy and keep inviolate this our firm friendship. May God always preserve your Highness in safety and prosperity."

The English-Russian political and trade matters were thus put in order for a while, but Ivan continued until the end of his life to dwell upon two other matters that were intimately concerned with Elizabeth—the possibility that he might have to ask her for refuge and his desire to have an English wife. Elizabeth had graciously offered him asylum should the need arise, and Horsey related that, especially after the Tatar burning of Moscow in 1571, Ivan did indeed plan to flee to England and that was why he "builds a treasure of stone, great barks and barges, to convey and transport upon sudden occasion treasure to Solovetsky Monastery, standing upon the North Seas, the direct way to England."

However, in spite of Horsey's assertion, there is serious doubt that Ivan took such definite steps in preparation to flee the country. Ivan was haunted from childhood on by the fear that attempts would be made to kill him or that the situation in Russia would force him to flee the wrath of his enemies. Most of this fear was of his own making, for there is no occasion on record when a definite plot was uncovered to kill him, although Ivan insisted innumerable times that such plots were being hatched. Elizabeth's offer to give him sanctuary in England meant a great deal to him, and was an important factor in his favoring treatment of the English.

Ivan's desire to have an English wife was of long duration, too. This desire might have sprung from Ivan's own Anglomania, or the germ of the idea might have been planted inadvertently by Jenkinson in conversation with the Czar about the Virgin Queen during his first visit to Russia. More possible, however, though open to grave suspicion, is Horsey's account of the efforts of Dr.

Elysius Bomel to ingratiate himself with Ivan by deluding him with the suggestion that a marriage with Elizabeth was possible.

Bomel, whom Horsey called a "skillful mathematician, a wicked man, and practicer of much mischief," was a charlatan of great cunning. He was born in Westphalia, but at an early age went to England. He studied medicine at Cambridge, but gained a reputation as an astrologer and sorcerer. During part of the time of Savin's ambassadorship in England, he was confined in prison. Through his own cleverness, he managed to convince the Russian ambassador of his value as a doctor and astrologer, and got Savin to promise to take him with him to Russia when he departed. Lord Burghley was happy to see him leave England, and readily consented to his release from jail on the condition that he join the ambassador upon his return to Russia. Savin promised Bomel that "he would receive good pay" for his services to the Czar, and did indeed take Bomel and his English wife, Anne Richards, with him.

In Russia, Bomel spent much time in Ivan's court, both at Moscow and at Alexandrov. It was during this time that Bomel is supposed to have deluded Ivan into thinking, as Horsey put it, "that the Queen of England was young, and that it was feasible for him to marry her; whereof he was not out of hope."

Eventually, Bomel was accused of "engaging in a conspiracy with other persons in favor of the Kings of Poland and Sweden." Ivan ordered that Bomel be tortured to death. As Horsey described it, Bomel "upon the rack, his arms drawn back, disjointed, and his legs stretched from his middle loins, his back and body cut with wire whips, confessed much and many things more than was written or willing the Emperor should know. The Emperor sent word they should roast him. Taken from the *pudkie* and bound to a wooden pole or spit, his bloody cut back and body roasted and scorched till they thought no life in him. Cast into a sled, brought through the castle. I [Horsey] pressed among many others to see him. Cast up his eyes naming Christ. Cast into a dungeon and died there."

Towards the end of his life, Ivan's desire for an English wife became an obsession. Convinced that marriage to Elizabeth was impossible, Ivan decided on second-best; he would marry a daughter of a British nobleman. But whom? The answer was supplied in 1582 by a Dr. Robert Jacob, a physician who had been sent by

Queen Elizabeth, at Ivan's request, to attend to the Czar's ailments. Ivan asked the good doctor if he knew of a young woman of royal blood in England who would make a suitable wife for him. Dr. Jacob replied that he did indeed, and gave the Czar the name of Lady Mary Hastings, the daughter of the Earl of Huntingdon. With his customary impetuosity, Ivan decided to send an envoy, Pissemsky, to England to plead his case for Lady Mary's hand.

Perhaps now at long last, Ivan hoped, he would find a woman he could love dearly and with whom he could feel the same closeness and companionship that he had felt with Anastasia. It is possible that he thought of his father who had married a foreign woman, Helena of Lithuania, and of his grandfather who had married the princess from Constantinople, Zoe Paleologus. From the time of Anastasia's death, Ivan's marital life had been divided between feverish gratification and emptiness. By 1579, he had accumulated a total of six wives, including his two mistress-wives, and, except for Anastasia, had loved none of them. His marriage to his second wife, the Tatar princess Maria, can possibly be interpreted as a political marriage, an attempt to appease the Tatar groups by aligning himself with one of their princesses. But his other marriages were occasioned by impulsiveness, whim, boredom, and a desire, in the formal marriages at least, for propriety.

All these women lived isolated, lonely lives in the *terem* of the austere Kremlin or the fortified Alexandrov palace. They had neither prestige nor influence. They dared not raise their voices in protest when the Czar surrounded himself with his harem and took to his bed the virgins that Adashev and, later, Basmanov and others recruited for him.

Ivan accepted each of his wives for a while as a convenience, and when he tired of them he disposed of them by one means or another. There is no evidence that he was outwardly cruel to them or even that he beat them in the typical Russian manner of the time. However, at best he tolerated his wives; at worst, he ignored them.

In 1580, Ivan married for the seventh time, or the fifth time if his two mistress-wives are not counted. His bride was Maria Nagoi, the daughter of a boyar. Horsey, who possibly had the opportunity of seeing her, described her as "a very beautiful young maiden, of a noble house and great family." Ivan seems to have had some affection for her, possibly because her gentleness reminded him a little of Anastasia. However, his affection was not deep, and did not deter him from his intention of winning an English bride.

At the same time that Ivan took Maria for his bride, Feodor, his youngest son, married Irina, the sister of Boris Godunov. Ivan, the oldest son, by now had married his third wife, Helen Cheremetiev; his first wife, Eudoxia Saburov, and his second, Praxevna Solov, having been sent to nunneries.

The marriage ceremony that united Ivan and Maria was interesting not because of the traditional pomp that surrounded royal marriages but because in attendance were three individuals who were destined to become Czars of Russia: his younger son Feodor, Vasili Shuisky, and Boris Godunov. Ivan's oldest son and heir was also present, but he did not live to became Czar. In 1581, Ivan killed him in a towering fit of rage, under circumstances, as we shall see later, that are not completely understood but with results that were to have far-reaching consequences for Ivan personally and for the Russian state and people.

In September, 1582, Pissemsky arrived in England with specific instructions from the Czar to negotiate a close alliance between Russia and England. He was also to communicate with Queen Elizabeth, in a private audience, Ivan's project of marriage with Lady Mary; to gain an interview with Lady Mary herself and to get her portrait painted on wood or paper so that Ivan could see for himself what she looked like; to make a detailed report to him about Lady Mary's age, complexion, height, and if she was pleasantly plump; and to obtain information about Lady Mary's relationship with the Queen, her father's rank in court, and the composition of her immediate family. In addition, Pissemsky was instructed to tell the Queen in case she raised objections to the proposed marriage because Ivan had a wife that Maria was neither a king's daughter nor a princess of a royal family. Pissemsky was to impress upon the Queen that Maria did not please the Czar, and that he would immediately repudiate her if a marriage could be arranged with Lady Mary. Furthermore, Pissemsky was instructed to insist that Lady Mary embrace Ivan's religion; that in case of his death, his son, and not Lady Mary, would become head of the Russian state, but that offspring of their marriage would receive special provinces and rights befitting children of the Czar; and finally that none of the conditions could be altered in any way, and that if the Queen refused to agree to them Pissemsky was to return home.

Pissemsky was well received in England, but his progress was slow. It was several months before he could get an audience with the Queen, who was in no hurry to throw Lady Mary into the arms of the seven-times married Czar whose reputation for the qualities that made him Ivan the Terrible had become firmly established. At the interview conducted in Elizabeth's private chamber, the Queen tried to dissuade Pissemsky from pursuing his objective. Tactfully she refrained from raising the question of the Czar's ferocious character or that he was already married; she used the strategy of belittling the looks of Lady Mary. When Pissemsky insisted that he would like to see her for himself, and also to have her sit for a portrait that could be sent to his Master, the Queen replied that Lady Mary had just recovered from a severe case of smallpox and that her face was full of blemishes. Pissemsky dismissed the Queen's objections. Finally, Elizabeth agreed to having the ambassador see Lady Mary and also to having her portrait painted. To Ivan, however, she wrote the following:

"I do not find her [Lady Mary] beautiful, and I cannot imagine that she would be found so by such a connoisseur of beauty as my brother Ivan. She has but lately had the smallpox and our painter has been obliged to depict her with a red face, deeply pitted."

Although Lady Mary was described by one of her contemporaries as a "swarthy, pock-marked" young lady, Pissemsky thought she was an "angel" when he finally saw her. An account of the meeting stated:

"Her Majesty caused that lady to be attended on with divers great ladies and maids of honor and young noblemen, the number of each appointed, to be seen by the said ambassador in York House garden. She put on a stately countenance accordingly. The Ambassador, attended with divers other noblemen and others, was brought before her Ladyship, cast down his countenance, fell prostrate to her feet, rose, ran back from her, his face still towards her, she and the rest admiring at his manner. [He] said by an interpreter it did suffice him to behold the angel he hoped should be his master's espouse; commended her angelical countenance, state and admirable beauty. She after was called by her familiar friends in court the Empress of Muscovia."

In his report to Ivan, Pissemsky described Lady Mary as "tall, well-built, and slender, possessing a pale face, grey eyes, and flaxen hair, and long and tapered fingers."

As for Lady Mary herself, at first she was intrigued with the idea of marrying the Czar of All Russia. She was thirty years old and, even with charity, far from attractive. However, as she heard more about the fifty-two-year-old Czar and his character, her interest cooled considerably. She pleaded with Elizabeth not to agree to the marriage and, as one account put it, "succeeded without difficulty in persuading the Queen to save her from the proposed honor."

In the meantime, word was received in London that Maria had given birth to a son, Dmitri. When Pissemsky was confronted with the news, he was not in the least disconcerted. He simply refused to believe it, insisting that it was a "malicious invention of opponents of the Russian-English alliance."

Queen Elizabeth, although she privately assured Lady Mary that she would not give her consent to the marriage if Lady Mary did not desire it, did not dare to refuse outright to Pissemsky; English trade in Russia was too lucrative to endanger by such forthrightness. Pissemsky would not yield, but insisted that Lady Mary's appearance and character would certainly please the Czar. Pissemsky's job—and head—was at stake. His task was to find an English wife for Ivan, not to set up standards of beauty.

In the autumn of 1583, Pissemsky made arrangements to return to Russia to report to the Czar on his progress. The Russian ambassador was given an elaborate farewell party at which he assured the Queen that Ivan preferred her to all other sovereigns in Europe. Elizabeth graciously replied in the full presence of her court that "I love the Czar with all sincerity, and I keenly desire to see him one day with my own eyes."

In addition to being a diplomatic gesture of friendship, Elizabeth's remark was probably made "with all sincerity." Ivan intrigued her. For twenty-five years, she had kept up a correspondence with the remote and mysterious Russian monarch. There had even been the hint of a courtship, which she had cleverly parried to her own—and her merchants'—advantage.

Pissemsky was accompanied on his return to Moscow by Sir Jerome Bowes, the new English ambassador to Russia. Before leaving England with his party of forty, Bowes was given definite

instructions by Elizabeth to apologize to Ivan for the Queen's refusal to sign the treaty as presented by the Czar. He was told to tell
Ivan that regarding the offer of a defensive and offensive alliance
Elizabeth believed it "requisite both in Christianity and by the law
of nations and common reason, not to profess enmity or enter into
effects of hostility against any prince or potentate without warning
first given to the party so procuring enmity to desist from his
wrong-doing or cause-giving of hostility." Other instructions were
given on trade matters. Bowes was to inform Ivan that Elizabeth
was willing to act as arbitrator between Sweden and Russia and
instructed Bowes to tell Ivan that "a dear disadvantageable peace
is more worth than an advantageable and victorious war, all things
duly considered." The British Queen on this occasion, as on others,
could not resist giving Ivan advice on the conduct of governmental
affairs.

For almost twenty years, Elizabeth had been dangling before
Ivan the bait of her consent to his request for English refuge. And
now, though there was no cause to bring up the subject again, she
instructed Bowes to tell Ivan that "touching his 'self' repair hither,
you shall declare to him that as occasion shall minister to him and
he shall so think good, he shall be as welcome as any prince confederate whatsoever, and receive at our hands the best offices our
small means can yield him."

As for Lady Mary, Bowes was to handle the matter most dis-
creetly, for Elizabeth was well aware that it touched upon Ivan's
personal pride and desires, and that if anything could disrupt the
good relations between them it was this. The Queen carefully detailed written instructions to Bowes on this affair:

"Having in this sort delivered our meaning to him upon the
treaty of amity, you shall declare to him, touching the secret messages and requests he made to us by his minister, for and touching
the matter of marriage, how the lady 'mentioned' is fallen into such
an indisposition of health that there is small or no hope she will
ever recover such strength as is requisite for that state, especially
considering the long tedious voyage she 'were' to make, in case
she should upon the report of his ambassador and view of her picture have any disposition to proceed therein. You shall use all the
best persuasions you can to dissuade him from that purpose, laying
before him the weakness of the lady when she is in the best state

of health, and difficulties that are otherwise like to be stood upon by the lady and her friends who can hardly be induced to be so far separate one from the other; whereby the greatest comfort of them that are near of blood are [sic] cut off. Unless their consent might be procured, which is a matter very doubtful, the match could not in any sort be brought to pass; considering that in those cases, as over the rest of our subjects, so especially over the noble houses and families, we have no further authority than by way of persuasion, to make them like such matches as are tendered them by good apparent reasons, may tend to their advancement."

Bowes' assignment with regard to Lady Mary was not an easy one, and Bowes himself was scarcely qualified to carry off so delicate a matter with such a person as Ivan. The ambassador was overly conscious of his high rank and of the great power he represented. He was haughty and arrogant in bearing and brusque and unpleasant in his manner of speech. He knew nothing of Russia and its ways, and was completely unsympathetic to what he considered Ivan to be—a tyrannical, barbarous Czar of an ignorant and savage people.

Upon his arrival in Moscow, he immediately made himself unpopular by sneering at the breed of horse that was sent to him by the Czar, and insisted upon a better one, to match the Czar's. Moreover, he was late for the elaborate banquet Ivan had prepared for him, and was dourly informed that the "Czar had stayed for him."

Ivan spared nothing to impress the ambassador with the wealth and power of Russia, and on the day of Bowes' reception at the Kremlin "the streets were filled with people, and a thousand gunners, clad in red, yellow, and blue garments, set in ranks by the captains on horseback, with bright pieces, harquebuses in their hands, from the ambassador's door to the Emperor's palace."

Suspicious that Bowes' mission was not favorable to his plans, the Czar had arranged that the ambassador be given a "spontaneous" demonstration of his people's displeasure. As Bowes traveled from his house to the Kremlin, the people lining the streets yelled derisively at him, calling him "spindleshanks" and other derogatory epithets.

At the Kremlin, however, Bowes was given the usual elaborate welcome and display of the Czar's wealth. The gold coats were brought out of storage, and nobles and merchants were outfitted so that when Bowes entered the palace he saw throughout its magnificent corridors and halls hundreds of expensively dressed gentlemen. Ivan himself was in all his imperial splendor.

"The Emperor sets in his majesty, richly clad, with three crowns before him," Horsey wrote, "four young noblemen, called *rindeys,* shining in cloth of silver, with four scepters or bright silver hatchets, on each side the Emperor; the prince and other his great dukes and noblest of rank setting round about him. The Emperor stood up: the ambassador makes his courtesies and speech, delivers the Queen's letters. The Emperor . . . asked how his sister Queen Elizabeth did. The ambassador answering, sat down upon a form at the side of the Emperor. . . . After some little time of pause and view of each other, was dismissed in manner as he came, and his dinner of two hundred dishes of meats sent after him by a gentleman of quality, which, being delivered and rewarded, left Sir Jerome Bowes at his repast."

The subsequent sessions that were held between Ivan and Bowes were most unsatisfactory from Ivan's point of view. Bowes' arrogance and haughty bearing made him personally unpleasant to the Czar, and the disappointing news that he brought from Elizabeth concerning Lady Mary angered him. At one such interview, as Horsey reported it, Ivan became so furious that "with a stern and angry countenance told him [Bowes] that he did not reckon the Queen of England to be his fellow: for there are those who are her betters."

Bowes replied "that the Queen, his mistress, was as great a prince as any was in Christendom, equal to him that thought himself the greatest, well able to defend herself against his malice whatsoever, and counted no means to offend any that either she had or should have cause to be enemy unto."

"Yea," said Ivan, "how say you to the French king and the king of Spain?"

Bowes replied, "I hold the Queen, my mistress, as great as any of them both."

"Then what say you to the Emperor of Germany?" Ivan asked.

"Such is the greatness of the Queen, my mistress," Bowes replied, "as the King, her father, had the Emperor in his pay, in his wars against France."

Bowes' answers so infuriated Ivan that he told him that if he weren't the Queen's ambassador he would throw him out of the palace.

As for Lady Mary, at first Ivan would not take "no" for an answer, in spite of Bowes' protestations of Mary's ill health, her wish not to leave England, and that the Queen could not force Mary, against her will, to marry the Czar. Ivan asked Bowes if it were indeed true that a subject in England could defy the Queen by not marrying one whom the Queen had designated, and that the Queen had no more power over her subjects than "persuasion." Bowes replied that in England such was the case. Angrily, Ivan wrote the Queen a note that contained the following harsh passage:

"We had supposed that you were a sovereign in your state and in possession of the supreme power in the state, that you had regard for the honor of your rank and was heedful of the advantage of your realm. But now we see that in your state other people rule, independently of you—and what sort of people, at that? Common tradesmen, and you are nothing but a common wench."

Finally, convinced that the "common wench" Elizabeth had no intention of forcing Lady Mary to marry him, even after he had offered to make a child of their marriage the heir to the throne of Russia, Ivan agreed to seek out another English noblewoman for marriage, and that he would send an ambassador to England for this purpose. The Czar then told Bowes that if this mission did not prove successful, he himself would go to England and would "carry his treasure with him, and marry one of them there."

All through Ivan's negotiations with Bowes, the various relatives and advisers of the Czar, especially the forceful and ambitious Boris Godunov, who was by now Ivan's chief adviser, tried to dissuade the Czar from his intention of marrying an Englishwoman. According to Horsey, they even "plotted a remedy to cross and overthrow all these designs."

However, whatever plots were in the making proved needless. Before Ivan had the opportunity of appointing another ambassador for a mission to London, he died. Shortly after Ivan's death, Boris Godunov, who became regent, dismissed Bowes. The English ambassador was not displeased to shake the dust of barbarous Russia from his haughty person, and return to his civilized England.

XXV

Death and Legacy

THE LAST few years of Ivan's life were filled with tragedy, frustration, and bitterness. For more than two decades he had carried on an intermittent war to push Russia's borders farther into Europe by capturing Livonia. He succeeded only in destroying tens of thousands of Russian lives and dissipating Russia's wealth. Russia remained landlocked in the west. The conduct of the war had created a certain amount of national consciousness, but it was too amorphous to give Ivan a sense of achievement. He had destroyed almost all of his associates and was friendless. High nobles avoided his court as if it were infected with the plague. His Oprichnina "experiment" had ended in failure. His personal life had been filled with tragedy; he could not even succeed in the relatively simple task of inducing an Englishwoman to marry him, even though he offered her marriage to one of the great monarchs of the time and the throne itself to their offspring. He felt alone, betrayed, disillusioned, and weary. From the depths of his being, he wrote, with pathetic candor:

"The body is exhausted, the spirit is sick, the cords of my soul and my body have been stretched too tight, and there is no physician who can heal me. I waited for one capable of suffering and mourning with me: but nobody came to console me, they all returned evil for good and responded to all my love with hatred."

He spent a good part of his time brooding in the privacy of his apartment, though on occasion he still indulged himself in such wild ravings and head-pounding against the walls and floor that, when he came out of his rooms, the court fled from his battered and bloody appearance and his wild, distraught temper.

He ceased to be the same overbearing, powerful monarch that he had been. A good deal of the fire had died down, and in its place there was an abjectness that was revealed in his stooped appearance and his hanging head. His self-pity became so abnormal that it robbed him of his haughty demeanor and made him appear a pathetic figure, more to be pitied than feared. His dream and ambition to be the inheritor of the mantle of the Caesars had been destroyed by harsh political and military reverses and by the brutalizing effects of a life that he had lived too hard, too severely, and too demandingly. Now, instead of seeing himself as a glorious conqueror, he viewed himself as a miserable sinner, albeit a repentant one. His prayers to his God to save him became more hysterical as, now in ill health, he saw the avenging sword of his Maker ready to strike him in retribution for the tortures he had inflicted and murders he had committed. The greatest—and most profound—of his fears was God's anger with him for killing his son and heir.

The murder of the Czarevich Ivan was accidental; a consequence of Ivan's unbridled temper. As Possevino, who was at Ivan's court at the time, reported it, the incident that caused Ivan to lose control of himself was trivial. The Czarevich, twenty-seven years old, was living with his third wife in the Kremlin, in quarters close to the Czar's. One evening Ivan entered the Czarevich's apartment and was greeted by his daughter-in-law, who was pregnant, in a dress that Ivan considered too revealing and daring for a woman in her condition. Prudish to the extreme in many ways, Ivan condemned her harshly for her immodesty. The Czarevich, who was present at the time, deeply resented his father's fierce condemnation of his wife, and defended her. One word led to another, and soon they were verbally abusing each other. As the argument continued, Ivan became more and more furious at what he considered his son's lack of respect, and suddenly, at the peak of his anger, he struck the Czarevich in the temple with the iron-pointed staff he always carried with him. The Czarevich fell to the floor, mortally wounded. Five days later, on November 19, 1581, he died.

Ivan was crazed with grief and remorse. The Czarevich Ivan had been his favorite. Together they had trod the bloody road to Novgorod and had participated in the destruction of the city and the people. They had sat together on the platform at the Place of Skulls outside the Kremlin walls as the Oprichnina leaders were tortured and executed. They were similar in tastes and temperament; it was gossiped that they even shared the virgins that were brought to the Kremlin and to Alexandrov. The Czarevich resembled his father in physical appearance. Moreover, he, like Ivan, had intellectual interests, and was said to have written a book, "The Life of St. Anthony."

For weeks after the tragedy, Ivan cried out his misery and pleaded with his God for forgiveness. He tore out his hair and beard. He prostrated himself, and beat his head on the floor. He wandered through the corridors and rooms of the Kremlin calling upon his dead son to return to life. He lashed out at courtiers with his iron-pointed staff, and then fell at their feet pleading for forgiveness. He took no notice of his appearance, and looked more like one of the proverbial Russian vagabonds than the Czar of All Russia. He ranted and raved, threatening to do all kinds of dire things to those about him and to himself. He debased himself, hoping that by surrendering his pride he could wash away his guilt. Over and over he swore to the frightened boyars that he called before him that he would abdicate the throne and enter a monastery. Nothing or no one could console him, for he realized, even in his grief, that he had not only committed a horrible sin that no amount of praying and head-banging could wash away but that he had plunged the entire Russian nation into a situation that might prove disastrous. For now with the Czarevich dead, the heir to the throne was his younger son, Feodor, a feeble-minded, almost idiotic, weakling, whom Ivan himself characterized as "a sacristan, not a Czar's son," and whose only capability, as Ivan himself stated, was as a bellringer in a monastery, an occupation that Feodor aspired to throughout his life.

As it turned out, Ivan's fears for the future of Russia were justified, for the tragedy had a long-range effect of plunging the boyars into a suicidal struggle for the throne of Russia: the result was a condition of chaos for the state and the people that lasted a generation and became known as the Time of Troubles. By killing the Czarevich, Ivan, in effect, wiped out the direct Rurik line, for Feodor had no offspring, and Dmitri, the child of Ivan's last marriage and the only other living son of the Czar, was murdered at Uglich under mysterious circumstances in 1591, during the regency of Boris Godunov.

Ivan never recovered his full, vigorous powers after the death of the Czarevich. He was a broken, humbled man. Politically and militarily he had been defeated and now with this personal tragedy, he waited, almost resignedly, for death. He stopped persecuting his enemies, and during his last years the executions ceased. Though he was only fifty-one at the time he killed the Czarevich, Ivan looked—and acted—like an old man.

Still, when he fell ill, possibly of a kidney ailment, and death was no longer a wish but an immediate, stark reality, he fought against his fate with all the vigor and determination that he had formerly used against his foes. He was incapable of facing death as he had advised Kurbsky to do. "If you are just and pious as you say," Ivan had written, "why did you fear a guiltless death, which is no death but gain. In the end you will die anyhow!"

He called in wise men, soothsayers, magicians, astrologers to seek for the propitious signs. He had his treasures brought to him, and as he pressed his most precious jewels to his breast, he hoped that in some miraculous way they would cure him. He tried to interpret every phenomenon as intimately connected with his battle for life or as a foreboding sign of impending death. While standing on the Red Stairway, so legend has it, he saw a comet with a tail in the shape of a cross, and Ivan lamented, "It portends my death." But if any of the soothsayers or magicians dared to interpret their signs as unfavorable to him, he dismissed them and employed others who would give him hope. On days when depression assailed him, he spent all his time in consultation with his astrologers and wise men; when he felt better, he laughed at their arts, and dismissed them, jeering at their pretense of being able to read the future.

The Czar, as he had so humbly protested to Kurbsky, was indeed "only a human being," and, on March 28, 1584, he died. The deathbed setting was dramatic and significant. On the day of his death, he had his priceless jewels brought to him, and then, surrounded by his treasures, he played a game of chess with Boris Godunov. His son and heir, Feodor, was at the Czar's side, but Ivan did not deign to look at the idiotic weakling that he had fathered; his eyes—and his hope for the future of Russia—were on

Boris Godunov. As the Czar set the king in place, he fell back in a swoon. The end had come.

The Metropolitan Dionysius was immediately summoned, and, knowing Ivan's oft-stated wish, he performed the ceremony in which the Czar was given the monastic tonsure. Czar Ivan IV, known as The Terrible, now became simply the monk Jonah.

When the news of Ivan's death was announced to the court, there was a feeling of deep sorrow. It seemed impossible that the fierce monarch who had been their nominal head for fifty-one years and their Czar for thirty-seven years was dead and that no longer would they witness his fierce temper and the ominous pounding of his iron-tipped staff on the floors of the palace.

The court's grief, however, was as nothing compared to the people's sorrow when Ivan's death was announced to them. The entire nation went into a mourning more profound than had ever before been seen in Russia. When he was buried beside his son Ivan in the Kremlin's Cathedral of the Archangel, and his coffin of cypress was covered with a red cloth, even the wives and children of his thousands of victims wept. For all his tyranny and terror, Ivan had not alienated the Russian people from him; they willingly submitted to him, and, in spite of—or, strangely enough, because of—his ferociousness, admired, imitated, and loved him.

Almost all visitors and observers in Russia during Ivan's time, even the English, who despised Ivan's form of government by terror, admitted, as Best did, for instance, that "he is not only beloved of his nobles and commons, but also held in great dread and fear through all his dominions, so that I think no prince in Christendom is more feared of his own than he is, nor yet better beloved."

Even the Poles of Ivan's time, who were dedicated enemies of the Czar, could not help wondering at the Russian peoples' devotion to him. Reinhold Heidenstein, a squire in Batory's army, observed that "those who study the history of his reign should be all the more surprised that in spite of his cruelty the people should love him so strongly with the love which other sovereigns can acquire only by indulgence and kindness, and that their extraordinary devotion to their sovereign could last so long."

The folk songs and tales of Russia are full of adulation for the terrible Czar. In songs and poetry, Ivan is admiringly quoted as saying, for example, "All the masters and princes I shall flay them alive," or "I shall have you cooked, everyone, boyars and princes, in a cauldron."

The few who could reason politically might have seen him, rightly or wrongly, because of his persecution of the boyars, as their defender against their immediate oppressors. But most of the common people loved him because in him they saw themselves. He was the prototype of all Russians. If they were brutal, sinful, coarse, so was their Czar. If they tormented their fellow man, disregarded the rights of their wives and children, so did their Czar disregard the rights of his people. If they washed away their sins and crimes by debasing themselves before their God and their fellow man, so did their Czar. If they were human beings endowed with all the frailties, so was their Czar. If they ripped and clawed at their souls to find understanding and meaning in a confused and brutal life, so did their Czar.

Ivan had the stuff that heroes are made of; he had dash, daring, and vigor. Everything he did was on a large, almost gigantic, scale, whether it was dividing all of Russia into two parts, destroying the people of a great city, or attempting the conquest of an entire section of Europe. Even in his personal life, he did nothing on a restricted scale. He married more times than any other Russian sovereign, had a harem that rivaled those of Eastern potentates, and the number of virgins that entered his bedroom is legend. As a popular hero, his terror, crimes, rages, and sins somehow lost their horrible aspect and became manifestations of a strong, determined leader's way of meeting fire with fire.

In the popular mind, Ivan is the last, and greatest, of those medieval, almost legendary Russian figures—Vladimir the Saint, Alexander Nevsky, and Dmitri Donskoi.

In Russia, Ivan is no Nero or Caligula, a vicious rapist and hardened murderer; he is the perplexed, erring human being whose battles against the vicissitudes of life and fortune are the battles of all poor sinners who lose the way but seek the light and wish to repent. Count Alexei Tolstoy in his "Death of Ivan the Terrible" has the sinful Czar cry out as he is about to die:

> I allowed the devil to rule my deathless soul.
> I am no Czar; rather a wolf, a cur!
> I have loved tortures and torments. I slew
> My son, a crime greater than the guilt

> Of Cain himself! I am in mind and soul
> A man of sin! My heart's iniquities
> Cannot be numbered by man's feeble powers!
> O God! O Christ! Heal me and comfort me!
> Forgive me as you forgave the robber!
> Cleanse me of all the filth with which my soul
> Is spotted and defiled, and thus make me worthy
> To be enrolled among your saints!

Ivan's cry of pain and anguish was believed by common people and poets alike. And because he could—and did—cry out his pain, the people took him to their bosoms and wept with him for his pain as well as for their own. The terrible Czar was not only their Little Father and their scourge but he was their fellow-sufferer, and even in the magnificence and grandeur of his exalted position he was, in the final analysis, a pathetic bug like each of them, crawling for a brief, allotted period of time upon a cruel and bitter earth.

Ivan was the mystic, the visionary, the avenger, the hater, the brooding intellectual, and the conqueror. His personality was, on a grand scale, every Russian's; his spirit, the spirit of Russia itself.

Yet he was more than a symbol of identification of the Russian people and nation. He was, beyond any other czarist Russian leader, the seeker of new forms, new ways, new horizons, and the fact that he sometimes failed to find and establish the new was due to the age in which he was born as much as to the limitations of his own character and intellect.

Ivan was less God's angry man than His restless one. Nothing seemed to please him or satiate him. He was a man constantly pursued and constantly pursuing. Nothing in life gave him pleasure, and the cruelties he inflicted on others were matched by the cruelties he inflicted upon himself. In many respects, Kurbsky's condemnation of Ivan in one of the letters he wrote to the Czar was justified. Quoting Cicero, Kurbsky wrote:

"You are crushed by all wretchedness and hardship, who think yourself blessed and prosperous. Your lusts torture you, you are in torment day and night; you who are not content with what you have and who fear lest even that very thing which you have may not be lasting; the conscience-pricks of your ill deeds goad you on . . . wherever you gaze your unjust acts encircle you like furies and do not even let you take breath."

Ivan, like all men, had a need for love and friendship. His constant grasping for friendship, whether from a Vorontsov when he was a boy, a Sylvester and an Adashev in his early manhood, or even from brutal bullies such as Skuratov and Basmanov was pathetic to see. But he could not hold on to a friend, much as he needed and wanted one, his suspicions always getting the better of him. He clutched and pushed away at the same time. Even his advice to his sons in later life reflected this. "Love men and reward them," he told his sons, and then in the next breath warned, "but always guard yourselves against them."

Ivan was of an unstable temperament, but he was not mad, if the word mad means that he was deprived of reason. He was no more mad than dozens of other violent despots in history whose madness consisted of inhumanness, unconcern for human dignity, and an insatiable desire for power irrespective of the means used in achieving it.

How much a leader affects the course of history is an old, unanswered question. However, if ever a leader influenced his nation's history, such a leader was Ivan. He gave Russia a consciousness of its national destiny and introduced many forms and methods of government that have remained manifest throughout the years until today.

His vision of the greatness and power of Russia, and the political and military means to be used to realize his vision, were matched only by those of Peter the Great, who followed Ivan's methods and vision in all ways, from imitating his terrorism to carrying on a relentless struggle "to open a window to the West." Moreover, Ivan set a pattern for state-people relations that in essence still prevails.

All this was genius, not madness, though it was in so many respects an evil, vicious genius.

Bibliography

EXCEPT for a few sketchy Church records and official State documents, there is no written record of Ivan the Terrible's reign by the Czar's Russian contemporaries. Fires that periodically ravaged Moscow destroyed some of the documents, and turbulent events of the kind that characterized the Time of Troubles account for the destruction of others.

The best—and an invaluable—contemporary Russian source is the correspondence between Ivan the Terrible and Prince Kurbsky. An excellently edited edition of the correspondence was issued by the Cambridge University Press in 1955—*The Correspondence of Prince A. M. Kurbsky and Tsar Ivan IV of Russia,* edited and translated by J. L. I. Fennell.

The most revealing account of Ivan and his times by a Russian historian is in V. O. Klyuchevsky's *A History of Russia* (London, 1911–31). The Soviet viewpoint on Ivan's reign is contained in M. M. Pokrovsky's *History of Russia* (New York, 1931).

By far the most important contemporaneous sources are the various accounts written by foreign ambassadors and travelers. An extremely observant picture of Russian life is by the early-sixteenth-century Austrian ambassador to Moscow, S. von Heberstein, in his *Notes Upon Russia* (London, 1851–52). British sources include Giles Fletcher's *Of the Russe Common Wealth* (London, 1591); the Hakluyt Society's *Principal Navigations* (London), which contains material from Richard Chancellor's journal, Anthony Jenkinson's narrative, Jerome Bowes' account of his ambassadorship to Moscow, and descriptions of the various dealings of the Russia Company; Jerome Horsey's *Travels* (in *Purchas, His Pilgrims,* London); and the *State Papers of the Reign of Queen Elizabeth*.

There are only a few biographical studies of Ivan IV in English. One of the most interesting, though confusing, is the translation from the French of K. Waliszewski's *Ivan the Terrible* (Philadelphia, 1904). The Soviet view of the Czar is contained in the translation from the

261

Russian of R. Wipper's *Ivan Grozny* (Moscow, 1947). Others are the sketchy late-nineteenth-century *Ivan the Terrible,* by A. Pember (London, 1905); the translation from the German of *Ivan the Terrible,* by H. von Eckardt (New York, 1949); and *Ivan the Terrible,* by S. Graham (New Haven, 1933).

Index

INDEX